COMBAT
CHAPLAIN

COMBAT
CHAPLAIN

The Personal Story of the

World War II Chaplain

of the Japanese American

100th Battalion

ISRAEL A. S. YOST

*Monica E. Yost and
Michael Markrich, editors*

*A Latitude 20 Book
University of Hawai'i Press
Honolulu*

Printed in United States of America

11 10 09 08 07   6 5 4 3 2

Library of Congress Cataloging-in-Publication Data

Yost, Israel A. S., 1916–2000
    Combat chaplain : the personal story of the World War II :
chaplain of the Japanese American 100th Battalion / Israel A. S. Yost ;
Monica E. Yost ; Monica E. Yost and Michael Markrich, editors.
        p. cm.
    Includes bibliographical references and index.
    ISBN-13: 978-0-8248-3023-6 (hardcover : alk. paper)
    ISBN-10: 0-8248-3023-7 (hardcover : alk. paper)
    ISBN-13: 978-0-8248-3082-3 (pbk : alk. paper)
    ISBN-10: 0-8248-3082-2 (pbk : alk. paper)
    1. Yost, Israel A. S., 1916–2000. 2. United States. Army. Infantry
Battalion, 100th. 3. World War, 1939–1945—Personal narratives,
American. 4. World War, 1939–1945—Chaplains—United States—
Biography. 5. United States. Army—Chaplains—Biography. 6. Japanese
American Soldiers. 7. World War, 1939–1945—Campaigns—Italy.
8. Chaplains, Military—United States—Biography. I. Yost, Monica
Elizabeth, 1942– II. Markrich, Michael. III. Title.
    D810.C36U69 2006
    940.54'78092—dc22

                                                    2006007355

Maps in this book are from *The Story of the 442nd Combat
Team: Composed of 442nd Infantry Regiment, 522nd Field
Artillery Battalion, 232nd Combat Engineer Company.*
Information-Education Section, MTOUSA, 1946.

University of Hawai'i Press books are printed on
acid-free paper and meet the guidelines for permanence
and durability of the Council on Library Resources

Designed by Liz Demeter

Printed by The Maple-Vail Book Manufacturing Group

CONTENTS

FOREWORD

Monica E. Yost

For me this book is a tribute not only to my father, but also to the men of the 100th Battalion. Reading my father's memoir and other materials about the 100th that he saved was an emotional experience for me not only because of the picture I saw of him, but also because of what I learned about the men with whom he served. I was touched deeply by their bravery, their stamina, their strong bonds of camaraderie, and their kindness to an outsider from Pennsylvania. Every time I read certain pages as I worked on editing the manuscript, I felt sadness for the men who died, the families who never saw their loved ones return, and the men who did return but with disabilities and traumatic memories. I am pleased that this book will add to the historical record about the exceptional men of the 100th. And I have an overwhelming sense of how fortunate I am that my father was one who did come home in good health.

I thank Michael Markrich for his enthusiastic help in editing the manuscript and the members of Club 100 for their contribution of information and photos. I also thank my husband, LaVern D. Rasmussen, for his patience and constant support while I worked on this project.

PREFACE

Michael Markrich

THERE WERE many famous regiments in World War II, but none received greater recognition and honors than the 100th Battalion and the larger force of which it became a part, the 442nd Regimental Combat Team. The 100th Bn and the 442nd RCT stood out from the other units because they were brave, highly motivated, and successful soldiers who were predominately Americans of Japanese ancestry (AJAs) from Hawaii. At a time when Japanese Americans were considered officially suspect by the U.S. government, the sacrifices and proud combat record of these soldiers, mostly in Italy and France, bore testimony to their loyalty and belief in American ideals.

Among the men serving with the AJAs from Hawaii during some of their most difficult and dangerous times was Israel A. S. Yost, a young army chaplain from a small town in Pennsylvania. What follows is the manuscript he wrote in 1984, several years after he retired from the ministry.

Chaplain Yost's memoir of his time with a battalion of men from Hawaii is the account of an outsider who is able to express his private thoughts candidly about those with whom he served. His request to serve as a combat infantry chaplain led to a chance assignment to the 100th Bn, which was essentially a reconstituted National Guard unit from Hawaii. He soon found himself, a white Lutheran minister, sent to serve as a spiritual adviser to a battalion of young Japanese Americans whose families were overwhelmingly Buddhist. Some had never even heard of the Lutheran faith. A few, because of his first name, assumed he was a rabbi.

Little could Yost have imagined that the 100th Bn would be assigned the role of advance guard in an American military campaign in southern Italy. The men suffered terribly from enemy fire, from unrelenting rain and snow, from the strain of being in nearly continuous combat, and from some senior white officers who thought of them as expendable.

Yost was with them all the time. He laughed at their jokes in Island pidgin that at first he found incomprehensible. He ate their food. With them he dodged bullets and shrapnel. He listened to their complaints about their officers. He picked them up when they were wounded. He comforted them when they were sad. He put them in body bags when they were dead. He preached Christian sermons in foxholes and tried to interest the men in his faith. From his preaching he won few converts. However, for his unflagging energy and deep concern for his fellow man in a time of nearly unrelenting tragedy he earned the love and devoted admiration of his fellow soldiers.

In this book we meet the future U.S. Senator Spark Matsunaga, librarian Kent Nakamura, future Hawaii Supreme Court Justice Jack Mizuha, dentist Dr. Katsumi Kometani, and others as young men. Yost tells the story of the AJA men and their haole (white) officers such as Farrant Turner, a future secretary of state for the Territory of Hawaii, with empathy, sensitivity, and understanding. The memoir is made up of parts of the journal he kept between 1943 and 1945 as well as excerpts from the letters he wrote home every day to his beloved wife, Peggy.

As a child in eastern Pennsylvania, Israel Yost suffered greatly when his father, a traveling salesman for an agricultural equipment manufacturer, was killed by a drunk driver. He went through trying times as he adjusted to his beloved father's death and his mother's struggles as a single parent during the Depression. The protective calluses he developed to survive the hurts of his youth were balanced by an empathy for others' pain that became a part of his ministry. His sensitivity to others would be severely tested by the brutality of the experiences to which he would bear witness.

✳ ✳ ✳

After arriving in North Africa, the men of the 100th Bn had been assigned to General Eisenhower's command but were told initially that they were not wanted. A place was found for them in the 34th Division of the Fifth Army under the command of Gen. Mark W. Clark. They would serve in Italy under General Clark for all but a few months during the war.

In his book *Calculated Risk,* General Clark described the combat they were up against. "The rain came down in torrents, vehicles were mired above their hubcaps, the low lands became seas of mud and the German rear guard was cleverly entrenched to delay our progress" (Clark, 226, 228). The terrain of southern Italy is made up of jagged peaks, steep gullies, and narrow mountain valleys usually crossed by rocky mountain trails and narrow roads. When this terrain was defended during a harsh winter by skilled German troops and fortified with concrete forts in three lines of defense with rifle pits, interlocking machine-gun fire, mines, rocket launchers known as Nabelwerfers, tanks, and artillery, it became nearly impregnable.

To the young men from subtropical Hawaii this combat in freezing temperatures was a nightmare. Not only was their unit ill equipped to fight under these kinds of conditions, without winter uniforms or the proper weapons, but their officers also lacked experience and expertise for this kind of combat. It was often said that the men of the 100th had the highest average IQ of any infantry division in the entire U.S. Army. In contrast to the uneducated rural poor who filled much of the ranks of World War II U.S. Army infantry regiments, the 100th was made up of the top AJA high school and college graduates of Hawaii. In a personal war in which they often fought as the advanced guard for the entire Fifth Army, they would need all of their intelligence and cunning to survive. Because of the harsh terrain that made large-scale troop movements difficult, this was a war fought by small units of infantry on both sides in which the most important decisions were made not by generals but by lieutenants, captains, and lieutenant colonels.

It was a dark, difficult, and costly effort that some at that time, and later, would complain had no strategic purpose. The main thrust of the Allied strategy to end World War II against Germany called for two invasions across France: a northern invasion in Normandy called Overlord and an invasion in the south called Dragoon, on the French Riviera. Overlord and Dragoon were years in planning and drew the highest priority in terms of planners, leaders, and materiel.

In comparison to these efforts, the war in Italy was an impromptu campaign never fully planned, never really intended, and fought under a mistaken perception. In 1943, Ultra, the super-secret decrypt of Japanese and German codes, indicated that following the surrender of the Italian government to the Allies in 1943, Adolf Hitler planned to evacuate German troops from Italy. The Allies, it seemed, had only to land in Italy, seize Naples, and take Rome and the war there would be over. They anticipated that they would be welcomed by fervent Italian crowds happy at being liberated.

Expecting minimal resistance, they faced instead a well-trained, ably led, and highly motivated German army intent on their complete destruction. The 100th landed at Salerno on September 22 with 1,300 men. Chaplain Yost would join them on October 5. By the middle of February, he would note that their ranks had been reduced, through almost continuous combat, to 521 soldiers. The 100th was continually reinforced, and their contribution to the war effort was seemingly without end. They would fight in Italy, be sent on a special mission to France, and then, just before the war's end, be ordered to frontally assault an impregnable mountain fortress in northern Italy.

It must be said that other units suffered severe casualties during World War II, but few (or none) for as long and sustained a duration as the 100th Battalion and the 442nd Regimental Combat Team. Nor did the other units suffer the indignity of having family and friends interned in relocation camps.

By war's end, Yost, like the men he served with, wanted to go home. He hated violence. He was tired of the army and wanted only to resume life with his wife and loved ones. He went back to Pennsylvania and worked hard at putting the war behind him. His life would be spent as a minister and teacher in service to others. However, he would be forever tied to the people of Hawaii because the bond he forged with the men of the 100th Bn and the 442nd RCT during World War II would never leave him. This book is Yost's personal testament because he could never let the story go. It was an immensely difficult thing to preach a message of love and compassion in a daily atmosphere of war and brutality. This book is his effort to explain what happened to him during that difficult time. It is a unique window to a past we must never forget.

LIST OF ABBREVIATIONS

AAA	antiaircraft artillery
AJA	American of Japanese ancestry
AWOL	absent without leave
Bn	Battalion
BSO	Battalion Supply Organization
CIB	Combat Infantry Badge
CO	commanding officer
CP	command post
C ration	canned field ration
CWO	chief warrant officer
DOW	died of wounds
DSC	Distinguished Service Cross
EMT	emergency medical treatment
GI	enlisted soldier
GRO	Graves Registration Officer
GRS	Graves Registration Service
KIA	killed in action
K ration	lightweight packaged ration
LCI	landing craft infantry
LST	landing ship tank
MIA	missing in action
MISLS	Military Intelligence Service Language School
MP	military police
OCS	Officer Candidate School
OP	observation post
POW	prisoner of war
PX	post exchange
RCT	Regimental Combat Team
ROTC	Reserve Officer Training Corps
V-Mail	Victory Mail (enlarged, microfilmed letter)
WIA	wounded in action

PROLOGUE

WHEN I was a young man, a few months after my twenty-seventh birthday (I am now sixty-eight), association with a remarkable group of men was suddenly thrust upon me: I was assigned to the 100th Infantry Battalion (Separate) as chaplain.

The men were Americans of Japanese ancestry (AJAs), and all save a few of the original unit were from the then Territory of Hawaii. Their officers, both haole (Caucasian) and Nisei (AJA), were also from Hawaii. Committed to combat with the Fifth Army in southern Italy in September of 1943, the 100th soon distinguished itself. It earned the title of "The Purple Heart Battalion."

★ ★ ★

In June of 1944, the 442nd Regimental Combat Team, composed of AJAs from both Hawaii and the Mainland, arrived in Italy; the 100th Battalion became the 1st Battalion of the 442nd but kept its own special designation as the 100th.

Except for the 100th's first week in combat, I participated in all of the military campaigns of the AJAs in Italy and France. I have written down the story of this unique experience, using the letters I sent my wife almost daily, the little journal I kept part of the time, and the accounts I have read and heard these past forty years.

Who in 1943 could have foreseen that a Lutheran pastor from rural eastern Pennsylvania would be blessed to live and tell such a tale?

Israel A. S. Yost
Spring of 1984

ONE

The Assignment

"CHAPLAIN ISRAEL Yost," said the colonel, adding an unmistakable emphasis to the name "Israel." Why was he laughing as he returned my salute? Embarrassed, I stood at attention as the other officers seated around the room joined their guffaws to that of their superior officer, Lt. Col. Farrant L. Turner![1]

"Chaplain, you're not Jewish, are you?" he asked.

"No, sir, I am Lutheran."

"We were wondering," he continued in a more serious manner, "why the army was sending us a rabbi when we have only Buddhists and Christians." Both he and I had been in the service long enough to know that the military often made decisions just as ludicrous as the one he was suggesting.

"Chaplain Yost, what do you know about the 100th?" His tone was quite serious now. "What do you know about our boys? What do you know about Japanese Americans? What do you know about the Japanese?"

"Sir, I only know what General Ryder told all of us of the 34th Division: not to judge the 100th until you men had a chance to prove yourselves in combat. About Japanese Americans I know nothing and about as little about the Japanese."

"That's fine. Then you won't be like the chaplain we had back in the States. In his sermons he kept making references to Japanese customs and to Japanese history. The men didn't like to hear such things; they're Americans. In fact, I got tired of listening to his kind of sermons, too."

"Sir, I expect to treat your men just as I would treat any other Americans, regardless of their background."

"Good, good! Then you'll get along with our boys. Now I'd like to introduce you to some members of my staff." He began with Maj. James Lovell, the executive officer.[2] Thus, on October 5, 1943, in southern Italy, my service began with Americans of Japanese descent.

Had anyone asked me how I felt about my new assignment, he would have learned that I was less than thrilled with it. Only a month before, I had joined the 109th Engineer Battalion of the 34th Infantry Division. Many of these combat engineers were Lutheran like me. The officers and men had quickly made me feel at home, no doubt because they had been without a chaplain for some time. Their executive officer had briefed me on the history of their contingent. The 34th was the first American division sent to the European Theatre in World War II, to Ireland and then to fight in North Africa.

I had looked forward to a pleasant relationship with this officer; he was interested in many of the same nonmilitary pursuits I was. I had especially enjoyed the visit he arranged for a small group of us to explore the ruins at Paestum, Italy. So congenial were these men and officers that I had quickly forgotten that I was on duty with them only until a combat infantry battalion of the 34th needed a padre. I admired the daredevils of the unit's reconnaissance troop, many of them Pennsylvanians like me. One of their tasks was to drive a jeep down a road toward the enemy until stopped by mines exploding, or gunfire, or a blown-out bridge. I had anticipated a busy and worthwhile life with these engineers.

Now I had been ordered to work with a much different group of soldiers. Who were these AJAs (Americans of Japanese ancestry) of the 100th Infantry Battalion (Separate), now attached to the 34th Division 133rd Infantry Regiment to replace its 2nd Battalion, which had been detached to remain in Algiers as the special military guard at General Eisenhower's headquarters?

I remembered seeing them boarding a troop ship in New York Harbor the same day I embarked for overseas; I realized then that they were Orientals of some sort, but I did not even make a note of them in my diary at that time. I saw them a second time when they moved to a bivouac near that of the 109th Engineers near Oran [Algeria]. With the rest of the Allied forces in North Africa I learned that they called themselves AJAs. Otherwise they were a mystery to me.

The first AJA I met personally was Capt. Katsumi Kometani;[3] he was leaning on a jeep at the spot near the command post of the 100th where I and my gear were dropped off by an engineer officer in the afternoon when I reported to my new assignment. He introduced himself to me as the 100th dentist and volunteered to present me to Colonel Turner. During my short walk to the farmhouse serving as headquarters, I began to like the guy.

After my interview with Turner, Kome[4] (for I soon began to use his nickname) took me under his wing and commenced familiarizing me with the men, the officers, and the history of my new unit. I discovered that he was also the battalion's morale officer. In fact, he had talked his way into becoming a part of the 100th; an infantry battalion is too small a group to have its own dentist, so the other position served as the reason he could be with his compatriots. Since Kome and I were the two officers who during combat normally had no specific duty assigned to us, we became a team up front, roving about and making ourselves useful wherever we saw a need, as noncombatants, of course, for neither of us ever carried weapons.

By the evening of the first day I was beginning to feel at home with my new parishioners. All but a handful of the enlisted men and noncommissioned officers were from the Hawaiian Islands, as were most of the commissioned officers, both Caucasians and AJAs. All had the aloha spirit and all sprinkled their speech with the pidgin of the Islands.[5] They were resting after their first battle experience since landing at Salerno on September 22.[6] Three men had been killed in action, twenty wounded, and thirteen injured in accidents (five when a medics jeep overturned). I had "hit the beach" with the 109th a day earlier, but I had not yet been with troops in actual combat. Little did I guess that I would stay with this distinctive outfit until the end of the war, engaging in all of their campaigns, taking short leaves only when the unit was in rest areas.

I met the chaplain I was replacing, Earnest E. Eells. We had been on the same ship in the convoy that had brought us and the 100th to the war zone. He had been assigned to the AJAs soon after I was ordered to the engineers. Here was another example of an army snafu:[7] since Eells held the rank of major, he should not have been assigned to a battalion, for such a unit's table of organization calls for a chaplain no higher in rank than a captain.

Ordinarily only lieutenants are assigned to the battalions; if they serve long enough they may be promoted to captain. As soon as somebody in authority became aware of the mistake, the major was ordered out and a lieutenant (in this case me) was ordered in. In my October 6 letter to my wife, Peggy, I wrote, "I am replacing a chaplain that was quite popular, so I hope I will be able to measure up to his standard."

The day had begun with C rations [canned field rations], specifically hash and the accompanying hard crackers and powdered coffee. The evening meal was 5-in-1 rations, more like a meal from home, especially since someone had gotten fresh vegetables from local sources and cooked them with the army chow. That night I slept in a pup tent.

The next morning, my first full day as chaplain of the 100th, I awoke early to the cacophony of church bells and cannon fire. This time my C ration featured baked beans with crackers and coffee powder. I started making my rounds among the men. Our oversized battalion had six line companies instead of four, as well as several attached platoons. I wanted to mix with the officers and men before the next engagement with the enemy. I sent off a letter to the Red Cross on behalf of an Italian prisoner of war I had met the day before. I wrote my wife, calling her attention to my new address. In my stumbling Italian I managed to make a *paesano* understand that I wanted to buy some white wine for Holy Communion.[8]

The army booklet on Italy pointed out that anyone who knew Latin would find the ablative form of the Latin noun was the word used in Italian. This was helpful to me for I was using the local language every chance I got. Before long the CO [commanding officer] was calling me in to translate for him until an Italian American officer joined us.

Chaplain Eells had scheduled a memorial service for the two men of B Company, Sgt. Shigeo (Joe) Takata and Pvt. Keichi Tanaka, killed in action on September 29th. I assisted him with the hymns and responsive reading at the solemn ceremony at six o'clock. This was my first official act in my new parish, bringing me face-to-face for the first time with the stark reality of what war is all about: death. I went to bed early.

The next day it rained. We prepared to move but sat around all day waiting. Some of the boys shared their mulligan stew with me. In the afternoon I joined our CO in the farmhouse, a very dirty place, and we sat there drinking coffee. In the evening, the woman of the house brought the colonel a quilt for him to drape around his shoulders as he sat in a chair trying to get some rest. "You remind me of my uncle in New York," she told him in Italian. I, too, sat at the table all night long, but without a quilt.

"Old Man" Turner was idolized by his men. He was a true "kama-aina,"[9] born in Hilo on the Big Island of Hawaii. He had implicit faith in the loyalty of the American-born Japanese. He had pulled strings to be appointed their CO, had on many occasions stood up to army brass to ensure fair treatment for his men, and continually challenged them to make their unit one of the very best in the army. Because of his age (forty-eight in 1943) and his emotional identification with his soldiers, many of his command wondered how long he would be able to continue as their leader in combat. It was generally agreed, however, that if Colonel Turner lost his position, the 100th would continue to perform well under its executive officer, Major Lovell.

Jim Lovell had been selected by Turner as his right-hand man because Jim had the confidence of the Islanders. Although not born in the Islands, he had taught and coached athletics at Honolulu schools that were predominately Nisei[10] in enrollment, and he had worked well with them as an officer in the Hawaiian National Guard. Like Turner, Lovell was interested in all aspects of the welfare of the men. He suggested that I mimeograph a sheet with worship items such as the Lord's Prayer, the Apostles' Creed, and a few hymns.

"Many of the men," he explained, "are not Christians, but they want to participate in the services. Until they can memorize what we use in worship, they'll need such sheets." I followed his advice; later, when as the Graves Registration Officer [GRO] I supervised the collection of the bodies of those killed in battle, I found that many had these worship sheets tucked away in a shirt pocket. The major was also a fine soldier; it was he who had worked out the changes necessary to convert our oversized battalion for use as a special unit.

The next day after breakfast, which for me consisted only of some hot cocoa, we trucked up closer to the front. Many of the bridges had been blown up by the retreating Germans, but the engineers had quickly constructed bypasses for the traffic. We met five Greeks from the island of Crete who had been held as prisoners by the Italians and arranged transportation toward the rear for them. We passed many Italian women carrying heavy loads on their heads. At our bivouac area I spread dried corn shucks on the floor of a building to ready it for sleeping. In the afternoon I partially dried out my wet pup tent, after eating more mulligan stew. For supper the headquarters mess crew heated some C rations. In the late afternoon I shaved, using water from a nearby well; large cups on an endless belt, powered by a bullock walking around the well, raised the water to the surface.

Saturday I received a request from the captain of D Company to conduct a memorial service in his area for the one man of his command killed in action some days before. Colonel Turner, briefing me about his personnel, had told me that I would find just about everyone cooperative, with one possible exception: D Company's Capt. Jack Mizuha.[11] "Just remember," he had counseled me, "Jack is rougher on the outside than on the inside." Therefore I was approaching this first solo memorial service with some trepidation.

When I arrived at 11:15, Captain Mizuha assembled his men and introduced me with a speech to this effect: "Chaplain, I don't believe the same things you do, but my men want a memorial service for their buddy, and I want them to have it. Just go ahead and I'll listen." I stayed afterwards and ate with the company.

At 2:30 at the 133rd Regimental Headquarters, I conducted a Protestant service to which six soldiers came. Since the chaplain of the regiment was a Roman Catholic, he had asked me to come to his area to care for his Protestant men. Right after my worship, he said Mass for those of his faith. Whenever possible an army chaplain must arrange for those who are not of his faith to be ministered to by pastors of their faith. This was also true for Jewish soldiers; at this time there were none in the 100th. Later on, when we had a single Jewish officer, I had to arrange transportation for him to attend Hebrew rites with the rabbi-chaplain of a larger echelon.

However, during World War II no provision was made for the spiritual care of Buddhists and Shintoists, the faiths of many of the men of the 100th. Although I had no orders to provide special worship for these religious groups, I was aware during my general worship service of their presence. I also encouraged our Mormons to use my wall tent for their meetings.

Every month a chaplain must fill out a report form about his activities; it is sent through military channels and eventually reaches the Major General Chief of Chaplains in Washington, D.C. During each month, therefore, I kept a record of such items as baptisms, attendance at worship, extra duties assigned to me by my line officers, equipment available (or not available) for my use, "excuses" why some duties could not be performed because of the exigencies of the service. I kept duplicates of all my monthly reports.

On Sunday at nine o'clock, for the first time I led worship for my battalion. About 300 attended out of a total of some 1,000 who were probably free to come had they wanted to. Always some men must be on duty, others have been on duty and are catching up on their sleep, some (many of mine) are not Christians, still others think it is too much effort to participate. I sent the following V-Mail [Victory Mail] to my wife.

> Just finished this morning's services. About a third of the men came out for the general services; that's a real good start. The colonel was there and said he thought I'd always be getting that many at least. Afterwards, eight

asked for Holy Communion, mostly Episcopal; but a Mormon or two also took it. My hymn books arrived from the other battalion just in time, so we had some good singing by the group. I am sure glad to be working with these men. . . .

This afternoon I guess I'll practice on my organ a bit and see how it works. I must also write out some notices of communion to be sent to the home churches. The fellows always seem to appreciate that. I'm invited to a chicken dinner at noon. Some of the men have acquired some chickens and are preparing a feast. So I guess I'll join in and enjoy it with them. They are always offering this or that to the chaplain—a good crowd to be around.

The War Department authorized the quartermaster to provide each chaplain in a combat zone with the following items: field desk, chaplain's flag (Christian or Jewish), portable folding organ, 150 service books, and a metal chest as a container for hymnals. For transportation, the chaplain has a jeep (a quarter-ton truck) and a quarter-ton trailer. Because the chaplain must write many letters, such as the notices of Holy Communion mentioned above, he is provided with a portable typewriter and case.

In bivouac he has his own wall tent in which he can set up the portable organ, his field desk (a large box with a side that drops down as a desk top), and a folding cot. Eight to ten men can crowd into the tent for a worship service. At times a sergeant led a few Roman Catholics in the praying of the rosary in my tent when conditions prevented transporting these worshipers to a chaplain-priest's Mass nearby. Most denominations provide their chaplains with a portable altar set; mine from the Lutheran church resembled a small suitcase with space for a small cross on a stand, two candlesticks, containers for bread and wine, a chalice, a paten,[12] a cassock and surplice,[13] and a small supply of New Testaments and religious tracts. Even though I am not a trained musician, I often practiced on the foot-pumped organ and sometimes played hymns for the worship services on it. More often a headquarters officer who was an accomplished pianist volunteered as organist on Sundays.

Each chaplain had to decide on his own policy in providing for the spiritual needs of his men. The general rule implied that at no time should he break any rule of his own denomination or violate his own conscience. Before communing worshipers with the bread and wine, I always explained that Lutherans teach that first sins must be confessed, that Christ is really present in a very special way with his body and blood, and that he does forgive us.

Those who believed those doctrines I welcomed to the Lord's Supper. Usually my sermons were based on the lessons appointed for a given Sunday as printed in the Lutheran *Common Service Book;* these were often the same as those appointed by the Roman Catholic and Episcopal Churches. I never attempted to conduct a Roman Catholic or a Mormon or a Buddhist religious rite. I prayed with any soldier who wanted a prayer and answered every question about the Christian faith as honestly as I could, witnessing to my own faith but also explaining how others taught differently.

On Monday morning Headquarters Company served pancakes. Then I washed my dirty clothes. Next I visited the nearby town. Good food, a bath and clean clothing, catching up on sleep, writing letters home, playing cards (many of my comrades played cribbage as well as cards), and talking with the local citizens all had priorities during rest periods. On this day I made three trips to town, one with Colonel Turner.

On Tuesday the battalion moved on foot to a new location. Customarily I marched with the men, now with one company and then with another, for I wanted to get to know as many men of my parish as possible. They differed in a number of ways from the typical GIs [enlisted soldier] of the Fifth Army.[14] It was rare to hear anyone curse or swear. Although highly motivated to make a good record for their racial group, they were easygoing in their relationships with each other, their officers, and the local Italians. Very quickly I became aware that they did not think of me as a haole[15] but as one of them; as a result I quickly forgot that they were in any way Japanese. Unless individuals told me I could not differentiate between the Christians and Buddhists among them.

Wednesday, I visited each company to find out how many persons needed items such as soap from the Red Cross. On a trip into town to check on repairs being made to the colonel's watch, I helped the local watchmaker sell a pistol to a soldier. Even though both the Italians and the GIs made fun of my spoken Italian, I was determined to learn the language. That evening I ate with A Company, where the special treat was an apricot jam sandwich of freshly baked bread.

Afterwards I led an impromptu hymn sing with the boys of A Company. When offered a taste of Vermouth wine, I took a sip and pronounced it terrible. It became my policy to always taste any new alcoholic beverage offered me, and then declare I did not like it. In this way

I avoided being considered prissy and also let it be known that I was not a drinking man.

This week General Ryder gave us a big boost in morale: we received permission to sew the Red Bull shoulder patch of the 34th Division on our uniforms.[16] By the end of the month the War Department sent a memorandum to the Army Ground Forces in the United States praising our battalion for its exceptional performance in its initial combat with the enemy in Italy. Instructions to commanding generals were specific: all AJAs in training should be told of the 100th's record.

The highlight of Thursday was the time I spent in the evening at the command post with Capt. Jack (John A.) Johnson, as he told me story after story about Hawaii. After graduation from Punahou, the Honolulu school for haole kamaaina,[17] Jack attended the University of Hawaii, where he was captain and star of the football team as well as student commandant of the ROTC [Reserve Officer Training Corps] regiment. He was called to federal service from his position as an assistant agriculturalist of the Hawaii Sugar Planters Association.[18] Day after day I was learning how really special all of the soldiers from Hawaii were.

On Friday, another moving day, I was up at 5:15. I hiked all of the fifteen miles save one, which I rode with the division chaplain in order to talk over our mutual concerns. He volunteered the information that the (Pennsylvania) engineers had hated to see me leave them.

On the march our battalion CO (Colonel Turner) scolded me for walking out of column, alongside another soldier and not in single file, for safety reasons. He didn't ask me for my reason for this action; I was trying to get to know more of the men as I moved up the long file of marchers. Usually I carried a full pack and always my Bible and communion set. Though never burdened by a weapon or ammunition, I made sure that the weight I carried equaled that of an infantryman. Often I carried extra blankets for the medics to use, as well as extra rations to share with others. I wore officer's bars, but I also wore the chaplain's silver cross and had a small, white cross painted on the front of my helmet. Always I was addressed as Chaplain and never as Lieutenant; I was as much a doughboy as I was a gentleman.[19]

En route we passed monasteries and convents, Franciscan brothers in their brown habits, army jeeps coming and going, refugees hurrying to the rear. Country folk handed us juicy apples as they waved us toward the front. Ahead in the distance we spotted antiaircraft batteries—our own, of course.

We camped in an apple orchard. When my driver arrived with the jeep and trailer, we set up the wall tent. Because of lack of cover (from the view of the enemy) it was too risky to assemble a group for a hymn sing as I had planned. By seven o'clock I was asleep in my tent.

Saturday morning I typed letter no. 28 to Peggy. We had agreed to number our letters in order to discover if any failed to reach her at home or me overseas. In part it read,

> I just had a fine breakfast (pancakes and coffee, as noted in my diary). Now I'll start getting ready for the services tomorrow. I'm basing the sermon on the Gospel for the Day but will bring in the Sermon on the Mount, showing how Jesus brought principles as opposed to laws: the Sabbath made for man, not man for the Sabbath.
>
> The cigarette supply keeps up with the troops, and now they are given to all free. We get another issue today. I find that mine are good for trading for other things. So far as clothing goes in this outfit, I'm about the best supplied. My bedding roll is kind of heavy, but I'm hanging on to all that I have. If it gets cold, I'll be well taken care of. Is that muffler on the way?

Toward evening of this same day I typed another letter home; this one was on the stationery supplied by the Service Commission of the National Lutheran Council. One of our artists had made a three-by-four-inch woodblock, which he then printed on the letterheads I supplied him. It portrayed a helmeted, barefoot AJA wearing a lei around his neck and a grass skirt over his uniform and carrying a large Santa Claus sack with "One Puka Puka" printed on it. At the bottom were the words "Mele Xmas." This cartoon took up the top half of the sheet. Below it I had written this explanation for my wife.

> The above is our Christmas greeting. You can see the three dictators (Hitler, Mussolini, and Tojo) in the bag. "Puka" is Hawaiian for "hole" or "zero." In childhood, Hawaiians go barefoot, so the soldier likewise. And he greets you, saying, "Merry Christmas." Our men, however, speak good English and always wear shoes. Many are university men.

On the back of the sheet I continued my message home.

> Today I rode a bit on a motorcycle; don't worry I take things easy. Today a village priest talked with me and invited me to spend the night at his place. I had to refuse. Then he invited me for dinner on the morrow, but I don't think that will be possible either. It was nice of him.

When orders were received this Saturday to move closer to the front the next day, our battalion worship was held that Saturday evening. Both the commanding officer and the second in command attended. Again the turnout was good.

Sunday morning we advanced on foot about eight miles, crossing the Volturno River on a pontoon bridge. Dead horses (not all German transportation was motorized) lay here and there. For the first time I saw our men using minesweepers. The bells of Italian villages were calling the faithful to Mass. Up on a hill, our mess crews had prepared a hot meal. I met an Italian farmer who as a young man had lived in Schenectady, N.Y.

After dark the battalion moved to a new position; this time I rode in my jeep. For the first time I heard artillery shells flying overhead both ways. I recorded in my diary that I was not particularly worried. It rained, and my blankets got a bit wet.

During the night two men of D Company, the heavy weapons company, were killed by shell fragments. By field telephone I contacted the regimental GRO; when he came I helped him load the bodies for transportation to an American military cemetery for proper burial by a rear-echelon chaplain.

For breakfast I ate K rations [lightweight packaged rations], which came in a cardboard box, waxed to make it water proof; I found it more palatable than the canned C rations. At noon I had more of the same menu. By tearing the waxed cardboard into strips and burning them, enough heat resulted to warm a canteen cup of water in which the canned meat of the rations had been placed. Then the warm water was used to dissolve the powdered coffee for drinking. In the afternoon, when our unit moved forward, I accompanied Headquarters Company. I would long remember this Monday, for we were moving into combat.

No one had ever instructed me on my specific duties when the fighting began, not even with what part of the battalion I was to associate myself. The only advice given to me was that of an older padre tagging behind his men as they passed through our sector. He stopped in front of me to catch his breath.

"Chaplain, I'm getting too old for this kind of life," he said. I guessed that he might be approaching the age of forty. "I just can't keep up with the boys. I'll have to ask to be assigned to something other than the infantry."

"You've seen a lot of action, haven't you?" I asked. "From your experience, tell me where a chaplain should be when the shooting starts."

"Well, you have three choices," he answered tiredly. "You can stay at the motor pool with the vehicles. Or you can attach yourself to the commanding officer's staff. Or you can stick close to the medics at the battalion aid station." Without further comment he shuffled off to catch up with his infantrymen.

One of his suggestions I dismissed immediately: I would not remain at the motor pool, for such conduct would look like cowardice. I decided to try out his recommendation to move with the battalion command post.

Thus, when on this memorable Monday our command group moved out after dark, I took a place in the line of march about eight spaces back of the colonel. At first we simply walked ahead on a cobblestone lane. When a machine gun began to chatter in front of us, everyone hit the dirt, and a whisper was passed from man to man, "Dig in, dig in." With some difficulty I got my trench shovel out of its sheath on my web belt and tried to burrow into the earth, but the cobblestones were immovable. Quickly, I grasped the handle, turned the scoop sideways in order to use it as a pick, and began swinging the tool with all my strength against the pavement. The clang of metal against stone rang out into the night.

"Who's making all that noise back there?" demanded the colonel from up front, his angry whisper sounding like a shout to me.

"It's the chaplain," whispered someone in reply.

"Tell him to stop his racket," commanded the CO urgently. A deathly silence followed. No machine-gun chatter, no whispering, no sound of any kind of movement.

When the column moved forward again in the darkness, I quietly and gradually allowed others to pass until I was well out of earshot of Colonel Turner. We walked along the river; there was no enemy opposition. We were ordered to dig ourselves slit trenches close to a hill, but before my hole was very deep, we were ordered into a ravine and began to dig in there. After a few scoops of dirt, I noticed an unpleasant odor. I continued until I realized that I was uncovering a German latrine. I moved across the road and began another foxhole, my fourth attempt of the night. I got so tired that I stopped digging, lay down in the shallow trench, and promptly fell asleep. I was rudely awakened early in the morning when some shells of a German barrage began falling close by.

I decided that I would feel better if I shaved. Taking the liner out of my helmet, I used the metal shell for washing and shaving. A kindly lieu-tenant shared his K rations with me. I was still more or less attached to the CO's staff but not within his sight. I moved into a safe gully at the side of the road and fell asleep again. At noon, I pulled my Bible from my pack and read a chapter from the book of Exodus.

Peggy and I had agreed to read a chapter of scripture daily, going straight through the Bible books and thus reading the same verses even though we were separated by thousands of miles. We even tried to coor-dinate the time, allowing for the six-hour difference between Italy and home. For lunch I ate a can of cold beans (C rations), supplementing it with tasty grapes from a nearby vineyard. The snores of the sleeping staff officers reassured me that all was well with the war. Probably we would move again at night.[20] It was prudent to get rest while it was possible. At dusk I ventured forth to locate the battalion aid station; there I got the medics to promise to keep a fine-looking German box for me to use to store hymnals. The afternoon I had spent watching Nazi planes attack-ing a nearby town.

Shortly after dusk, battalion headquarters moved along the Volturno River. Again I was in my self-appointed spot near our CO but not within sight of him. At midnight, after removing our socks and pants, we waded across the river. What a way to be captured had the enemy coun-terattacked during our crossing! On the far bank I dried my feet and legs with a towel out of my pack. We filed into a nut orchard and dug in. This time I completed a deep hole, not for safety but to get warm, for it was a cold night. Capt. Jack Johnson came along and, without digging a hole, lay down without so much as a blanket and promptly fell asleep. What a man!

On Wednesday I had a new experience: I talked with a frightened soldier. At noon in a letter to my wife I wrote,

> As I see Italian families evacuating and returning, I am so thankful that you and our babies need not go through the like; and also that Nazareth will not become the shambles some Italian towns have become. In mod-ern warfare the civilian population in battle areas suffers most of all—even more than the soldiers themselves.

About seven p.m., the 100th set out on a mission, met machine-gun fire, advanced under it, and then dug in. I happened to be at the end of the headquarters file, which was at the tail end of the line companies and just in front of the medical detachment. When I saw that the medics needed help in evacuating the wounded, I volunteered as a litter bearer and for the first time came under enemy fire. It suddenly dawned on me that I had discovered the proper spot for the chaplain to be. From this night on, most of my time in combat was spent with the medics: in the forward aid station, forward of the aid station acting as a litter bearer, or ranging out with Captain Kometani looking for the wounded.

On this occasion, Kome and I took the same route the attack company had taken. As we cautiously groped our way through a barnyard, the kitchen door of the farmhouse opened and a ray of light caught us in its beam. We were startled. There stood an aged Italian woman, smiling and rattling away in Italian as if she were welcoming us as we made a social call.

We proceeded ahead until we caught up with the battalion staff. We hunkered down with the group and listened as the officers discussed what the next step of the pinned-down advance should be. A company lieutenant was reporting that after his men had dug in, the several who crawled ahead to locate the enemy machine-gun nests had been killed; he advised the colonel that it was impossible to advance any farther.

I was astounded that as he concluded the report, he pulled out a cigarette, struck a match, and lit the smoke. He had taken some precautions: he was squatting, he cupped his hands around the flame, and he was turned away from the front lines. That he would take such a chance of being spotted by the enemy appalled me. When I reprimanded him, he lamely excused himself by saying he was so upset he had to have his pacifier.[21]

Kome decided that we two should advance farther. We soon discovered that the battle was not far ahead; we fell flat and, with Kome in the lead, began to squirm toward our troops. A burst of machine-gun fire barely cleared our prostrate bodies.

"Kome, get your backside down," I whispered. "You'll be hit."

"I can't get it any closer to the ground," he whispered back.

Then I realized that since he was stouter than I, he was in greater danger. In fact, he formed a good protection from the bullets so far as I was concerned. We kept looking ahead, but we slowly inched back out of the range of the firing. I had learned a lesson: when there is any kind of firing going on, a noncombatant should stay under cover unless he is taking care of the wounded or carrying a casualty on a stretcher.

Before dawn our companies were withdrawn from the battle. The higher brass had decided to bypass the heavily fortified section our battalion had failed to capture. I assisted in bringing the wounded to the house where our battalion surgeons treated their wounds and from which ambulances transported them to a field hospital.

Thursday, October 21, I spent in the vicinity of the battalion aid. Two soldiers near me were hit by shrapnel; I ran and brought one of our doctors, who performed a tracheotomy on the one, but he died before evening. Artillery shells fell near our position, some of them our own.

That night several of us slept on beds on the second floor of an Italian house. Shortly after I fell asleep, a shell exploded very close to our quarters. Kome shouted for me to get out of the building, but I would not leave until I had found my shoes, my helmet, and my glasses. I had taken them off before retiring and in the darkness—and the excitement of awakening under danger—I could not locate them. The four of us calmed down, boiled some chicken and vegetables, ate, and went back to sleep. Thereafter, I followed a set procedure about bedding down: glasses inside my right shoe and shoes nestled up against my helmet. In the morning we joined the battalion in bivouac on the outskirts of Alife.

On Friday morning, Captain Kometani and I returned to the battlefield with some of the medics to tag the bodies of the dead. I telephoned the regimental headquarters for vehicles to transfer the corpses for proper burial. One of the surgeons, Capt. Isaac Kawasaki, wandered away from the group, and Kome and I spent an hour and a half looking for him. Many of our dead lay directly in front of the Nazi machine-gun pits, some of them very close to the nests. It was not difficult to see why the enemy had been able to stop our attack: their pits were deep and their lines of fire covered every section of the almost level terrain. Even so, grenades tossed by the Americans had been partially effective; in one emplacement we found three German corpses.

During the fighting the night before, word had come to the aid station that one of the company aid men, easily identified by his Red Cross brassard, had been shot and killed by the enemy. We had also heard how one complaining American had vowed, "We'll get one of their aid men, too!" We did indeed come across a dead German wearing a Red Cross armband.

In the afternoon only my driver, Toshio Yoneyama, and I remained at work locating corpses and transporting them two at a time on stretchers on top of my jeep, down a country lane to a collecting point in a small village. This was an extremely distasteful task for my assistant. He drove with one eye on the bodies as if expecting them to suddenly rise up and do him harm. Nothing I said allayed his fears.

At dusk we made our last transit of the area to make sure we had completed our job. For some reason "Yone" turned off the jeep engine, and in the silence I thought I heard someone calling off in the distance. I was sure we were the only Americans in the vicinity, and I was certain that there were no Americans directly ahead of us toward the enemy's new positions. For my helper, the unknown voice was the final straw to break his failing courage; he wanted the two of us to get out of there fast. He was not at all inclined to agree with me that someone was calling out for help. As I stood listening in order to locate the source of the call, he insisted that this was some kind of Nazi trick.

I heard the human voice again. I ordered Yone to wait near the jeep; I walked toward the sound, yelling that I was a chaplain and that whoever was shouting should identify himself. Crossing a small knoll, I saw someone lying on the ground, but the distance was too great to distinguish friend from foe. I went no closer until the man answered my questions about his name, serial number, and outfit. He was, indeed, a wounded Caucasian infantryman.

When I knelt by his side, I realized that he was disoriented. He had no idea how long he had been lying there, drifting in and out of consciousness. The upper bone of one leg was fractured. He was hungry. He had drunk all his canteen water. I made splints from some saplings growing nearby and bandaged them to his leg. I went back over the knoll and roared for Yone to bring the jeep. We put the GI on a litter and lifted him to lie across the rear of the vehicle.

By the time we got off the field and to the lane, it was dark. On our last trip out to the battle area we had seen a number of our units, including one of tanks, bivouacking for the night along the lane. Now we realized that we would be approaching them in the dark from enemy territory. The jeep did not have regular headlights, only cat's eyes, which served solely for warning anyone directly in front that an army truck was coming. I walked several paces ahead of our jeep so that the noise of the motor would not interfere with the words I kept calling out: "Somebody challenge me! I'm an American chaplain bringing back a wounded soldier! Somebody challenge me!"

Several times I was challenged by posted guards, recognized, and passed through. What a relief it was to deliver our wounded buddy to the medical unit in the village! He was from one of the battalions of the regiment to which the 100th was assigned.

The next day, uncertain that all of our KIAs [killed in action] had been removed from the battlefield, I took a detail back to the area and

found too many for our crew to move. We also came upon seven German dead. I instructed my men to assemble the corpses and properly
identify them so that the regimental GRO could complete the task.
Meanwhile, our battalion had again been committed to action, and I felt
strongly that my chief responsibility was to the living rather than the
dead. I was irked that one of the detail wandered off and did not return
for an hour—irked because he delayed my return to the battalion.

In less than a month, I felt that I had become an essential part of the
One Puka Puka.[22] Already I was intensely proud of being associated
with these sunburned soldiers from Hawaii. Even though I had never
visited their sunny isles in the Pacific, I had a feeling for their aloha spirit
and their humorous pidgin. I felt that all the people in the United States
ought to get to really know and appreciate their history.

Notes

1. Farrant L. Turner (1896–1959) was a former executive for Lewers and Cooke, a
once large hardware store in Honolulu, as well as a lieutenant colonel in the Territorial
Guard. After the war, he was appointed secretary of state of Hawaii during the Eisenhower administration.

2. James W. Lovell (1907–2001) was originally from Nebraska and came to Hawaii
as a young teacher. He was well known to many young AJAs because of his role as a
coach at high schools such as Roosevelt and McKinley, which had large AJA populations.
He was severely wounded at the battle of Cassino. After the war he returned to Hawaii
and began work as the manager of the lumber department at Lewers and Cooke. He rose
from that position to become president of the company. Later he became president of
Mid-Pacific Airlines.

3. Katsumi Kometani (1907–1979) had a successful dental practice after the war. He
was also chairman of the Board of Education and owned a Japanese semi-pro baseball
team in Honolulu.

4. Pronounced "koh-mee"; most of the enlisted men called him "Doc."

5. Blend of English, Chinese, Japanese, and Hawaiian used as a mixed language
among different ethnic groups on the sugar plantations of Hawaii.

6. Salerno, Italy, was chosen as the principal landing beach site for the first large-
scale invasion of Europe by Allied forces, as Salerno was considered the most direct route
to Naples, which would afford the Allies a resupply port on their advance to Rome.
Between September 3–9, 1943, the British Eighth and American Fifth Army troops
began landing. They were faced by the German 16th Panzer Division and the 79th Panzer
Grenadier Regiment. The Germans numbered 135,000 men and nearly broke the
Allied assault on the fourth day of the battle. Gen. Mark Clark, the head of the Fifth
Army, later would describe the Salerno landing as a "near disaster." On September 28,
the Allied troops broke through German lines and took Naples.

7. World War II acronym for a glitch, as in "Situation Normal—All Fouled [euphe-
mism] Up."

8. Ritual sacrament in which Christians receive bread and wine as the Body and Blood of Jesus; also called the Eucharist and the Lord's Supper.

9. Hawaiian word meaning "born in Hawaii."

10. Second-generation Japanese Americans; American-born children of Japanese immigrants.

11. Jack Mizuha (1913–1986) later became a Hawaii Supreme Court justice.

12. A shallow dish on which bread is laid at the celebration of the Eucharist.

13. Clothing worn by a minister during services: an ankle-length, long-sleeved, black robe beneath a shorter, white garment with wide sleeves.

14. The Fifth Army was made up of the 36th Division, the 34th Division, of which the 100th Battalion was part, the 45th Division, the 82nd Airborne, as well as a ranger and commando force. The leader of the Fifth Army was Gen. Mark Clark.

15. Hawaiian word used to refer to Caucasians, which can be used in a derogatory way.

16. This was considered significant as the 34th Division, made up largely of National Guard troops from Missouri and other states in the Midwest, had distinguished itself in battles in Tunisia before the invasion of Italy.

17. An elite private school in Honolulu that was initially for missionary children.

18. The Hawaiian Sugar Planters Association represented the interests of the sugar industry in Hawaii. During World War II it was the dominant economic, social, and political influence on the civilian population of the Islands.

19. The term "doughboy" was coined in World War I to refer to an infantryman; "gentleman" refers to an officer.

20. The Germans had fortified the mountain ridges and the men of the 100th were under constant observation. The only safe way to avoid accurate bombardment was at night.

21. The men were suffering a high casualty rate. They smoked to deal with the stress.

22. As "puka" means "hole" in Hawaiian, the number 100 was described as a 1 followed by two holes.

TWO

The Making of the 100th

O N **DECEMBER 7, 1941,** 158,000 persons of Japanese ancestry lived in the Hawaiian Islands[1] and 127,000 in the continental United States. The Japanese attack on Pearl Harbor horrified not just a majority of these people but almost every one of them, whether they had emigrated from Japan or had been born American citizens. Few, if any, could foresee how profoundly their lives would be changed as a consequence of this single day in history. The AJAs,[2] both of Hawaii and the Mainland, became suspect of disloyalty by many other Americans, some in high positions in the government.

However, the treatment of the ethnic Japanese in the Territory of Hawaii differed radically from that administered to their counterparts in the States, where most of them lived on the West Coast. Most residents of Hawaii accepted their AJA neighbors as loyal subjects of the country in which they lived, and both civilian and military leaders knew how much the economy of Hawaii depended upon this largest of the racial groups there.[3]

Such was not the case with the very vocal special interest organizations, primarily in California, who had long sought to expel all Orientals from their society. They whipped up antagonism against all the Issei (Japanese immigrants) and Nisei (American-born children of Japanese immigrants), drowning out the voices of a small minority who called for fair treatment under the law.

On the day Pearl Harbor was attacked, more than fifteen hundred Nisei were serving in the army in Hawaii, most of them in the two infantry regiments of the National Guard,[4] which had become a part of the regular army in 1940. In December of 1940, selective service boards began to process inductees; in the twelve months before the war began, of the three thousand called up, about fifteen hundred were Nisei, many of them volunteers. In addition, AJA students had joined ROTC units of Oahu schools and of the University of Hawaii. After the Japanese bombed Pearl Harbor, infantrymen were posted on the beaches to repel the expected invasion; many of these defenders were Nisei.

Before long, questions were raised in Honolulu about the advisability of having in the U.S. Army men who looked like our Pacific enemies. In particular, navy brass protested the presence of AJAs. In January of 1942, the 317 Nisei soldiers of the Hawaii Territorial Guard were discharged without explanation. Some of these dischargees petitioned the military governor to accept their services in whatever way he saw fit to use them; within a month 150 of them, almost all University of Hawaii graduates, became a labor contingent under the Army Corps of Engineers.

By the evening of the day after the attack on Pearl Harbor, 370 Japanese had been arrested because they were Buddhist or Shinto priests, or Japanese-language school officials, or commercial fishermen, or Kibei (American-born Japanese who had spent some time in Japan attending school), not because of any acts of sabotage or disloyalty.[5] Eventually only 981 aliens and citizens of Japanese background were sent to the Mainland for relocation as under suspicion, but not for committing any illegal acts. The great majority of the persons of Japanese ancestry in the Territory (40,000 of them were aliens) remained there and, like other Americans, threw all their resources into the national effort against a common enemy. Rumors notwithstanding, not one single act of sabotage was ever performed by any Japanese American in Hawaii. Indeed, after long investigation on the Mainland, the verdict was the same there: no act of sabotage by any AJA on the West Coast.

Induction of Nisei was discontinued by the end of March, both in the Islands and on the Mainland. During April, troop replacements (from the West Coast) displaced the AJAs who had been guarding Hawaii. In May, the War Department ordered the formation of an all-Nisei battalion from Hawaii to be transferred to the continental United States.

Staffing of this segregated unit was left in the hands of the Hawaiian Department of the Army. The commanding officer of the infantry regiment in which the AJAs were assembled recommended an officer of his choice as the CO of the new battalion. His executive officer, Lt. Col. Farrant L. Turner, objected and insisted that he wanted the position. The chief of staff had the final say; he appointed Turner, who then selected James A. Lovell as his plans and training officer and executive officer.

This procedure indicates Turner's prestige in Hawaii, even in military matters, and also his aggressiveness in questions about which he had strong convictions.

All the officers of the newly designated Hawaiian Provisional Battalion were from Hawaii, both haoles and AJAs. Thus, even on the surface, it appeared to be a homogenous contingent. Many observers have written about the uniqueness of the Paradise of the Pacific: its aloha spirit, its pidgin speech, its easygoing pace of living—all contributed to an overall homogeneity. A special segment of this close-knit community now became Hawaii's own fighting brigade, and this microcosm was even more homogenous than the larger group from which it came.

It was almost entirely Japanese but limited to second-generation men.[6] (The first immigrants from Japan were young, male contract workers, and none came before 1885.) The men were all young and with similar experiences, backgrounds, and schooling. The Caucasian officers were men who had worked closely with the Japanese community.

Less obvious factors made this battalion distinctive. The enlisted men's average score on army intelligence tests was 103, only seven points below the minimum needed to enter officer candidate school. Their average age in 1942 was twenty-four years, older than normal for the infantry. About 85 percent had attended Japanese-language school. Only a few had ever traveled outside the Islands. Almost all were sports minded, and most of them actively participated in sports. Ancestrally they were predominately from the farmer caste of old Japan and imbued with something very much like the American Protestant work ethic. The Caucasian officers had a gut feeling about the uniqueness of their men.

Their homogeneity did not make them any less individuals. Although most were small of stature (average five-feet-four inches), some were tall and robust. Two percent had studied in Japan. Some were college graduates, but a few spoke only stumbling English. Some were Buddhists, some Christians, some Mormons, some uncommitted.

One characteristically Japanese trait marked just about every one of these soldiers: they clearly understood the concept *"on"* and intended to carry out its application in their role in the army. U.S. Senator Daniel K. Inouye, a decorated Nisei veteran of the 442nd Regimental Combat Team, in his autobiography *Journey to Washington,* explains that his father sent him off as a soldier by reminding him that he must prove himself as a real American by making every possible sacrifice for the welfare of his country, the United States, because the Inouyes had great *on* for America. Inouye writes, "*On* is at the very heart of Japanese culture. *On* requires that when one man is aided by another he incurs a debt that is never canceled, one that must be repaid at every opportunity without stint or reservation" (Inouye, 85).

Even though the laws of the United States prevented alien Japanese from becoming citizens no matter how long they had lived here or how well they had served this country, these alien parents taught their American-born-citizen sons that they had a moral obligation to fight for their native land. The sons were resolved to make a record as soldiers that would convince all Americans that they were, in fact, as American as others, and that, therefore, their brothers and sisters, parents, and children should be fully accepted without any shadow of suspicion as to where their loyalties lay.

On June 5, 1942, these 1,432 infantrymen (from whom all weapons had been taken!) sailed on the SS *Maui* from Honolulu, headed for the West Coast of the Mainland. Most had received no leave to bid their families good-bye; many had no idea what might happen to them in the States. On docking at Oakland, California, the unit was designated the "100th Infantry Battalion." Three troop trains taking different routes carried the men eastward. Many of them wondered if their folks might soon be relocated to the Mainland, too, in internment camps.[7]

The troop trains carrying the AJAs of Hawaii from Oakland arrived at Camp McCoy, Wisconsin. On June 13, 1942, a Second Army Headquarters officer came to impress upon CO Turner that his unit, now designated a "separate" battalion, had to be carefully trained and their morale kept high.

The Second Army's June 21 report to Washington of the inspection of the 100th Infantry Battalion (Separate) predicted that the all-Nisei contingent could be committed to a "highly efficient state of combat training" very quickly. In effect, this was the unit's first of many official recommendations.

The men were in high spirits, with every individual bent on doing his very best so that he would be a vital part of the best combat outfit in the U.S. Army. Because the eyes of the country were upon them, all wanted to be better-than-average soldiers. They also carefully cultivated good relationships with the haoles in the nearby towns. They marched in parades; they fielded a crack baseball team with a Hawaiian troop of singers and dancers to accompany it; they made friends everywhere. At first some AJAs passed themselves off as Hawaiians, but Turner threatened to punish any who did not introduce themselves as Americans of Japanese ancestry.

When asked if they would "fight the Japs," they replied without hesitation, "Yes!" They pointed out that they had family and friends to avenge since most of the civilians killed in the attack on Pearl Harbor were of Japanese descent.

As a "separate" battalion, the 100ᵗʰ had to organize itself to function without the support normally provided by a larger regimental unit. Instead of three rifle companies, it had five: Able (A), Baker (B), Charlie (C), Easy (E), Fox (F), and the customary heavy weapons company, Dog (D). It maintained its own medical section, a service section, a transportation platoon, and an antitank platoon. Additional officers were needed; Turner asked for twelve more lieutenants, "former residents of Hawaii if possible." Turner briefed each new arrival. When one learned that he had been assigned to an all-AJA force, he sputtered, "My God, I didn't know I was getting into this!"

"Your name is Schemel, isn't it?" Turner asked.

"Yes, sir."

"I see that your first name is Kurt. Born in Germany?"

"Yes, sir, in Berlin. I see what you're getting at, sir. If you'll have me, I'll be glad to join this outfit" (Murphy, 75–76).

Another lieutenant, reporting from Officer Candidate School (OCS), was greeted with the words, "Young Oak Kim! A mistake has been made. I'll see that you are reassigned to another unit." Turner recognized the name as Korean and assumed that since many of Korean ancestry hated the Japanese for occupying their homeland, a Korean American would not want to work with any men of Japanese descent.

"No, sir, I want to serve with this outfit," responded the young looie [lieutenant]. The colonel looked the young officer over and decided he could use such a fellow.

When six of the new officers, overage in grade, were promoted to the rank of captain, AJA lieutenants with longer service in the 100ᵗʰ resented taking orders from them. After they discovered that the older men were better qualified, they gracefully dismissed their resentment. Not until much later did they learn that Turner was obeying an order that no AJA might lead a rifle company. He was quietly waiting for the time when a Nisei would be the best qualified; at that time he would appoint his own man and then argue with his superiors that they were wrong. Such an action was typical of the "Old Man."

Colonel Turner constantly boosted the morale of men and officers by confiding in them: news sessions, pep rallies, lectures, scoldings, commendations, fatherly advice, orders, and explanations. He forbade the use of Japanese, explaining that to show their Americanism, they must use English or pidgin. He abounded in self-confidence, was accustomed in civilian life to dealing with business executives, had associated in Hawaii with high-ranking military officers on a social basis, and was never intimidated by regular army brass. He considered his boys first-class citizens and first-class soldiers; he would not allow anyone to treat them otherwise, nor would he permit them to act otherwise. At Camp McCoy, everyone came to feel that he was an important part of a close-knit team.

In December, personnel from the Military Intelligence Service Language School (MISLS), Camp Savage, Minnesota, visited the battalion and selected sixty-seven men who were reasonably fluent in Japanese. These were the first Hawaiian AJAs to join Mainland Nisei and Kibei at the school. By the end of the war, some five thousand AJAs would serve as interpreters, interrogators, translators, and cave flushers, many also doubling as infantrymen with front-line troops in the Pacific. General Willoughby, MacArthur's chief of intelligence, credited the work of these Yankee samurai as shortening the war with Japan by two years.

On a December day with the temperature at sixteen degrees below zero, a number of generals observed the battalion in action. On the last day of 1942, orders came to move south to Camp Shelby, Mississippi. This was good news for men reared in Hawaiian sunshine. They were happy to be finished with winter training, sleeping outdoors one night each week in November and December; they had not looked forward to the seven consecutive outdoor nights planned for January.

On January 1, 1943, Chief of Staff Gen. George C. Marshall, with the consent of Secretary of War Stimson, approved the formation of an all-Nisei combat team in addition to the 100th Battalion. For several months a group of officials had been urging this action. The implementation of this decision would radically alter the government's policy toward AJAs.

Induction of Japanese Americans in the days immediately after the Pearl Harbor attack had been left to the discretion of local draft boards. On March 30, 1942, an order of the War Department had discontinued the induction of all Nisei on the West Coast. On June 17, the department had announced that it would no longer accept anyone of Japanese descent, regardless of citizenship, except for special cases. On September 14, the Selective Service had reclassified all registrants of Japanese ancestry as IV-C, the status of enemy aliens! Some Nisei citizens in the relocation camps had begun to fear that the prediction of some Issei that even American citizens of Japanese descent would be expatriated to Japan might, after all, become fact. Hopefully, the new proposal for the creation of the Nisei Regimental Combat Team signaled fairer treatment of AJAs.

The new unit would be made up of volunteers, for the government recognized the injustice of imposing a military draft on persons who were locked up in relocation camps. The excellent record of the 100th Battalion in training and of the Nisei in the intelligence language school had not gone unnoticed. Increasing numbers of Americans believed that most Nisei were loyal. Furthermore, the project was a good propaganda device.

In the relocation camps on the Mainland, 1,208 Nisei volunteered for the army out of an estimated 10,000 eligible (3,000 had been expected). In Hawaii, where AJAs had not been interned in relocation centers, the call for Nisei volunteers was answered by 10,000, one-third of all those of draft age; approximately 2,500 were inducted to fill the quota. Additional AJAs were permitted to volunteer from noncombat units in the Islands. In early April, 2,855 enlisted men and 25 officers sailed for the Mainland, arriving at Camp Shelby on April 13.[8] These new AJA recruits from Hawaii, along with Nisei from the Mainland, formed the newly created 442nd Regimental Combat Team, which, though it trained at Camp Shelby alongside the 100th Battalion for four months, was not merged with the 100th at this time.

In Mississippi, early in January of 1943, the 100th had been attached to the 85th Division for training and within two weeks drew favorable mention from the division's commander. Early in March, eleven OCS graduates joined the outfit, among them George H. Grandstaff. During the D-Series Maneuvers in March, the battalion was attached now to one regiment and then to another.

The Hawaiian AJAs were shocked by the color-line practices they saw in the South, even though they themselves were treated as whites. They did not attempt to become a part of the community as they had in Wisconsin. They did, however, resolve to do their fighting in combat for the America of the North, not for the America of the South.

In April, the two-month-long war games began for them at the immense Louisiana Maneuver Area: chiggers, ticks, heat, poisonous coral snakes and water moccasins, hiking (once twenty-five miles in one day), a one-quart limit of water on some days.

On June 13, at Camp Claiborne, Louisiana, they began two days of intensive firing of all weapons. When they returned to Shelby on June 16, they were considered prepared for overseas duty. On July 20, the 100th Battalion received its colors with the motto "Remember Pearl Harbor." On August 11, the unit departed for Camp Kilmer, New Jersey. On August 21, at Staten Island the contingent from Hawaii boarded the *James Parker* and set sail as part of a large convoy destined for North Africa.

GIs of other units shared the crowded transport with the 100th personnel. The normal activities of soldiers during forced inactivity occupied the twelve days at sea: bull sessions, singing, card games, crap shooting, movies. Twelve received Christian baptism. On this voyage, all carried their weapons, along with packs and two barracks bags. When an artillery general asked to borrow the 100th's arms for his unarmed battalion in the case of an aerial attack, Turner answered that his boys would do any shooting that became necessary. The general acquiesced. But no Nazi planes were seen.

After landing at Oran, the contingent camped several miles from the port at "Goat Hill." The hot winds, dust, sand fleas, and strongly chlorinated alkaline water made life unpleasant. Soon the men were buying wine that was locally produced in preference to drinking the tainted water.

Turner soon learned that his unit was slated to become part of the 34th Division, a National Guard outfit that had performed exceptionally well in the recently completed North African campaign. Its commander, Maj. Gen. Charles W. Ryder, assembled the sixty commissioned and forty noncommissioned officers and warned them that soon they would see combat and many buddies would be killed and wounded. He promised that he would expect no more and no less from the 100th than from any other of the division's battalions. The AJAs were replacing the 2nd Battalion of the 133rd Regiment, which had been detached to guard General Eisenhower's headquarters in Algiers.

Veterans of the division immediately began training all the AJA companies in the lessons the 34th had learned while fighting the enemy in the Tunisian campaign. On September 19, the regiment, with the 100th attached, shipped out, with Italy as its destination. Instead of heading for Naples as originally planned, the convoy proceeded to Salerno (Naples

The 100th Bn landed at Salerno on September 22, 1943. Chaplain Yost joined the battalion near San Martino a few miles southwest of Benevento on October 5. Through the months of September and October, as the 100th moved north toward the Volturno River, they suffered their first heavy casualties. After crossing the Volturno and engaging in grueling fighting in the hills during November, they rested nineteen days at Alife during December. After Christmas, Yost was given five days' leave in Naples.

was still in German possession). The AJAs, on board the SS *Frederick Funston,* climbed down into landing barges and then hiked six miles inland, except for E and F Companies, which were assigned to guard duty near the beach, the first at an ammunition dump and the second at a temporary airstrip. This was on September 22.

The next day the Allied troops advanced out of the beach area. On September 25, when the 34th Division joined in the pursuit of the retreating enemy, the 100th, with the 133rd Regiment, moved twenty-five miles east by truck. At this time, officers of all the components of the Fifth Army received this communiqué.

> There has recently arrived in this theater a battalion of American soldiers of Japanese ancestry. These troops take particular pride in their American origin. Your command should be so informed in order that during the stress and confusion of combat, cases of mistaken identity may be avoided. (Murphy, 125)

The next night the 100th, in vehicles, moved 106 miles, past Lioni, and camped in the mud. On September 27, the GIs waded a river (the bridge had been blown up) and bivouacked in the rain near Montemarano. The next morning a B Company squad took the 100th's first prisoner, who thought his captors were Chinese. Here, too, the first casualty was suffered when a jeep ran over a land mine from which a fragment gave a squad leader a slight face wound.

On September 29, B Company, the advance guard of the battalion, passed through the village of Castelvetere on foot, moving toward Chiusano. Seconds after the two lead scouts rounded a turn in the road, one of them turned around and raised his rifle horizontally above his head, the signal that he had sighted the enemy.

Almost immediately, the Jerries [Germans], who had zeroed in on the bend in the road, laid down a barrage of machine gun, mortar, and artillery fire. Squad leader Sgt. Shigeo (Joe) Takata shouted, "It's the first time so I'm going first," and walked forward, firing his automatic rifle at a machine-gun nest he had spotted. Shrapnel hit him in the head, but before dying he told a buddy who had crawled up to him where the emplacement was. Before the enemy positions were taken, another soldier, Keichi Tanaka, was killed and seven others wounded. Thus at about ten a.m. on this day, the One Puka Puka actually contacted the enemy. Sergeant Takata was awarded the DSC (Distinguished Service Cross) posthumously.

At noon, a blown-out bridge slowed down the advance; the Germans shelled the area, but no casualties were suffered. The retreat pattern of the enemy became clear: motorized infantry and self-propelled cannon covered the orderly withdrawal of the main force northward. The rear guard stopped the American advance at easily defended locations, and then the foot soldiers ran to troop carriers to be speeded to the next defensive position.[9] Roads and areas around demolished bridges were heavily mined, and enemy artillery concentrated on both roads and bridge sites.

In the afternoon, the 100th was ordered to move off the road and to cross fields in order to cut off the enemy on a highway leading north out of Chiusano. Enemy shells rained down on them, hitting a number of the GIs, but by seven p.m., men of the 100th were on the high ground, thus cutting off any use of the designated road. Leaving A Company on the spot, the rest of the battalion set out in the dark for Montefalcione, three miles away, traveling most of the way cross-country through gardens and vineyards. By midnight the objective was reached without encountering any of the enemy. In the morning the 1st Battalion passed through, allowing the AJAs to rest in the little town.

On October 1, the Nisei moved on to Montemileto and the next day, in the rain and mud, continued north to San Giorgio, thus protecting the regiment's right flank. That night the battalion continued on foot toward Benevento, passing through the outskirts of the town in single file at one a.m., to reach higher ground and dig into positions to provide supporting fire when another battalion of the regiment crossed the Calore River. On October 4, the 45th Infantry Division pushed through, and the 34th moved into assembly areas near San Martino.

It was here that I joined the Hawaiian Japanese Americans. Though at the time I did not realize it, this was the assignment that made possible for me the kind of service I had hoped to be called to when I volunteered to become an army chaplain late in 1942.

Notes

1. Japanese Americans, numbering approximately 160,000, made up nearly 40 percent of the population of Hawaii prior to World War II; 25 percent of the Japanese American population (about 40,000) were foreign-born nationals.

2. The background information in this chapter about Americans of Japanese ancestry and the formation of the 100th Battalion is taken primarily from Murphy 1954.

3. They played dominant roles in agricultural labor, fishing, and the construction industry. Although widely discriminated against in civil service positions, they played an important role in the Territorial Department of Education.

4. The 298th and 299th Hawaii Territorial National Guard.

5. Some Japanese community and business leaders were also arrested.

6. There were a few men from other ethnic groups, including native Hawaiian.

7. One hundred twenty-thousand Japanese Americans on the West Coast, including those who were U.S. citizens, had been forcibly relocated to ten internment camps in other parts of the United States. In the relocation centers, surrounded by barbed wire and armed guards, they were incarcerated in very substandard conditions solely because of their Japanese ancestry, not because of any criminal acts.

8. Murphy, 111–112.

9. The German defense was organized by Field Marshall Albert Kesselring. The Germans had the advantage of being on high, rocky ground looking down on the Allied advance from concrete bunkers.

THREE

From Parson to Chaplain

W**HEN WAR** was declared after the attack on Pearl Harbor, I felt no inclination to become personally involved. No one in my family had any connection with the military, and it had no appeal for me. A graduate of The Lutheran Theological Seminary at Philadelphia, I had been called to the pastorate of a rural, two-congregation parish near Bethlehem, Pennsylvania, in September 1940, and in September of 1941, I married and settled down to what I hoped would be a life in one spot.

In September of 1942, our first child, Monica, was born.[1] I intended to keep busy as a good pastor, a good husband, and a good father. Then the world conflict began to impinge upon our comfortable world: more and more of the young men of the parish were entering the armed forces, and a number of older pastors were answering the call to fill the quota of Lutheran clergymen needed in the army and the navy. My conscience began to bother me; I was unable to shake off the growing conviction that it was my duty to volunteer as a chaplain. Growing dissatisfaction with the parish situation made me consider ministerial work with soldiers as an alternative to regular parish service. Would I be more satisfied if I had to make some sacrifices with others of my own age? With the approval of my wife Peggy, I wrote to the army, asking about the procedure for getting a commission.

The reply was quick and to the point: ministers do not apply directly to the government; first they must be approved by their own denominations, and then they can be considered only after they have completed three years in a parish. Shortly after receiving this information, I learned that the three-year rule had been modified to two years. I immediately applied to the United Lutheran Church in America;[2] its committee approved my application and recommended me to the army. Instructions came for me to report for a physical examination at Philadelphia on December 15, 1942.

So far as I knew, I was in excellent physical condition except for one ailment: hemorrhoids. At the army dispensary I was passed along from booth to booth, each physician handling in an impersonal fashion only one specific detail of the overall process, until I came to the section handling vision. I recognized the examiner at first glance.

"Will Rogers. Imagine meeting you here!" I exclaimed. "I haven't seen you since we were in college at Muhlenberg."[3]

"Izzy Yost, my old buddy," he replied. "So you want to get into the army." Throughout the testing we chatted about our alma mater, the professors, and classmates. He didn't say a word about the condition of my eyes, and I was so glad to meet someone I knew that it never entered my mind to ask him any questions about how good my eyesight was according to army standards. After all, I was concerned only if my rear end would pass the exam.

Finally I came to the cubicle where the medic said matter-of-factly, "Drop your pants! I want to see if you have hemorrhoids."

"Doctor, I have hemorrhoids," I answered, beginning my prepared speech. "But they are not bad and they rarely give me any trouble. I've had them checked by my own doctor and even asked him to operate on them if he thought they were bad. He said an operation was not necessary. You see, they are really not a problem at all for me."

The examiner looked at me as if to say, "What kind of nut do we have here?" Then he spoke. "Stoop over and let me take a look. Hmm. If we kept everyone who has hemorrhoids out of the army, we wouldn't have any army."

"Does that mean I pass?" I asked anxiously.

"Of course. Unless you have something else the matter with you."

I left the dispensary in a jubilant mood. I would soon be in the army. According to the regulations I would receive two weeks' notice of my appointment so that I would have enough time to settle my personal affairs before reporting for duty.

However, when I received my copy of the physical examination, I was shocked to discover that I was being accepted "FOR LIMITED SERVICE ONLY" because of defective vision. As I scrutinized the report, I noticed that the officials at Philadelphia had recommended that I be accepted for general service in spite of the disqualifying defect and that the Surgeon's Office of the Headquarters of the Third Service Command on December 19 had agreed, but that on December 23, the Office of the Surgeon General had decided I was fit only for restricted service. If only I had known about this when my friend, Dr. William R. Rogers, was examining my sight.

Meanwhile I alerted the members of my parish that before long I would be ordered to active duty in the Army Corps of Chaplains. My appointment came very soon, dated as effective on January 16; with it was a form for the oath of office, which, when executed and returned to the War Department, signified my acceptance of the position as chaplain, first lieutenant, in the Army of the United States "for the duration of the war and six months thereafter unless sooner terminated."

On Thursday, January 20, another envelope came from the War Department; it had been missent to Kutztown, Pennsylvania (we lived in Butztown), and thus had been delayed by at least two days. Inside was an official communication with the label "RESTRICTED" at the top. By the direction of our president I was to report to the Chaplain School at Boston to receive training, and General Marshall was expediting the matter. This was the first of a number of such orders I would receive during the next two and half years, all to be stowed away in my 201 file and carried to each new assignment.

Unfortunately, the incorrect address on the envelope meant that I lost several days of the time I needed to straighten out my civilian affairs, primarily those pertaining to the parish I was serving. I had to contact my synodical president,[4] visit the sick and shut in, arrange for neighboring pastors to provide spiritual care in emergencies, instruct volunteers in specific tasks, plan for the special service to be held on January 31 for those already in the armed forces. I purchased my officer's uniform, wrote out my resignation from the parish, transported our piano to my mother's home, and moved my wife and infant daughter into her parents' house.

During these hectic eleven days as I brought the parish records up-to-date, I discovered to my amazement that one of my predecessors, Pastor Christian Streit, had left this parish to serve in the army of George Washington during the Revolutionary War. Apparently I was the second parson from Trinity Lutheran Church in Hecktown[5] to answer the call to the colors.

On the last day of January, 375 attended my last civilian worship service, compared with the 234 who had been there the previous Sunday.

In the evening 400 turned out for the special ceremony when we dedicated the Service Flag for the forty-seven members of the parish already in uniform.

Traveling from Bethlehem, Pennsylvania, to Boston was an easy matter in 1943 when railroads operated on schedule and had frequent passenger service. I reported in on time at the Chaplain School on the campus of Harvard University on February 1.

First of all I had to buy my chaplain's crosses and lieutenant's bars, for I had not been able to get these when I purchased my uniform. On the train coming north, I had sat in the rear of a coach in a corner with my overcoat collar turned up so that no one would notice the absence of insignia. But there was no time; directly after breakfast we had to report to the medical officer for inspection, and in formal dress. Several of the newly appointed chaplains preceded me in the lineup outside the office of Lt. Col. David H. Keller. Those coming out passed the word: "The colonel is a martinet, a stickler for regulations. . . . He's sure to bawl you out for something."

To avoid being lectured for appearing "out of uniform" because I had no crosses or bars, I removed my dress jacket and reported in my shirtsleeves. I was promptly reprimanded for improper dress and ordered out of the room and to return in full uniform. Embarrassed, I tried to explain my predicament. The colonel listened to my excuse but without much grace. He remarked that he could not lend me his insignia and commanded me to get the bars and crosses as soon as he had finished with me.

The experience was my introduction to the army; the examination at Philadelphia did not count, for then I was still a civilian. I must admit that I never did get used to the authoritarian system of the armed forces when it was used to put down an individual rather than to get a job done properly.

At the Chaplain School all the students were, of course, officers, but during the one month there we were treated like enlisted men: we marched to classes, shouting out the cadence; we checked the bulletin board twice a day, and anyone who missed a posted assignment suffered restriction to quarters over the weekend; we drilled (but without weapons); we saluted every officer in sight—at first some of us were also saluting all the noncommissioned officers too. We learned about military courtesy, how to orient and use a field map, the importance of the monthly chaplain's report, that we were responsible for the spiritual welfare of all the men of our unit, that our consciences and the regulations of our individual denominations should guide us in our work.

We became friends with chaplains of faiths other than our own; roommates were assigned so that we bunked with ministers not of our own persuasion. We learned how to use gas masks in a special building filled with gas; just before leaving the chamber each of us had to remove his mask and take a whiff of the fumes on our way out to the fresh air.

Some chaplains went through cultural shock. One young Protestant was surprised to learn that he would not be able to spend several days a week preparing his Sunday sermon. A staunch Southern Baptist who believed that communion was only for the close circle of members of a local congregation had no idea how he himself would be able to receive the bread and grape juice from another chaplain or how he could in good conscience offer the elements to other soldiers. Some, unaccustomed to much physical exertion, hoped for an assignment to a post that was not beyond their capacity to fulfill. Others thoroughly enjoyed all the activities and seemed anxious to complete the course so that they might get on with the real work of being chaplains with the troops.

On February 25, each of us received a twenty-nine-page booklet labeled "RESTRICTED." At the top of the first page my name had been typed in, and I was referred to paragraph 10, which ran in fine print from page 2 through page 7. There at the end of a long list of orders for officers to report hither and yon, I saw my name, the last one in the alphabetized list. I was to report to Camp Davis, North Carolina, on or about March 3. Once again my orders carried the notation "for limited service only."

At Davis I was assigned to a chapel in the Officer Candidate School, the assembly line for turning out "ninety-day wonders" (second lieutenants) for antiaircraft units. Any who could not take the rigorous demands on body and mind during the intensive three months of training went back into the ranks of the enlisted men. Candidates had little time for anything except the accelerated course. The chaplain, however, had little to do except conduct the Sunday worship, but he had to be at the chapel all of every weekday. Only occasionally did a soldier come for counseling, as did a black soldier one day.

He wanted to know why the color line was still in force at the camp theatre, why he was required to sit in the rear of the auditorium. I made a quick telephone call to the officer in charge of recreation without identifying myself. Apparently thinking that his caller was a white officer, the recreation officer at first indicated that he was keeping the colored men in their proper place. When I identified myself as a chaplain and threatened to make an issue of racial discrimination, right up to the post commandant, the junior officer promised to stop any segregation at the movie house. Most of the time, however, weekdays were boring.

One day I accompanied the candidates on their long and final hike of the course. It was an especially hot and humid day, and a number of the men began to straggle. I passed one group gathered around a pump, pouring water over their heads in an effort to cool off. I continued to overtake and pass small groups of men and I finished the march feeling in good shape. I knew from my experience as a Boy Scout that drinking too much water on a hot day could be dangerous. After I returned to my chapel, I heard the report that one of the hikers had died from heat exhaustion.

Quite unexpectedly the Lutheran chaplain assigned to the school with me received orders to report to a new assignment within twenty-four hours. At once I became concerned that I might be the next one moved without warning.

Peggy and daughter Monica had come down south to be near me, living first in a two-room cottage in Scotts Hill and then in new, concrete rooms of a hastily constructed housing project quite near the main entrance of Camp Davis. Soon orders came; I was to report to Camp Croft, South Carolina, on July 16. I applied for and received four days' delay en route, time enough to escort my family of two back to Pennsylvania.

We three, with what little baggage we had, traveled north by train from Wilmington, North Carolina. Although we had been promised that our coach would go straight through to Pennsylvania, at Rocky Point, North Carolina, we had to change trains. We waited several hours in a station crowded with service personnel and their families; like the rest of the travelers, I checked every train that pulled into the junction. When ours arrived, I hurried Peggy and little Monica into a coach and then went back for the rest of our luggage. In the meantime the conductor, because of the people already crammed aboard, closed the trap doors over the steps and refused to allow anyone on board. In vain I pleaded with him to permit me to join my family. As my panic was increasing, a captain touched me on the shoulder and motioned for me to follow him. When we came under an open window of a coach, he boosted me up and catapulted me through the open space right into the lap of a startled passenger.

With a hasty "Pardon me," I reached out the window and pulled in the pieces of luggage the kind stranger handed me. The next morning I noticed my rescuer sitting at the far end of our coach. When I approached him and asked him how he got on the train, he smiled but offered no explanation.

At Camp Croft, I was attached to an infantry training battalion. It was a short-lived duty, for on July 24, I was transferred, on paper, from the Fourth Service Command to the War Department and thus alerted for further movement orders, probably for duty overseas.

On August 6, I received an airmail letter informing me that I would be equipped for extended field service with summer and winter clothing, blankets, mattress covers, canteens, a first-aid packet, and a gas mask. I was told that relatives could not accompany me to the port of embarkation, which would be either Brooklyn, New York, or Newport News, Virginia.

For someone like me who had volunteered with the hope of serving overseas, this should have been good news, and in a sense it was. But the timing was poor: we were expecting the arrival of our second child almost any day. If I followed the orders precisely, I could not spend any time at all with my wife; our new baby might even be born before I would go overseas, but I would not be able to see him for many months, even years. Why should I not be allowed to go home on leave and wait there for the exact date for reporting to the port of embarkation? The more I thought of this, the better the idea seemed. I decided I would try to convince the commander of the camp to my way of thinking, even though I had never met him.

At camp headquarters, I explained my situation to the sergeant major, an old regular army noncom [noncommissioned officer]. He was sympathetic and helped me convince Colonel Griffith that my plan to await orders at Nazareth, Pennsylvania, made good sense. The CO agreed to telephone me as soon as definite word came about which port I should proceed to. His instructions were clear: stay near the telephone. That same day he issued special orders granting me four days' leave beginning the next day. After I arrived at Nazareth, he granted me three additional days' leave via the phone. Orders arrived at his office on August 9 for me to report to Fort Slocum, New York, by August 14.

How special it was for me to be home with my family of two! I conferred with the physician who would deliver our second child at home, in the residence of Dewey A. Landon, father of my wife. As Peggy and I wanted the new arrival to be baptized as soon after birth as possible, I contacted a nearby pastor who had been my classmate at college and seminary, and he agreed to come to the house to perform the sacrament. My mother lived but a few miles away; she would come to help my wife's mother take care of all three members of my family. Peggy and I had already agreed on both a boy's name and a girl's name for the expected baby. We also promised each other that until I returned from overseas each of us would read each day a chapter of the Bible, beginning with Genesis.

Saturday, August 14, I left Nazareth, taking a train from Bethlehem, Pennsylvania, to New York City, a short distance from Fort Slocum. Wife Peggy was in fine health, but the baby had not yet arrived. We knew that no message could be phoned out of the overseas staging area or into it. As soon as I reported in I learned that I could have stayed home a day longer; psychologically this information depressed me.

That evening I wrote a brief note to my wife; when she received it, there were nine censor-cut holes in the message! At least she learned that I had gotten to where I was going, by taxi and train and army ferry from the metropolis. My note written the next day got through the army mail with only four "windows" cut out.

The letters I sent the next two days passed without any deletions, but they didn't include any real information, except that my address was now APO #7126, New York, New York, and that she should call the Red Cross just as soon as the baby came in the hope that such an organization could get the news through to me.

On August 19, we fifty chaplains assembled with our baggage and, after a brief physical examination, left the fort by truck, heading for the Staten Island ferry. On the way we passed the *Queen Mary* and the *Normandie;* from the ferry we saw the Statue of Liberty; we unloaded at Pier 16. After a bag lunch, prepared by the Officers' Club at Fort Slocum, we boarded NY 176, military designation for the *Hawaiian Clipper,* where twelve of us were assigned to Stateroom 10 on D Deck, an interior cabin without a porthole. After receiving instructions for loading the men the next day, we watched the cargo being loaded.

The next morning I anxiously contacted the transport chaplain, but he had received no word about my wife. I helped prepare the bunks in the hold for the troops; theirs were five tiers high with little aisle space, compared with ours, which were only three tiers high. In the afternoon on the aft gangway I helped direct the men coming on board. Although I remember that Oriental troops were boarding a nearby ship, I did not record the fact in my diary. I hailed one of the stevedores and had him bring me seventy-five-cents worth of candy bars.

On August 21, I came up on deck at six a.m. because I thought the ship was moving; this was my first ocean voyage and I did not want to miss any of it, but I was wrong. After an excellent breakfast, I watched the last of the cargo loading, the gangplank lifting, and the antics of some girls on the pier bidding farewell to their soldier friends on board.

A tug came alongside, and at noon we left the pier. Our ship took its place in a large convoy, the second vessel on the left side. I remained on deck all afternoon, except during the lifeboat and fire drill at four o'clock. At 7:45, all personnel were cleared off the decks. Throughout the day I had been thinking a lot about my wife, for this was the date the doctor had set for delivery.

August 22 was a Sunday. For breakfast at 8:15 we had apricots, two eggs with potatoes and bacon, buns with butter, and coffee; we could go back for seconds. I attended the 9:30 Mass in the officers' mess; only a handful of white officers, black troops, and priests-in-transit were present. In the early afternoon, the gunners fired some practice rounds from a gun mounted on the rear of our civilian cargo ship. At 2:15, a black chaplain conducted a Protestant service over a forward hatch.

Even though no mail could be posted during the voyage, I began the practice of writing my wife daily, sharing with her my thoughts and commenting on my activities. Now I wrote of having parsnips for a meal, of my short haircut with only an inch of brush above my scalp, of the need for her to send two copies of all important letters in case some mail should be lost, of how much I loved her and needed her for my "balance wheel," of which chapter of the Bible I was reading on a given date so that she could adjust her daily reading in order to keep our devotions the same. I also shared my gripes with her: how I objected to the senior chaplain when he invited a Jewish chaplain to lead our Protestant devotions; how disturbed I became because our group devotions seemed to lack spiritual depth; how anxious I was to get my permanent assignment where I would be able to work without any interference from the hierarchy of the Chaplains Corps. At this time I sent her a V-Mail for the first time: a one-page letter that was reduced on film, sent back to the States, and then developed and printed a bit smaller than the original.

The enlisted men sailing with us were not well organized; apparently, like us, they were replacements and therefore without their own officers and noncoms. On August 23, all chaplains and other unassigned officers were requested to assist with the troops. The next morning I was directed to help with the troop mess from 9:00 to 10:30; then I volunteered to also assist with the second meal of the day, from 3:00 to 5:15. By this time many of the soldiers were dirty and sick, no longer taking much care of themselves in the hot and crowded holds of the tossing ship. Spilled coffee ran down from the mess tables onto the floor and then dripped on the cargo below.

Since I was an officer, conditions for me were much better. I could shave and shower without difficulty. I slept on the open deck when I wanted to, with my raincoat beneath me, my pack for a pillow, and my trench coat as a cover; at daylight I could go below to my bunk and continue sleeping until eight a.m. Magazines and books were available for reading, and I played cribbage with some of the chaplains.

On August 25, we received a booklet about North Africa; we now knew our destination was Oran. We also lined up for our second typhus shot. No debris had been thrown overboard to attract Nazi submarines to our position. We had become accustomed to the naval escort ships bobbing up and down on the flanks of our convoy. On August 26, when I went through the holds talking to the men, I discovered that C Hold, the hottest of them all, was no warmer than my stateroom; but of course, I had been out on the cool deck most of the nights at sea.

On September 1, the ships of the convoy lined up in two columns to go through the Strait of Gibraltar. What looked like a cloudbank low ahead gradually became hills as the vessels zigzagged forward. Then we saw the Rock itself. That evening, after a duck supper, I took Atabrine, a malaria preventive, for the first time. At 9:30 I suffered a violent attack of vomiting and blamed it on the medicine.

The next morning I found out that a number of others were ill; the doctor blamed the illness on the food rather than the Atabrine. The Mediterranean Sea was as calm as a pond. We all packed and prepared for disembarkation after thirteen days at sea. Late in the afternoon we docked at Oran. We trucked to Castel through the filth of the city that was swarming with Arab beggars. Each group of eight chaplains was assigned to a tent with double-decker cots. After a supper of chicken potpie, peas and carrots, bread and jam, and spiced ice tea, we enjoyed an outdoor movie.

For the first time I washed up using a helmet for a basin. I wrote Peggy that she should change her time for devotions to four p.m.; I did not tell her the reason: the time difference between us was six hours. I would try to read our chapter a day at ten p.m.

On September 3, after a breakfast of scrambled eggs and bacon, bread, farina (a kind of porridge), and milk, all of us trooped to the finance office for pay vouchers. Then I left the others and hurried to the Red Cross headquarters. Since there was no news from home, I sent a cablegram to Nazareth, Pennsylvania, requesting an immediate reply; none came. At noon we had limeade with our steak. I mailed a stack of letters to the United States. Supper consisted of chili con carne, potatoes, bread and butter, and tea. Not yet assigned to duty, we were spending these few days at the First Replacement Depot.

The next day we were told that each of the fifty chaplains fresh from the States would meet individually with the top-ranking chaplain in North Africa, who would give each of us the opportunity to name the type of unit he would like to serve with. If true, this was new, surprising, and welcome. On the way overseas we had tried to determine how we had been selected for sending to the European theater and had decided that a noncom must have pulled our names out of a file at random and handed them to an officer who, without looking at anything other than the chaplain's religion, had sent us orders.

After a few months in the army, many officers and men gave up trying to understand the logic used in making decisions affecting them. That we would be asked to suggest where we wanted to serve seemed far out, unmilitary, and most unlikely. But I learned the report was true; when I was called in for my interview the area chief of chaplains began the conversation by saying, "Chaplain Yost, with what kind of a unit would you like to serve?"

"With combat infantry," I replied without hesitation.

"Why with infantry?" The look on the questioner's face indicated that he did not quite believe what he was hearing. Could the look mean that he thought the chaplain standing before him was a bit crazy to ask for such an assignment?

"Sir, an infantry chaplain stays close to his men even in combat. I want to share as completely as possible the life my men have to lead. But I have a problem, sir."

"Well, what is it?"

"Sir, I am on limited service, and I understand that because of that I cannot be assigned to infantry. I have my physical report with me." I reached inside my shirt and pulled out the official sheet and handed it to him. "It's only my eyes that disqualify me. And there at the bottom of the report you can see that it went to the surgeon general's office; it's a borderline case, so he had to decide. I want to take the eye examination over again. I'm sure I'll pass it and be reclassified for general service." I was thinking to myself, *I'll memorize the chart to make sure I pass.*

Turning to his assistant, the chief asked, "Are we bound by the physical exam over here?"

"No, sir, we are not," the assistant chaplain replied.

"Chaplain Yost," said the chief of chaplains, "you have asked for infantry and infantry you shall get."

That afternoon at a general meeting of the chaplains of the Fifth Army, I was told that I had been assigned to the 34th Infantry Division. Praise the Lord! I was finally getting the job I had volunteered to join the army to do.

Sunday morning I got up too late for breakfast. I attended the Protestant worship in a tent at Canastel; the officiating chaplain introduced us visiting chaplains by name and state of origin. In the afternoon in Oran I witnessed an Arab street fight, attended a Holy Communion service, recognized stores that sold horse meat, ate at a Red Cross Club, bought a leather bag at the exorbitant price of 225 francs ($4.50), and then started to walk back to our quarters, greeting the passing folks with "bonsoir!" Five kilometers from camp, our group hitched a ride on an army truck. An air raid alert highlighted the end of the day.

On September 6, I had my second bout with Atabrine; we now had to take it daily. I swallowed the pill at the noon meal, and, perhaps because I went out into the sun, at four o'clock I began throwing up into my helmet. (Of course, before using a helmet for anything except protection, a GI takes out the inside liner.) I was knocked out for the rest of the day. My buddies toured the area; when they returned at eleven p.m., they reported that they had visited the *Hawaiian Clipper* and enjoyed cold Coca-Colas there.

On September 8, the three of us assigned to the 34th Division were escorted from the depot to divisional headquarters, where we changed our APO to that of the new unit. Since at that time no infantry battalion of the 34th needed a chaplain, I was ordered to go to the division's 109th Combat Engineer Battalion with the understanding that as soon as an infantry battalion needed a chaplain I would be reassigned to such a unit. A command car carried me out to a cork grove beyond El Ancor, where the 109th was bivouacked.

After meeting my new CO, Lieutenant Colonel Coffey, and the S-1, Captain Miller,[6] I set up my pup tent with the help of two privates. At evening mess I met the officers of my new "parish," and then after the meal I walked around the area visiting my new "parishioners." I also paid a courtesy visit to Episcopal chaplain Krumm of the 109th Medical Battalion, camping next to us.

The next day, as I was coming into our area upon returning from a visit elsewhere, someone yelled from the headquarters tent, "Chaplain, you got a telegram from the Red Cross! It's a boy!"

"Hurray," I shouted back. "You don't have to tell me his name. It's Christian Michael." I dashed up the road to read the message for myself. It gave little information beyond the date of birth, August 29. That was when I was on the high seas on the way over. I went back to my tent, knelt down, and thanked God for his goodness. That night I wrote a letter to our firstborn son to be given to him at the age of eighteen in the event that I should not return from the war.

I settled down to the task of getting to know the officers, and the men, and the history of the battalion. The assistant assigned to me informed me that he had formerly been a cashier in a bowling alley, was of French-Canadian ancestry, and had been court-martialed for being AWOL (absent without leave). I put him to work making a roster of all the personnel in our contingent. I went to division headquarters to secure hymnals for worship and a schedule of all the services for the next day, Sunday.

The next morning I went to each company and got a runner whose duty it was to lead members of his company to the worship site at the appointed hour. I arranged the candles and cross on my opened altar kit, a gift from the National Lutheran Council; the kit I placed on top of a packing box. Forty-three attended the general Protestant service at ten a.m. At the service of Holy Communion that followed at 10:45, twenty-eight communed; I signed and dated the cards of the ten Lutherans who attended. Later in the day I wrote postals to the home pastors of twenty of the communicants.

For two days I was bothered with diarrhea, probably caused by using a mess kit that had not been properly sterilized in boiling water. From the division, in addition to forty-six large army and navy hymnals, I received a portable typewriter and a field organ. One evening I sat in on the court-martial of two men in a candlelit tent, the first and only time in my army career that I ever observed such a trial.

September 16, the engineers moved out of camp by truck and boarded the SS *Rajula* of the British India Steam Navigation Company Limited, docked in the harbor of Oran. I was to occupy room 64 on the port side. Diarrhea forced me to locate a restroom in a hurry; it was of the French type: instead of a commode there was a trench-like area along a wall that you backed up to in a squatting position. Somewhat later I found a men's room on board with our conventional style of fixtures. That afternoon Hindu servants invited the officers to tea. At seven o'clock the officers dined: bouillon, salmon and sauce, meat, cabbage and potatoes, pudding with sauce, and coffee. Alongside each plate was an array of silverware.

The next morning the *Rajula* pulled from its pier to anchor just outside the port. The officers' breakfast was served in style: rolled oats, fish, scrambled eggs, and coffee. The printed luncheon menu I saved and later on mailed home to Peggy as a souvenir: grilled rump steak and onions, boiled potatoes, Madras curry and rice, cheese and biscuits, and fruit. A boat drill was called in the afternoon; I had trouble using the Akron-Ohio lifebelt. Dinner was again a meal in proper British fashion. This was Peggy's birthday. At dusk we sailed away from the Algerian coast.

On September 19, four hundred men gathered on deck for Sunday worship, with Chaplain Ames presiding; I preached the sermon entitled "Eternal Life." I had gone below to circulate among the men, inviting them to attend. They were not receiving any "red carpet" treatment such as the officers were enjoying, and some of them were bitter about it. At twilight I led the worship, and the other chaplain preached. Both of these were general Protestant services. The next evening I conducted a communion service on deck, wearing cassock and surplice and lighting the two candles on the altar kit. About thirty communed, most of them Lutheran.

On September 21, our transport was off the coast of Salerno, where on September 9, the Fifth Army under Gen. Mark Clark had landed on the beaches against stiff German resistance. The Allied forces had not expected to be held back so long from the port of Naples. The plan was for units such as the one to which I was attached to enter the Naples harbor and unload just as easily as they had loaded at Oran. For this reason many reserve units were not prepared for a beach landing and approached Italy as if on a pleasure cruise. I even tipped our waiter on the ship two dollars and the room steward one dollar. What a way to fight a war! Most of us did not know just how matters had been handled until after the war.

The beaches were now safe for landing parties. We had two more meals on board ship, excellent for the officers, not as good for the men, and then climbed down into landing barges and from them either into the water to wade ashore or into "ducks" (GI term for DUKW, a two-and-a-half-ton, six-wheel-drive amphibious truck equipped with a propeller and a watertight hull), which landed personnel dry shod. I was with our major; he commandeered a duck and I did not have to get my feet wet. In addition to my field equipment, I hand carried my altar kit on the eight-mile hike to our assembly area. We ate K rations for supper and spent an uncomfortable night on the ground without blankets and annoyed by the mosquitoes, even though I had used a repellent on my neck, face, and hands. At least we were not disturbed by planes or artillery.

From September 21 to October 4, the 109th Engineers remained on the same spot. Since I had few assigned duties, I was free to use my time as I saw fit. I visited with the men and officers, talked with nearby villagers, read books supplied by Special Services for troops in rest areas, wrote letters, censored the outgoing mail of enlisted personnel, studied the Italian language, accompanied our battalion doctor when he visited sick civilians, and took care of my personal needs.

Sunday, September 26, sixty attended worship with no hymnals and no organ. Twenty-five turned out for the later service held for the 34th Reconnaissance Troop, and six stayed to receive communion. The following Sunday morning I conducted separate services for three units: divisional headquarters, 109th Engineers, and 109th Medics. That afternoon I held worship at the 776th Tank Destroyer bivouac. After most services I offered communion to those who wanted special assurance of forgiveness.

On September 30, I had a long talk with a local priest; I was the first Protestant minister he had ever met. I set up a pattern for my conversations with Italian priests, telling them, "I believe in the Trinity; I respect the Virgin Mary but I do not pray to her; I pray to the Father through Jesus; I do not believe in the pope."

Some days I had time to write down in my diary what I saw and did. Here is the description of September 22.

> I was up before dawn because I was cold. For breakfast I had more of the K ration. Then I lay in the sun and read last night's scripture. I accompanied the baggage detail back to the debarking area and had a cooked meal at noon with a black quartermaster unit. We saw many Brahman cattle in the fields. A bridge on the single-track electric railroad had been blown up. After returning to our own area, I walked to a farm and got some grapes. I gave a boy a penny and some Life Savers. I was surprised to see a brown snake on the way back since I thought there were no snakes in Italy. I cleared out an area of brush and thorns and stretched out my shelter half as an awning between trees; under it I laid my bedding roll and

attached my mosquito bar. For supper I had U rations (cooked food) with the staff and then shaved. When it got dark I bathed my feet, where else but in my helmet (I had used it for shaving water, too) because one of my toes had been rubbed open. I read a chapter of Genesis under my shirt by the light of my flashlight, for we still had to be careful since the Allied troops had not yet broken out of the beachhead.

This was the same day on which the 100th Battalion landed on the Salerno beach. At the time I did not know that very soon I would become their chaplain and stay with them during all of the war.

Notes

1. Monica E. Yost, one of the editors of this book.

2. Now called the Evangelical Lutheran Church in America.

3. Muhlenberg College, founded in 1848, is a liberal arts college in Allentown, Pennsylvania, affiliated with the Evangelical Lutheran Church in America.

4. Now called "bishop."

5. One of the two congregations Yost was serving.

6. Adjutant, staff record keeper.

FOUR

Back to Serious Business

W HEN THE story of the chaplain of the 100th was interrupted by the two flashbacks to Pearl Harbor, the day was October 23, 1943, and the hour was noon. My diary records the rest of the day's events thus.

> Ate K ration and came to front: walked last half of the way; went to Bat-talion Aid. In p.m. talked with shell-shocked boy. Helped carry out wounded men. Shells landed close; snipers fired two shots close; machine gun stray bullets close. Talked with men as they were put in ambulance. Received twenty letters, Peg's two copies of birth certificate of Chris. Ate C ration and Kome and I slept alongside haystack. Dr. Kawasaki com-plimented me on my work. Colonel Turner rightly scolded me for trip-ping on communication wire.

By this time I had established a definite pattern of life during combat: assist the medics in the battalion aid station as long as enough litter bear-ers were available to bring in the wounded; go forward as a litter bearer whenever needed; in lulls between skirmishes, circulate among the men in their dug-in positions, whenever this was possible without my move-ments drawing fire from the enemy; direct the evacuation of our own KIAs and, when possible, supervise the burial on the spot of the German dead; counsel with any GIs who were disturbed, usually at the battalion aid; set an example of cheerfulness and of faith in all my contacts with the men and officers. I always carried my Bible in my musette pack, a small Lutheran *Common Service Book* in a hip pocket, and stationery and envelopes in my map case. Almost every day I read a chapter of the Bible and wrote a letter to my wife. As a litter bearer I normally replaced two of the Nisei because I was so much bigger than most of them; down-hill I placed the front handles on my shoulders and two of the AJAs car-ried the rear. Until December 12, 1943, I kept a small diary of each day's events.

Here is the entry for October 24.

> Sunday, Oct. 24. Wrote Peg and Mother. Ate C ration. Came to battalion aid; things quiet. Had brief service at battalion aid and communed four men (one Mormon, one Catholic). Washed socks. Gave out all religious tracts I had to men in positions. Had "gully service" for seven men. Got detail of four men to get out bodies. Brought Yoneyama up and he almost ran over an Italian man when a shell fell close. Slept in house near San Angelo.

The V-Mail letter I sent to my wife on this day was important to me.

> Letter #35 October 24, 1943 Sunday Morning
>
> Dearest, dearest Mine,
>
> The two copies of the wonderful news of Chris's birth details arrived yesterday along with other letters I shall read today. But the two copies I read last night in the fading light. My heart was thrilled as I read how beautifully God arranged for Chris to come. Only the word of the unbearable pain hurt me. But what nicer for us, Chris, and Mother; how pleased I am that she could do the delivering; how pleased I am that you could experience it all, and so calmly. All these good things make up (almost) for my not being there. I shall also write the doctor to relieve his feelings. I like him really; I think things happened as they did for our good. My heart shall sing high praise to God our Father all this Lord's day, Peggy Sweet; how unsearchable are the ways of His goodness to our little family!
>
> By sticking to my job I believe I've won my men and officers to a deep respect for the chaplain. Pray God continue His grace and strength that I may continue to do the whole job over here as He would have me do it. God willing we shall soon be one again and then we shall live to the full the glorious life of those who trust our Lord (almost) completely. God bless us all.
>
> Your adoring Israel

It was a Sunday when Peggy began to feel labor pains; the physician, who had been alerted earlier in the day, could not be located. My mother came immediately and, in the absence of the doctor, delivered our son. Mother had assisted at other births and knew what to do with the "blue baby," born with the umbilical cord around his neck. She literally saved Christian's life.

★ ★ ★

During combat, washing socks was an important task. If men with wet, cold feet had to remain inactive in their foxholes when under enemy fire, they began to suffer with "trench foot." All of us were warned to carry extra socks inside our shirts, where wet ones would dry because of body heat, and to change into dry ones whenever possible.

Even though I never experienced as rough conditions as did the infantrymen, I carefully followed all good advice and took necessary precautions. I drank only safe water, chemically treated in lister bags or with halazone in my own canteen. I kept proper distance between myself and others when walking in front-line areas. I bathed frequently. I did not expose myself to enemy observation. I wanted to stay alive and healthy in order to serve my buddies; wounded, sick, or dead I was of no use to them.

The "gully service" is an example of "playing safe." Since these men were out of the sight of the enemy and clustered together, I could safely lead them in worship. Of course, I did not know all the safety rules in the early days of combat; I learned from experience. Sometimes the best I could do on a Sunday was to visit the men in their slit trenches and give some printed materials to the interested ones. In rest periods I scheduled company and battalion worship on any day of the week to "make up" for the worshipless Sundays.

To get to the men up front, I either accompanied a company runner returning to his unit from the CP or followed the telephone wire strung along the ground from the rear to a forward position. One day when I was following a wire, carefully picking my way up a hill and staying on the beaten path to avoid mines, I looked up and saw a sergeant coming downhill toward me, checking the wire. When he reached me, he asked, "Chaplain, what are you doing out here?"

"I'm on my way to Dog Company," I replied.

"Don't you know how dangerous it is out here?" he said, the words tumbling out of his mouth in a seemingly angry torrent. "And why isn't your assistant with you? Who's going to take care of you if you get hit? You should stay back at the aid station. Or if you insist upon coming up here, bring your assistant along."

I could have reminded him that I was an officer and that he was being insubordinate, but instead I posed a question: "Sergeant, what are you doing out here?"

He looked at me as if to say, "Are you so dumb you can't see what I'm doing?" but he answered, "I'm checking this wire for breaks."

"Don't you have an assistant?" When he nodded affirmatively, I continued, "Well, why isn't he with you?"

"Chaplain, there's no sense in two of us exposing ourselves out here, so I told him to stay in his foxhole."

"Right you are," I agreed with a smile, "and that's exactly why I didn't bring my assistant along." As I proceeded up the hill I felt good inside. Here was an example of a buddy showing his affection for me by being overly concerned about my welfare but completely unconcerned about any danger that might be a part of the task he had to perform.

My mission this day was to see how Captain Mizuha of D Company was getting along. Some days before, I had hiked with him as he led his company forward, because I wanted to find out why he put on such a rough front; he was one of the few AJAs who sprinkled all his speech with profanities. I was not convinced that he was as antagonistic to Christian beliefs as he appeared to be. Before very long I realized that Jack was indeed a fine man but that he had a gripe about the world as he saw it.

"They ought to use us in the Pacific, not here in Europe," he had growled at me as we walked together. "When the war is over, they'll say we were willing to fight white men but not people 'of our own kind.' I just wish they'd let us show them. We're Americans, not Japs." He repeated this theme in various ways, salting his words with a liberal dose of cursing. No matter; my respect for him grew, and I got to like him by the time we reached our destination.

When I visited him this day at the end of the D Company wire, he was still growling, but this time about the Germans. "Those Krauts can't hit a thing," he said, standing up in what I thought might be the plain view of the Jerries. And he continued to lambaste the enemy and to extol the competency of his own machine-gun and mortar operators.

On Sunday, October 24, I fired my driver. When Yoneyama was driving me in our jeep from the rear of the battalion aid station, a German shell exploded on the dirt road ahead of us. Yone ducked his head and made the vehicle swerve off the highway into a gully, narrowly missing a group of Italian peasants coming toward us. The shell had not landed close enough to do us any harm, but my driver just did not have enough nerve to act rationally under pressure. We sat still in the jeep until he had collected his wits.

"Yone, this is the last time you will drive for me," I told him. "You could have killed one of those Italians or wrecked the jeep and both of us. You are too nervous to be my assistant. Take the vehicle back to the

motor pool and tell the officer there that I'll get another driver later on."
I got out and walked the rest of the way.

Yone obeyed. As a motor-pool driver he was all right. Later on at
Cassino, when many of the rear-echelon personnel were pressed into
service as ammunition carriers, he was in the group and fulfilled his
duties during the emergency without reproach.

> Monday, Oct. 25, San Angelo. Spent morning moving dead men includ-
> ing one German. Lost patience trying to locate one corpse. Ate at regi-
> mental headquarters, good meal of Spam, peas, bread, catsup, butter and
> pears. Rested in p.m. Things quiet. Had chicken for supper at medics bat-
> talion aid. Spoke to and prayed for a wounded man; he said I should pray
> for others left behind. Slept on litter in house.

On October 25, the 100th was designated divisional reserve and
remained at San Angelo until October 31. The battalion had suffered
heavy casualties in the hills, but it had maintained its record of excel-
lence. However, Major Lovell had been hit by a fragment of a German
"screaming meemie" (rocket gun with six barrels, fired electrically), and
a complaint had been lodged at the division's headquarters against Colonel Turner for not securing a line of departure.

The latter occurred when a patrol sent out by our CO reported back
that no enemy troops were in the area through which the 135th Regiment would move forward beyond the 100th's position. German soldiers
put up a stiff resistance when the other regiment came forward, and on
the road our battalion vehicles apparently blocked those of the regiment
relieving us.[1]

> Tuesday, October 26. Breakfast of coffee and C ration hash. Shaved off
> much beard. Visited Command Post and Companies E and F, all quiet.
> In p.m., Kome and I went to cave on hillside by chapel near San Angelo
> where men on Observation Post had found 100 Italian refugees. Spoke
> to them in Italian and told them it was safe for them to go back to
> Naples. Brought canned milk and some food to children and candy and
> a few cigarettes: one baby of three days, three of three months, many
> small children, and several old folks and several pregnant, one ready to
> give birth. Men able to lead seemed spineless. Promised to contact Red
> Cross for gas for their truck. Ate German frozen apricots at supper. Vis-
> ited sick Italian woman near CP. Slept on litter. Captain Kome told tales
> of Japanese problem after Pearl Harbor, before retiring, and other stories
> as we lay ready to sleep. Before retiring I told a soldier of his brother's
> death.

To provide for people in need and to visit those who are sick and to comfort any who have lost loved ones are recurring tasks in the life of a parish pastor. Now as a chaplain in Italy I was involved in the same kind of ministry I knew as a pastor in Pennsylvania; I had changed the locale of my parish, but the work remained the same.

Wednesday, Dr. Kawasaki and I set out by jeep to visit the hospitals to which our wounded had been evacuated, but it took so long to get the necessary permit that we postponed the trip until the next day. Thursday, the two of us left the bivouac area early and spent time with men of the battalion at the hospitals in Caiazzo, Caserta, and Naples. In one of them, as I was entering a ward, I heard someone call, "Chaplain, Chaplain, over here!" It was Terry Lewis of Alabama, the GI whose leg I had splinted on October 22. [This incident is described in chapter 1.] He was doing fine. He reached under his mattress and pulled out the X-rays of his leg to show me that the fracture had not been a bad one. He thanked me for finding him and for knowing what to do about his injury. (The army had not taught me any first aid; I learned that and a lot more that helped me in the chaplaincy during my years in the Boy Scouts of America program as a boy and as a leader.)

Late in the day we shopped in Naples and briefly visited the ruins at Pompeii. It was only during rest periods that I left the battalion; on this first excursion away from the unit, the surgeon and I combined business and pleasure. The ride back in the rain took four hours. We were glad for the hot coffee "back home" at the end of our trip.

The next day, after getting up late, I gave Colonel Turner a report of our hospital visits. Then I made arrangements for worship services later in the day since another move was imminent. After the noon meal we got the bad news that our CO was relieved of his command and ordered to a hospital for a rest. How would the Hawaiian contingent get along without Lovell and Turner?

I had tried to stay out of Turner's sight after the fiasco of my first night with him near the Volturno River (when he was displeased with the racket I made with my shovel), but I was unsuccessful. One day at the CP, when he noticed that I was wearing a Boy Scout sheath knife, he barked, "Chaplain, let me see that knife you're carrying!" As he was examining it, he pontificated, "Get rid of this immediately. If you should be taken as a prisoner, the Jerries would consider you armed, and you'd be in for it."

Another time, when I was hightailing on a captured Italian motorcycle along the dirt road in front of his tent, he roared loud enough for me to hear him above the cycle noise, "Chaplain Yost, report to me over here." After I had dismounted and was standing stiffly at attention before his angry gaze, he ordered, "Chaplain, as long as I am in command of this outfit, I don't ever again want to see you riding that motorcycle. We don't want a dead chaplain in the 100th." And there was the time I was conducting an open-air service within sight of his CP when enemy planes swooped overhead. As we all scattered, I looked toward the colonel's praetorium and knew that he was blaming me for drawing enemy attention to his headquarters by gathering a mass of soldiers so close to it.

But always I and all the others in the One Puka Puka knew that our commanding officer loved us genuinely and bawled us out only for our own good. Now that he was leaving us, many in the ranks felt that they had let the Old Man down. Eventually mature judgment prevailed as we realized it was better for our idol to leave us at this point, for we doubted that he would have been able to bear the increasing strain of witnessing the mounting numbers of his "boys" killed, maimed, and suffering.

Before leaving, Colonel Turner called the battalion together for a last pep talk and a final "God bless." He surmised that he would be sent back to the States. He took the time to write a comment on my permanent military record: "This officer is <u>absolutely outstanding</u>." The underlining was the colonel's.

That afternoon men of Headquarters, D, and E Companies assembled for worship. German bombers overhead interrupted us, but we reassembled after the scare. I went to F and C Companies for scheduled worship, but these two units were moving out. I phoned Chaplain Hoffman and told him that his Mass announced for 4 p.m. was now canceled because of troop movements. With the other officers I met Maj. James J. Gillespie, our new CO. He knew how we all felt about Turner, and he said he shared our sorrow, but he warned us that we would be losing other commanders in the future. I tarried long enough at headquarters to eat a good supper, which included rice; meanwhile, the line companies had left the area. At 5:30, I joined other officers in the CP three-quarter-ton jeep to follow the men. A couple of hours later, when this vehicle got stuck in a ditch, I transferred to the C Company jeep. We got lost.

It took most of the night to travel a few miles. Two vehicles of our column went through bridges that had been blown; they missed the bypasses and two men were killed in the accidents. Toward morning our transport stopped, and we sat there, trying to sleep until dawn.

> Saturday, Oct 30. Arrived at new CP at 6 a.m. Ate breakfast of C rations
> in house. Moved out with troops over hill and dale (not far) to new loca-
> tion; CP in house. Had dinner and supper there; in p.m., light fixed, so
> read New Testament a bit and two officers spoke with me of the Bible.
> Slept on floor in house (near Pratella).

Officers, observing me at Bible study, talked with me about its teach-
ings. Some told me they carried New Testaments and read the scriptures
fairly regularly. My military parishioners thought it only normal for me
to have devotions and to talk freely about my Christian faith. Nevertheless, it was my policy to wait until I was asked questions before I delivered any informal sermons.

On Sunday I was up early, but it was not possible to have worship
with the troops up front. I rode back to the company in reserve (A) and
there breakfasted and shaved. At 9 a.m., one hundred of the company
came to the service. Then I hitched a ride to divisional headquarters to
get religious tracts, but none was available. After lunch at A Company,
I went to our rear CP to write up my October "Report of Chaplains"
for a clerk there to copy. Normally this was done by the chaplain's assistant, who was supposed to be a typist as well as a driver; thus far I had
been assigned a driver only. Leaving my bedding roll in the CP truck at
the rear, I went by vehicle three miles to the forward CP, passing some
of my former buddies of the 109th Engineers on the way. That night I
slept in the nearby town with the soldiers, first sleeping outside, then in
a jeep, inside a house on the floor, on a chair by the fire, again on the
floor. It was an uncomfortable night, for it was cold and every sleeping
surface hard. The night was like the day, nothing much accomplished.
What a way to celebrate Reformation Sunday, an important festival for
us Lutherans.[2]

And how prosaic the summary of the month's activities at the end of
the "Report" sounded.

> During the month troops were on the move three Sundays; therefore, one
> battalion service was held on a Saturday. On one of these Sundays a serv-
> ice was held in the battalion aid station and one in a gully; another Sun-
> day service was held for a company in reserve. Visits were made to the
> front to urge private devotions when public worship is not available; tracts
> were distributed at the same time. . . . Though I participated in no buri-
> als I supervised the proper removal of 24 men of my battalion killed in
> action. In combat I have stayed near the battalion aid station; in lulls
> between pushes I have visited the men in their positions.

On November 1, I moved with headquarters forward along a hill. I was not deserting the medics, but until we suffered casualties in number, I could get more information on what was going on by being near the command group. The battalion was still in reserve. When I heard of three men wounded in E Company, I went there and prayed with two hit by shrapnel. I stayed with this company all morning, first digging a trench for myself and then enjoying a K ration lunch. In the afternoon, I checked in at the aid station and after supper returned to the CP on the hill. When German bombers came overhead, our own antiaircraft fire wounded a Headquarters Company man; I went there to be with him. Returning to the CP, I heard that bombs had been dropped in A Company area and two or three Nisei killed. That night I slept in a building where there was a lot of hay. I enjoyed a fine, fine sleep.

The next day our outfit moved into Ciorlano. Here the eating habits of our buddhaheads got them into trouble. (Nisei from Hawaii referred to themselves as buddaheads and to the Mainland Nisei as kotonks.) They preferred rice to potatoes, and they liked an abundance of vegetables, and they especially enjoyed cooking their own combinations of foods. George H. Grandstaff, our supply officer, traded off standard GI chow for rice every chance he got. Whenever it was possible to buy or appropriate any kind of food from local *paesanos* to add to the army victuals, the men themselves did so. I quickly learned not to ask where all the extras came from; I simply relaxed and enjoyed the banquets of pork, chicken, fruit, wine, and vegetables. However, I refused to be an arbiter in their squabbles over food; once I came upon a squad cooking something in a helmet and was asked whether the steaming mess was of edible vegetables or weeds. I laughed and walked away.

At Ciorlano, an angry Italian stalked purposefully into the CP building and loudly demanded to speak with "Il Commandante" at once. It took a lot of motioning and guessing before the assembled officers understood the man's angry tirade. He identified himself as the local medical doctor and owner of several hutches of rabbits. These animals were solely for experimental purposes, he explained. But alas, he exclaimed, all these fine animals had been stolen by the American soldiers! He appeared to be more upset by the audacity of the thieves than by the monetary loss involved. He insisted that some action be taken to punish these uncivilized robbers.

Our CO's first reaction was concern that those who might eat the stolen animals could become sick. He wanted to know if they had been injected with any kind of disease that might affect those who ate them. When the local physician, after some unsuccessful attempts at translation, finally understood the question, he answered in the negative.

Relieved, our major sent out a runner to bring our own battalion surgeon to the CP. When he arrived, our commandant said to him: "Doc, I'm going to send a message to all our companies that whoever has eaten any of these rabbits in this town is in danger of getting the disease with which they are injected, unless he gets treatment right away. And I am ordering all such to report immediately to you for treatment." Doc got the message: he was to teach the petty thieves a lesson. He assured his boss that a dose of a laxative would make all of them uncomfortable long enough for them to repent of their evil deeds. And who appeared first in line for the remedial treatment? It was the Nisei captain of the rabbit-foraging company! No one let him in on the joke until he had swallowed his medicine and had begun to feel the effects of it.

On November 3, several of us visited the two local churches and met the priest still in the town. He invited us to his rectory, a nicely furnished home, and suggested that he would be honored if I accepted his offer of an overnight stay. Once again I had to decline a priest's courteous hospitality, for we were to move forward that evening. Hamburger on bread was brought up from the kitchens in the rear before we set out. As I hiked with headquarters personnel, one fellow asked me how it was that I was always in such good spirits; he said that I was passing it on to the men.

This gave me a chance to explain my philosophy of life: the Heavenly Father works all things together for the good of those who love him; we who are his children must simply strive each day to follow his will and trust him to take care of us in whatever way he sees fit.

At the Volturno River, I waded across with the litter bearers and became worried when German shells fell too close for comfort. Helping to carry a casualty back on a stretcher, I fell into the shallow water and got uncomfortably wet. The west bank of the stream was heavily mined, and there were many casualties, among them our first officer killed in action, Lt. Kurt E. Schemel, the German American who at first had reservations about joining the 100th.[3] It was here, too, that a platoon sergeant led a company bayonet charge over a stone wall to rescue Lt. Young Oak Kim. Also near the river, a wire team of six men and a mule carrying a reel of wire got off the advance route and ran into machine-gun fire. By dawn, the medics had brought the many wounded back across the ford to safety.

Thursday morning I took off all my wet clothing and spread it out in the sun to dry. I wrapped my naked body in a blanket and lay down on the ground to get some sleep. Awakened by planes overhead, I clutched the blanket tightly and dashed toward a nearby slit trench. The bombs fell a safe distance away. At noon I dressed and moved forward with the medics, crossing the Volturno in a jeep. Three of us proceeded along the dirt road skirting an orchard.

David Nakagawa, the aid man with Captain Kometani and me, decided that he would go into the orchard to put an EMT (emergency medical treatment) tag on a KIA he was sure had died among the trees. I tried to discourage him because it was probably a mined area, but he insisted that in the daylight he could pick out a safe path. After he started into the place, Kome decided that he had better follow David just in case the aid man had any trouble. As I watched the two, one several paces behind the other, I decided that, since later on I would have to bring a detail to recover the body, I might just as well follow the two and thus know how to get in and out of the grove safely.

When I was halfway along (David was already kneeling by the dead man and Kome was midway between David and me), I spotted a dark cord on the ground and opened my mouth to yell to the others that I had spotted a mine. But it was too late; my foot had already touched the wire and the mine exploded. I felt a stinging sensation in the lower part of the back of my neck, and I saw David falling forward. I looked down at the trench coat I was carrying over one arm; it was full of little holes. There were similar holes in the legs of my trousers and scuffmarks on my combat boots where shrapnel had hit but not gone through.

When I touched the sensitive area above my musette bag with my fingers, I felt a small piece of metal but I could not pull it out. Kome, closer to me than David was, had not been hit. Poor David, farthest from the exploding mine, had been struck by shrapnel and was bleeding; examination revealed that a nerve affecting the use of one arm had been severed. Kome stopped the bleeding, and the two of us got the aid man out to the safety of the road.

When I took off my musette pack at the aid station, I discovered that the top of it was also full of holes. Our surgeon refused my request for him to remove the pellet I could feel; he sent me back to the hospital collecting station where another doctor took out the steel fragment and handed me a Purple Heart. That night I slept on a cot at A Company of the 109th Medics, using five blankets.

The next morning, after a breakfast of pancakes and coffee, I went back to our aid station in the vicinity of Capriati. When Captain Kawasaki asked me, I accompanied him when he visited the collecting station to check records of casualties from the 100th. After a noon meal of hot C rations, the battalion aid moved a short distance forward to the CP in an orchard. Doc Kawasaki went on ahead to look for another location for the medics. After some enemy bombing, we all moved forward and found out that bombs had fallen close to our surgeon; he had a severe headache as a result. We fixed up a big building near the railroad, blocking the door so that no light could shine out at night and bringing in mattresses, straw, and water.

That night casualties poured in, including the executive officer, Jack Johnson, and Capt. Taro Suzuki, both hit by fragments of mines set off when some men wandered off the path that had been marked with strips of toilet paper. Late that night, 45th Division men brought in a wounded German. When I put a flashlight beam on the faces of our AJAs, he expressed surprise that any Japanese were supporting the Americans.

After breakfast on November 6, I met the GRO (Graves Registration Officer) and with him evacuated seven bodies of Americans and two of Germans. At the rear CP I talked with seven German POWs (prisoners of war). A bomb exploded about one hundred yards from us, killing three Italian mule drivers and one of our men, all part of a detail about to take food and ammunition to the front. I got the names of the dead Italians from another *paesano* and tagged their bodies. I returned to the aid station in the medic's jeep, in time to help move the medical materials forward on foot through the gullies, orchards, and open fields to a house near Pozzilli.

While I was helping with the wounded here, another bomb fell close at hand. Doc Kawasaki was hit in the leg while going to the forward CP and had to be evacuated as a casualty. We became aware that our location was on the extreme left flank of the 34th Division in a gap in the hills not protected by our own unit or men of the 45th Division. I put my valuables in a dispatch case and tied up my private communion kit in a sling and attached it to my web belt, just in case we would have to run from a German counterattack. Early in the night I helped carry a litter case to the rear. I returned exhausted and was grateful for the coffee Dr. Kainuma[4] had ready for me.

The next day was Sunday; I got up late, with my right ankle hurting even when I was not using it. I read the Gospel for the Twentieth Sunday after Trinity[5] to the walking wounded just before they started down the trail to the rear. In the late afternoon a call came for medics to come to the forward CP. Kome and I went along, carefully following the narrow trail up the hillside through a minefield. It took all the courage I had to keep stepping from stone to stone marked by toilet paper, aware that a step off the solid path would probably set off a mine. I was still in shock from my experience in the orchard a few days before. On the way we saw dead mules and a dead fox.

Empty ration cartons were strewn about. Wounded on litters were carried past us as their bearers inched slowly down the almost impassable trail. We saw one WIA (wounded in action) roll off his litter. In the helmet of a KIA along the way, I found a pornographic snapshot and destroyed it. When Kome and I reported to the CO, we were told that no more medics were needed. It was too late to make the return trip, for we could not safely follow the path in the dark. The two of us put down the litters we were carrying and each lay on one at some distance from the CP, hoping to get some rest. It had begun to rain, and soon a rivulet was running down my litter, soaking my back. Too wet and cold to just lie there, I got up, took off my raincoat, and put it over my head, and then sat uncomfortably on my helmet placed upside down on the ground.

Kome was soon fast asleep on his stretcher. I sat awake all the night long, meditating on the verse that reads, "My soul waiteth for the Lord more than they that watch for the morning, I say, more than they that watch for the morning" (Psalm 130:6). Occasionally shells flew noisily overhead.

Early the next morning, after greeting the officers at the CP, the two of us, weary and shivering, slowly and carefully retraced our steps on the slippery trail. We arrived safely at the aid station, drank hot bouillon, and then slept until noon.

I phoned the headquarters CO to send me a detail of four men to evacuate KIAs, but no one came forward. As I did quite often, I kept busy heating bouillon, coffee, and C rations for the wounded and the busy medics. A German WIA weighing over two hundred pounds was brought in; our little Nisei had carried him down the dangerous track, a job well done. He and I conversed in German. This Austrian, named Alois Schaner, confessed that he had not thought that he would be treated so well. He admitted that only by a miracle could Germany win the war. He told of Nazis who dodged being drafted into the Wehrmacht and of chaplains who were conscripts. We fed him well.

The next day I got to the nasty task of picking up the dead. An aid man went with me back over the route our men had used in their advance. We were told that the 120th Medics had evacuated five or six of our KIAs the day before. Someone else had taken care of another of our dead. We found two German KIAs. A guide from one of the line companies located three of our boys for us. In the afternoon the four men assigned to me moved two of our dead out of a gully near the aid station. A Caucasian soldier, seeing us bearing one of our fallen comrades toward him, stepped off the path, took off his helmet and beanie, and stood at attention as we passed by, a truly touching tribute! That night as I tried to sleep on the aid station floor, I had an attack of diarrhea. I sneaked out of the building, let down my pants, and cut away the soiled underwear.

November 10 was another day of removing corpses, and I enlisted the services of Sgt. Calvin Shimogaki, our expert on mines and demolitions. When first in the army, he had played a saxophone in the band; upon the formation of the Nisei unit, he specialized in the dangerous job of handling explosives. When he had heard that I had been hit when I tripped a mine, he had been quite upset and had bawled me out for not asking him to clear the area before entering it. Now I had him use his minesweeper to clear a lane into the mined area where lay the bodies of a Nisei and a 100th haole officer.

After locating each mine, Calvin had to dig it up and defuse it, a tricky business. Dead cattle and donkeys littered the minefields. I marked a spot in a gully where an Italian corpse was lying. We attempted to tie bodies on mules to bring them down the hillside, but the animals bucked the burdens off, and we ended up using manpower and stretchers. Twice during our work in the exposed areas, Luftwaffe bombers flew over us. Since I had eaten no breakfast, except for some hot cocoa, I came back to the medics area and ate two cans of C ration beans. I phoned regimental headquarters but could not locate the GRO.

Discouraged, I went up the trail and asked the companies on the line to gather their dead buddies in one area. Troops moving off the hill had to pass the assembled cadavers, a most depressing experience for them. I felt completely frustrated. My detail took four corpses to the road to be picked up by a truck. We put our mules in the mule train that had brought up rations and ammunition to the front. It was a terrible afternoon for me, but when I returned to the medics, they had soup and pork waiting for me. My second call to the GRO reached him, and I also talked over the phone with Colonel Turner, who was visiting regimental headquarters. A depressing day had an encouraging ending.

The next day a detail of more than twenty brought down nine dead on litters and one on a mule. The GRO finally arrived, and we removed all the known dead except one. This was an unidentified paratrooper who had appeared out of nowhere to guide our men on the first day of the attack. He had died in a minefield. To remove his body from its dangerous position I had the help of a detail of minesweepers, a medic, and a guide.

At noon I enjoyed a 5-in-1 meal at the CP in town. A PX (post exchange) ration caught up with us: five fig bars, a big Tootsie Roll, and a few chewy candies. CO Gillespie gave me a chocolate Mounds bar. We always had hard candy but not much chocolate. From time to time I asked my wife to send me Hershey bars and peanut candy.

Supper at Headquarters Company consisted of soup, frankfurters, vegetables, and crackers. That night I slept soundly in the medics quarters on a litter placed on top of a bed frame on the second floor of a house, using my own bedding roll, a shelter half, and five blankets. I, of course, did not have five blankets of my own; I simply borrowed extra ones not being used for the wounded. This was one advantage of staying overnight with the medics.

On Friday after breakfast in the F Company mess (the field kitchens had been brought up to feed us), I led a detail of four men and three medics to the top of the hill where our troops had engaged the enemy. We examined what had been the enemy CP and the deeply dug positions of the Wehrmacht. We conducted a tiresome search for German corpses. We found three partially buried Jerries, completed filling in the graves, and paused for a brief burial service. I was able to identify one of the three; the other two remained unidentified because we did not dare move their bodies for fear they had been booby-trapped. We found one Caucasian KIA; the detail carried him the long way back. As we returned, we saw shells hitting the F Company area. A bit later we saw the results of the barrage: shell bursts in the trees had killed two and wounded three.

This was a payday. I sent $175 home by a government finance check and kept $20 for my personal needs, which included giving $5 to Club 100, the battalion organization that planned to build a clubhouse in Honolulu after the war. My wife knew that during combat no one needed much money on hand. That evening I shaved off a twelve-day beard, took a helmet bath, and changed into winter underwear.

Saturday, after finding an Italian woman to do my laundry, I got three more bodies back to the GRO. I announced the services for the next day, rested, and put my personal belongings in order. War correspondents from *Life* magazine visited the battalion, now withdrawn from the front. When I picked up my laundry—underwear, pants, shirt, socks, towels—I was pleasantly surprised: everything had been carefully pressed with an iron with hot embers in it. The woman would not take any money; I paid her with food. One of the AJAs gave me a much-needed haircut.

On this day most personnel of E and F Companies were assigned to the other companies to replace their losses in combat. Even so, A, B, C, and D Companies had only 150 infantrymen each instead of the usual 187. Our overall casualties in Italy now totaled 75 enlisted men and 3 officers KIA or DOW (died of wounds) and 239 battalion personnel wounded or injured. The 100th sometimes received Caucasian officer replacements, but all replacements of enlisted men had to be AJAs.

In the evening I phoned Yone to bring my vehicle forward. About one a.m., a casualty was brought up to the battalion aid. Although I was tempted to stay in bed, I got up and held his hand as the massive shell wound in his leg was treated. Once he muttered, "The damn Jerries," and asked for a drink of water. I prayed with him briefly. When I went back to bed, I thought of how Christ had hung on the cross for three hours on such open wounds.

On Sunday, 150 from four companies turned out for a 9 a.m. service in a house in Pozzilli, men upstairs and down and on the stairs; outside it was raining hard. An officer suggested we sing "What a Friend We Have in Jesus." The other hymns were "Rock of Ages," "Now Thank We All Our God" (because we were so close to Thanksgiving), and "America." At 11 a.m., 98 from two other companies came to a house in their bivouac area for worship; here three requested communion after the service. (Although assigned to other companies, the men of E and F Companies had not yet moved to their new units.) I ate the noon meal with F Company and then listened to a lecture to all their noncommissioned officers. I phoned the one remaining company, C, about worship for them, but they were not ready.

In the afternoon, the chaplain of the 1st Battalion told me over the phone that Chaplain Hoffman of the 3rd Battalion was still alive. Father Albert J. Hoffman, recipient of the Silver Star in the African campaign, had tripped a mine while attempting to carry a wounded German out of danger several days before; the blast shattered one foot. He later received the DSC (Distinguished Service Cross) for this and other brave actions. In talking further with my brother chaplain, I began to wonder if I had found the right spot to be during combat. From what he said, he was normally farther forward than I most of the time. I hated to think that I was not doing as much as I could for my men. Perhaps the way in which Chaplain Hoffman had become a casualty was making all of us reconsider our day-by-day ministry with the troops. I had never really heard any discussion as to where a combat chaplain was supposed to be. Perhaps each man was expected to let his conscience be his guide.

At 3:30 p.m., I went to the C Company area, but it was still raining, and there was no house available for our use. At six p.m., in an upper room of the battalion aid, I held a communion service for ten soldiers. Four had come because they wanted to be baptized. I was called to the CP and left the group singing hymns. At the CP I took a message about the Mass scheduled for the next day. When I got back to the upstairs room, I asked each of the candidates, "What is the meaning of Holy Baptism?"

"A new life," answered the first.

"Following Jesus," said the second.

"I was raised a Buddhist," explained the third, "but now I want this better way."

"I have been attending church," said the fourth, "and now I want to be baptized."

Then I told the four, "Normally instruction takes place before a person receives baptism, but under these combat conditions I'll baptize you tonight and give you instruction later on. But let me explain simply that to be baptized means to become a Christian. Through it a person is forgiven all his sins and made a child of the Heavenly Father. Thereafter he lives each day as a new person, safe in the Father's keeping. He therefore tries to live the kind of life Jesus wants him to. And he is sure that he will always belong to God. Listen now as I read to you what Martin Luther wrote about baptism in the *Small Catechism*."[6]

After reading the Lutheran teaching to them, I invited the men who had been singing hymns to join us in the ceremony. I used the "Order for the Baptism of Adults" from the Lutheran *Common Service Book,* omitting only the section requiring a pledge of loyalty to the Lutheran Church.

Instead I asked each one to think about what church in the Islands he would like to join and urged each to write to that congregation requesting membership. I put water into the communion chalice and it became the font for the sacrament. Hideo Ueno, Nobuhara Allan Doi, Wallace Tadashi Onuma, and Marshall Sakae Higa (all of Headquarters Company) answered the questions of the rite individually. Isaac F. Akinaka and Torao Kawano served as witnesses. The date was November 14.

The requests for initiation into the Christian fellowship caught me by surprise. I had only three copies of the *Small Catechism* and no adult baptismal certificates. I wrote to my wife to have our church supply store in Philadelphia send me a dozen catechisms and a dozen certificates. I had no idea that very soon I would need more than twelve of each. I went back to the CP before retiring because someone there had prepared rice pudding for me. At this time I received a letter of commendation from Colonel Turner. It was dated October 29, the day he was relieved of his command, but it had gone through army censorship, which apparently delayed its delivery to me.[7]

Now the 100th was a veteran battalion, battle scarred but still undaunted. It had lost its top leadership: Turner, Lovell, Jack Johnson, as well as Captain Kawasaki. No longer over-strength with extra companies, it had become an integral part of a regiment in the fighting Red Bull Division. Nevertheless, the One Puka Puka retained its distinctiveness as the AJA contingent from Hawaii with its aloha spirit, Island pidgin, high morale, and dogged determination to take and hold military objectives. Officers and men could hardly realize that only three months less one week had elapsed since they had left the States.

Notes

1. The roads were very narrow and the U.S. Army had too many vehicles. The traffic was dangerous because the army was constantly under fire from German guns (Clark 1950).

2. The last Sunday in October, when many Protestant churches celebrate the sixteenth-century Reformation Movement in the Christian Church, led by Martin Luther and others.

3. After the war, Seitoku Akamine of the 100th Battalion and his wife, Shizuko, named their son Kurt in honor of Lt. Kurt Schemel (Yamane 2001).

4. Richard T. Kainuma.

5. Every Sunday in the Christian calendar has a name and appointed passages to be read from the Bible. At that time, the Sundays from late spring through late fall were named "Sundays after Trinity," in reference to a church festival called "Trinity."

6. Martin Luther's *Small Catechism,* published in 1531, is a little handbook that instructs by asking a question (e.g., what is the meaning of baptism?) and then giving the answer. This handbook, used for the instruction of people preparing for membership in the Lutheran Church, provides a concise explanation of basic beliefs common to all Christians.

7. See the appendix following for the letter of commendation from Colonel Turner.

Appendix

Typed Letter to Chaplain Yost from Lieutenant Colonel Turner

HEADQUARTERS 100TH INFANTRY BATTALION (SEP)
APO 34–U.S. ARMY

29 October 1943

SUBJECT: Commendation
TO: 1st Lt (Chaplain) Isreal [*sic*] A. S. Yost

1. On the occasion of my relief from command of the 100th Infantry Battalion (Sep) I wish to make a matter of record my profound satisfaction with the services you have rendered to the battalion in so many ways.

2. You have done things which no chaplain could be required to do. You have repeatedly assisted in the actual care of the wounded and have assisted in their evacuation under heavy shell-fire. Your skill and the comfort you have given painfully wounded men have aided materially in their recovery.

3. I can truthfully say that no man in the unit is more respected or loved than you are. It has been my pleasure to make a brief note on your qualification card which expresses my feelings toward you.

/s/ Farrant L Turner
FARRANT L TURNER
Lt Col, 100th Inf Bn (Sep)
Commanding

FIVE

How Long in These Hills?

THE RAIN continued on Monday, November 15, and rain makes mud. For the day my principal activity was a lack of activity, rest. In the afternoon I began instructing the four new Christians, outlining for them the content of the books of the Bible. I posted a box of gifts home to Peggy; V-Mail and surface mail cost members of the armed forces nothing, but we paid for sending packages and airmail letters. I overheard an officer asking one of the drivers if he would like to become the chaplain's assistant. "It's too risky," replied the soldier. "You are wrong," I interrupted with a laugh. "The safest place is with the chaplain."

A chaplain's job is not nearly as dangerous or frightening as that of most combat infantrymen, but the fellows liked to say it was and were making a sort of legend about the chaplain's activity. I certainly did not feel brave and daring. I wanted to get home from the war safe and sound and as soon as possible. It was only out of a sense of duty that I was trying to do what I could to be a good padre. The compliments they paid me often embarrassed me. In the evening I played the field organ and some of the men sang hymns with me.

The rain continued most of Tuesday. Bill Mauldin called his first collection of cartoons about the war in Italy "Mud, Mules and Mountains," and he was right about all three; they were making life miserable for all the GI Joes. Headquarters sent over my breakfast to the medics quarters. When the troops moved to a new bivouac area at Santa Maria Oliveto, I walked along with our CO, Major Gillespie. The medics set up the aid station in a small church. The sacristan informed us that the Germans had taken the priest along with them; he also expressed his concern that our men would use too much of his straw and hay. I had the men black out two of the church windows with blankets. At noon I wrote to Peggy, assuring her that the cold weather was not bothering me; I had borrowed an enlisted man's overcoat and gloves, and I was wearing a raincoat on top of everything else. After the evening meal at headquarters mess, I spoke in French with someone at the CP, but I cannot remember with whom.

Wednesday began with clear skies, but soon the rain returned. It was a good day for writing letters, and that's what I did. For supper we had tough beef; a local man had slaughtered an animal, and we bought the meat from him. Kome shared some homemade taffy he had gotten from home. The medics joined me in singing some Christmas carols. We tried to use a charcoal stove to heat the chapel but it smoked too much.

On Thursday morning I was finally able to hold worship with the only company I had not been able to meet with on Sunday. In the afternoon, Masaichi Goto, top noncom of the medics, accompanied me on a visit to E and F Companies. An AJA requested that we have more services than just the one on Sundays; I explained that whenever we were within reach of enemy shells and bombs we dared not risk assembling large groups. I arranged for a service with A Company for the morrow. I joined the others who were griping about not receiving our mail; rumor had it that at regimental headquarters a lot of bags were stacked up.

The next day, at 8:30 a.m., the service with A Company was held as scheduled. Afterwards one of the worshipers asked me to explain the difference between Roman Catholics and Protestants. At 4:30 p.m., seven of this company came to the battalion aid to request baptism. After I had explained the meaning of the sacrament, one who had been raised Buddhist questioned his right to change religions. He seemed satisfied when I explained what Christians mean by "free will." All promised to receive instruction. Using water in a canteen cup, I baptized all seven in the same manner I had baptized the four on November 14. In the blacked-out church, the light of a single candle added an impressiveness to the ceremony. We were in the midst of the paraphernalia of the medics: litters, blankets, opened chests with jars and bandages on the tops of trays. Captain Kometani and Isaac Akinaka stood as official witnesses that these seven AJAs were now Christians: Carl Kiyoshi Morioka, George Toshio Inouye, Seichi James Maeda, Shoichi Isaac Tengan, Robert Haruto Karasaki, Frank Isamu Ikehara, and Kenneth Tadahisa Okamoto.

This was a unique event: it took place in an Italian Roman Catholic church converted for the time into an American aid station; the pastor was a German American and the new believers were Japanese Americans; one of the witnesses, Sergeant Akinaka, was a member of the Church of Latter Day Saints (Mormon); the other witness, Doc Kometani, told the converts that this was the most important decision they had ever made. To my wife I wrote, "I had some difficulty with the Japanese names, but what an experience as they were brought into the Kingdom! It's worth the sacrifices, Peg, for this." That evening two of the medics sang Hawaiian songs to guitar accompaniment; they included two hymns in Hawaiian, "Leaning on the Everlasting Arms" and "Jesus, Savior, Pilot Me."

On this day Kent Y. Nakamura[1] became my assistant. A graduate of the University of Hawaii in the social sciences, he was both a clerk and a driver. Saturday began in a pleasant way: someone brought breakfast to me. When I reported to the CP to arrange for worship for the next day, I was told that one of our patrols had found a German KIA. With a detail of four men and a guide from B Company, I hiked to the spot, attached a long wire to the body, rolled it over (a precaution against a booby trap), and helped the detail bury the corpse. In my November "Report of Chaplains," I recorded the action thus.

> German soldier: half of identification disk already removed by someone else; half remaining read thus: 2/Ers Btl S13 5493 A Buried 20 Nov 1943 on hill west of S. Maria Oliveto, Italy, on east slope 50 feet from top of hill: from top took compass sights: to Venafro, 220 degrees and to S. Maria Oliveto, 100 degrees.

As an officer I usually carried field glasses, a compass, and the current operations map. As a Boy Scout I had learned to use topographic maps and a compass. If one of the detail was also trained in compass work, I had him verify my readings after I had taken them. On this occasion, since we did not have a minesweeper with us, I was very careful as we moved off the beaten path to perform our task. Back at Headquarters Company at noon, I dined on spaghetti, hot dogs, fish, bread and butter, and coffee. A member of D Company requested baptism; I arranged for it to take place the next day.

Even though we were busy with the details of the war, we found time to think of the future, as this letter I wrote to Peg in the afternoon explains.

> Last night two of the doctors and I got talking about the post-war world. They are strong for keeping an army prepared. I don't know; perhaps they are right. So long as the world is not Christian we can't expect Christian principles to keep the world from war.[2] But I do know that we need more than just military training for our young men; they ought also give some time to doing something constructive. Perhaps every lad of 18 ought to

spend six months in military training and six months on some project that will help toward world peace or better the country: slum clearance, hospital work, or the like. One year out of the life of each teenage boy would not hurt—they can put off marriage and the other things for their future welfare.

And I know that I will have a big task when I get home. This war is so much the result of selfishness. Even now we are all selfishly wishing that the war might end so that we can get back to our little family groups. We find that Poles and Czechs and Austrians who have nothing in common with the Nazis are on the lines over here against us. When captured they speak out against the full-blooded Germans. I suspect that the reason is that they are also thinking of their loved ones back home and know that not to fight would mean harm to their families.

So because they are selfish just as we are, they fight hard. When I get back, God willing, we must in season and out preach that it is as individuals neglect to think and act properly in little things that world events go haywire. If we neglect to vote, or speak on current issues, we allow the cheat and crook to get into office, until finally things get to the point where a Hitler or a Mussolini rules nations. It will be hard for me to soft-pedal when once I get back. If a man has no interest in the church and never attends, I'm going to talk turkey to him, and if he remains in his lethargy his name will go off the church roll, regardless of the five dollars a year he may give. There is an urgency about life and the work of the church; there's no time for fooling around.

On Sunday I was up at daylight; I woke up before dawn and did not get back to sleep. My new assistant went out to guide the Roman Catholics of the battalion to the location set for Mass. At 8:30, men from A, D, and Headquarters Companies joined those of B for worship. At 10:30, E and F Companies and the Battalion Supply Organization (BSO) worshiped. At 11:00, I had a separate service in the C Company area. During lunch at C, enemy shells fell too close for comfort, so we all moved up the hillside. At 2:30, fifteen, including those already baptized, came to the aid station for instruction in the meaning of the Apostles' Creed. At 3:30, with the altar kit set up on a low desk in front of the Roman Catholic altar, I donned cassock, surplice, and pectoral cross, lit the two altar-kit candles, and baptized Masato Charles Takashima and Kosuke David Shimabuku, both of D Company. Akinaka again served as a witness; Lt. Scott A. Wise was the second witness. In the meantime I missed the evening meal; thoughtfully, my assistant Kent had saved chow for me. This was the kind of Lord's Day, completely filled with activities, that I had been accustomed to in the parish back home.

Monday after breakfast I worked on baptismal records. The Corps of Chaplains expected each chaplain to keep precise data on pastoral acts. Here is the complete report for the first baptism I performed.

> Hidei NMI Ueno, 30100055, Hq. Co., 100th Inf. Bn., on 14 Nov 43 at Pozzilli, Italy; born 16 Oct 1917 at Honolulu, Oahu, T.H.; witnesses: Isaac F. Akinaka, 30100059, and Torao NMI Kawano, 30101801, both of Med. Det., 100th Inf. Bn. Parents: Jisaburo and Tsuneyo (nee Fujioka) Ueno.

Even under combat conditions the regulations pertaining to the monthly report had to be followed exactly; if it contained errors or if it omitted required facts, it was returned to be corrected. When I was unable to find out a mother's maiden name, I put "(mother)" after her name, anticipating that in the case of Japanese names most officials in the military would not know which of the parents' given names was that of the mother.

Before dark I walked about in the areas of three of the companies. I talked with two AJAs about baptism; one told me he was ready to become a Christian. I also made arrangements for services on Thanksgiving Day. On Tuesday I prepared a four-page worship bulletin to be mimeographed on a single sheet of paper; on it were the Apostles' Creed, a Confession of Sins, the Offertory, and the Collects for Grace and for Peace, all from the Lutheran liturgy.[3] Each member of the battalion would receive a copy. In my letter to my wife I requested that she send me face soap, heavy woolen socks, and chocolate candy. I was still looking for the muffler she had promised me, but I assured her that I had enough clothing to keep three, or at least two, men warm and that the winters in Italy were milder than those in Pennsylvania.

After supper I attended the Adoration of the Blessed Sacrament, a service in the Italian language conducted by a local priest in the second church in town (we occupied the first church building). Afterwards, at the CP, I sat in on the instructions for the next military operation. As a member of the battalion staff, I considered such briefings very important, for in this way I could locate the objectives of each company on my map and gain information on the trails and donkey paths to be used by the litter bearers and by myself as I visited the men on the front.

On Wednesday, because we were to be in combat on the next day, I held three Thanksgiving Day services a day early, all in the morning and covering all the units of the battalion. In the early afternoon some first-class mail arrived, including a letter posted on October 16 (this was November 24) with pictures of my wife and two children, a big morale booster. I replied immediately, lamenting that I was not able to send home any pictures of myself because ten days ago a new censorship rule had forbidden the taking of photos. Also included in this batch of mail were a September 20 telegram about the birth of our son and a V-Mail of November 8. We concluded from this evidence that even though V-Mail letters were difficult to read because of the small size of the writing (and worse, of the typing) and at times were printed almost too dark for reading, it was better to use them for our correspondence because they took so much less time in transit.

At three p.m. a hot meal was served in all the company messes. A bit later the medics had to take care of a soldier who had accidentally shot himself while examining an Italian pistol. The battalion trucked out; I rode in one of the ambulances. A half mile from the start, our vehicle got stuck and had to be winched out by a truck. I spent the rest of the trip standing on the running board on the right side, directing the driver so that we would not get stuck again. As we pulled into Colli, our destination, two shells zoomed overhead. That night we medics slept in what had been a hotel.

On Thanksgiving Day the companies moved into their positions in the hills. At 7:30 p.m., I joined the detail about to carry rations to the front, hoisting a box of K rations to my shoulder. In the dark, we crossed a narrow footbridge over a river and then climbed up a ladder on the far side; I had difficulty when the handle of the shovel hanging from my belt caught on the rung. (Years later one of our veterans told me that on the same ladder he had been unable to keep hold of the mortar barrel he was carrying, and it bounced down the ladder and was lost in the water below.) Then we stumbled up a rocky trail. After dropping my load at the forward aid station, I continued on with the ration crew to the forward CP, arriving there at one a.m. I spent the night at that spot in the cold, grateful for the overcoat I was wearing.

On Friday after a K ration breakfast, I accompanied a soldier going to his unit on Hill 1017. With help from nearby riflemen I buried a German just ten yards off the trail, breaking in half his identification disk and burying half with the body. At noon I ate at the forward CP, then checked in at the forward aid, and then returned to Colli. Here I gave my assistant the information about the burial and the half of the identification disk for him to send back to the GRO.

A letter from the chaplain of the division advised me that I might soon be advanced to the rank of captain. Better news was the arrival of some much-needed New Testaments from the division. The company kitchens had prepared turkey and filling and had packaged the food along with some nuts in a cardboard box; I had my share of the Thanksgiving feast. Gathering up my musette bag and blanket roll, I walked back across the bridge, climbed up the ladder, and plodded steadily along the rocky trail toward the forward aid station, all by myself in the dark.

Diary notes for Saturday, November 27, read,

> Leisurely breakfasted and shaved at the forward aid station. Walked to CP and then up to platoons on the side of Hill 1017. Intended to take marker to grave of German, but Hill 1017 was being shelled. At CP got forward aid station's share of turkey sandwiches and carried them down to them. Went to sleep on a litter in house there early. At 11 p.m. heard of wounded so went with litter squad to place to which wounded had walked. When he (the wounded soldier) saw me he said, "Chaplain, you didn't need to come up here." Guided squad back with litter.

Sending turkey sandwiches to the men on the line was a good idea, but the execution of the plan was poorly handled, according to the story told by some of the men. One unit received cardboard boxes containing only bread, and another received boxes with meat only. Those receiving the bread griped because, though the slices tasted good, there was no meat to make sandwiches. Those who got the turkey did not miss the bread too much, and they chuckled at the thought of some buddies trying to feast on plain bread. The next morning the situation was reversed: the turkey eaters got diarrhea because the meat had spoiled on the way up, and the bread eaters laughed because they were still healthy. Diarrhea is not cause for a man to be evacuated from the front, but it increases the chance of being wounded; indeed, cases of soldiers being killed while moving their bowels have been reported.

Diary notes:

> Sunday, Nov. 28. Breakfast at forward aid. Walked to CP and had brief devotions in M/C. Then moved on and had three other services with small groups on the side of Hill 1017. Read lessons for First Sunday in Advent and three hymns and spoke of (1) Jesus showing God's love by coming as a babe, (2) We ought to prepare for Christ's coming into our hearts, (3) We ought to serve Him.
>
> Dinner [noon meal] at forward aid. Walked down trail. Had similar

service with some of D at ration dump near footbridge. Reported at rear CP and went by ¾-ton truck to E and F and had service as above but longer: sang two hymns and I read the Venite and longer development of sermon. Then hitchhiked to BSO (Battalion Supply Organization) and had service there. Started back after dark in peep [small jeep] but got in troop movement, so at bypass set out on foot; finally got ride in engineer truck. Had service at rear aid station in upper room. Took my assistant and Frankie (medics runner) back to forward aid. And so to bed. (Felt nauseated when I retired.)

The events of November 29 are recorded in my little notebook and on two sheets of stationery. I was awakened in the darkness at five a.m. by the tinkling of the field telephone hanging at the top of the bed of Lt. John J. Dahl, the battalion surgeon who had joined us some days before as a replacement for Doc Kawasaki. We were sleeping on the ground floor of an Italian farmhouse, on beds with springs over which we had stretched blankets. We got up and aroused the litter bearers sleeping on the floor above. I had a mild case of diarrhea; I went outside and used the nearby slit trench latrine. Some ate a light breakfast, but I refrained, feeling that my stomach could not tolerate food.

We packed up; I carried a musette pack in which was stowed my private communion kit, several New Testaments, a Bible, a *Boy Scouts of America Handbook,* a *Soldiers Handbook,* a set of winter underwear, and mess gear; a dispatch case crammed full of writing paper and booklets; a suspender belt with canteen and cup, first-aid packet, and shovel; and an overcoat with two meals of rations in the pockets and a mattress cover stuffed into a sleeve, the last item for "sacking" a dead body before placing it on a litter. We followed a rocky trail down which water was trickling. I quickly got winded but managed to keep up with the others; the fresh morning air helped to take away the sensation of nausea. About four hundred yards up the hill we came to what had been our forward CP.

We had not taken the easier route across the fields because they were mined. Since mules had been carrying rations over the cobbled path for several days, many of the stones were loose. When we all stopped to drink from the spring near the CP, I went aside and dealt with diarrhea again. We rested here for some time; the CP was the last house on this trail to the summit of the hill. Then for several hundred yards we continued on the regular path. Upon sighting a stream off to the side and downhill, we sent the minesweepers across the fields to clear a path for the rest of us; they did not find any mines. As we traversed the open area we passed by a German dugout that looked as though a shell had hit it directly. In a gully below, a single dead German was lying on his back with his mess gear nearby. We came to some houses from which a cobbled path led to the stream. While we rested here, a shell exploded near us; we assumed that an enemy OP (observation post) had spotted our column as we crossed the open country. We kept under cover as we proceeded down to the water, cutting through a vineyard on the way.

Before reaching the stream we stopped at a group of houses. The one we selected for the aid station was locked, and none of the Italians in the area had a key for it. We broke into it and found the interior unsuitable. Beyond the stream were two houses that looked better the closer we got to them. Upon investigation, the medics found that the second floor of each farmhouse had tiled floors and a fireplace. The aid station was set up in one of these rustic buildings.

A member of the Ammunition and Pioneer Platoon, the ones who did the minesweeping, in "checking out" the buildings, found three hen's eggs and brought them proudly into the medics quarters. I told him that since I was sick, he ought to give me one of them. He thought it over as he boiled all three eggs and decided that he could spare one of them for me. The second one he had already promised to his lieutenant. After I had enjoyed mine, in came the owner of the building. When I told him I had just eaten my first fresh egg since leaving the United States, he looked at me in an odd manner and said that he had just bought three eggs. We immediately went to check on his eggs; of course he did not find them, for his eggs were the ones we were eating. He did not seem too upset at his loss; after all, he was smoking our cigarettes and soon would be eating some of our food.

A litter squad brought in Jack Mizuha; he had multiple wounds from German machine-gun bullets. When he saw me, he propped himself up with one arm and pointed a finger at me as he said, "Chaplain, don't go near those German heavies; they are deadly accurate." He was too seriously wounded for me to laugh at his remark, but I was remembering how some days before he had belittled the efficiency of German gunners. I gave Mizuha some of the bean soup I had just warmed up.

I went out to deal with diarrhea for the third time, and then I slept for two hours near the fire inside. When I got awake I learned that most of the medics had left to set up an aid station closer to the front. Doc Dahl insisted that I should stay put and rest, but after the next litter case came through our station, I loaded up all my gear and two blankets besides and set out for the litter squad and Sergeant Goto up the paved donkey path toward the forward aid a mile and a half ahead. Midway we passed several cottages; two women and some children greeted us from the door of one—so often the local people did not leave their homes to take refuge in a safer place but remained at home even in areas that were bombed and shelled. One of our boys gave the children some *caramelli* (candy). Farther along we passed walking wounded going to the rear and then three young German POWs guarded by two Nisei. Just as we were passing these two groups, "screaming meemies" hit to the front and side of us; everyone hit the ground—guards, prisoners, casualties, and medics.

After a rest behind a cottage, we continued our ascent, soon passing a lone wounded Jerry rearward bound. After we arrived at the forward aid station, one in a cluster of shabby cottages, the farthest up the hillside, I ate some supper and fell asleep. During the night I was awakened once by the noise of mules bringing rations forward.

When I got up the next day I was no longer ill. For the day's happenings, compare the two accounts that follow, the first a letter written to Peggy early in the day and the other the diary's record scribbled at the end of the same day.

Dearest Sweetheart. Letter #70 30 Nov 1943 Tuesday Morn Italy

I'm sorry that I didn't get a chance to write to you yesterday. It's one of the few days I've missed writing, and as on some days I've written twice or thrice, I know you'll forgive me. I was on the move (on foot) much of the day and also had slight diarrhea. When not hiking, I lay resting. Didn't even get to read my chapter of the Bible yesterday, though I did write a few lines in my notebook for you.

This a.m. I feel better; diarrhea almost gone. It's the last of the month and another chaplain's report to get in; but I won't be able to get to it for a few days yet.

Peggy, Italy is beautiful; if there were not a war going on we could enjoy the mountains and the little houses and barns nestling high up on the slopes with donkey paths winding up to them. The people must be rather self-sufficient, raising and making most of what they need for a simple life.

The towns we are seeing now have better homes. In one I saw a quite modern nursery: clean, well furnished with desks, pictures, washroom and toilet, small chapel, etc. Sometimes we get to stay in buildings; in fact, I haven't slept outdoors in the last month or more. That's because the aid station almost has to be inside a building and that's my place of duty. I therefore have it so much easier than the fighting soldiers; they really have tough going, Peg.

As I sit here writing I notice the door of the little house has a hole cut in it at the bottom, just big enough for the cat to enter and leave. And of course each cottage has a fireplace in it; usually we are able to use it too. So you see I have not much hardship to bear personally. The fighting man bears the brunt of war's sufferings. I cannot do much to relieve him of that; but I am doing the best I can to care for his soul.

Tuesday, Nov. 30. Near Scapoli. Breakfast. During a.m. many wounded came through. Many dead up on hill. Worked making hot drinks till afternoon. Got fine letter from Peg but had to wait several hours before got time to read it. Shell landed nearby, concussion felt in house. Late in afternoon, two 18-year-old German prisoners brought wounded 19-year-old German (Peter Schoeneberg of Bonn). They took one of ours on down and we gave Peter a unit of plasma. Could have cried as I watched the two German kids en route down the path: one Catholic, one Evangelical. Spoke in German with Peter: only child, father dead, said his mother had many sorrows. He had two years yet in school, studying engineering. In evening had fire as on night before. Several officers and men dropped in and chattered and ate. I finally suggested that we turn in; had tried to sleep but too much commotion. During night one cold fellow moved closer to fire and put feet in my face!

That the Allied attack in the hills was not faring well was evident. On December 1, our CO, Major Gillespie, stopped in at the aid station on his way forward, just as he had done on the day before. A litter squad went forward in the drizzling rain to the CP and by eleven a.m. had evacuated nine casualties, most of them only slightly wounded.

The CO returned from the front sick, mostly because of fatigue. All the companies were weak in numbers of active men. I helped in the battalion aid all day long. At dusk a call came to me to come forward to remove three KIAs. I rushed with a squad of four to the CP, but it was too dark to work, and there was no special reason for getting the bodies out that night. We returned to the forward aid station.

On Thursday after breakfast, I went forward by way of the CP to A Company in the vicinity of Hill 841. There a lieutenant showed me several of our KIA. He suggested that I use a trail others had not been using; it had been swept of mines, he said. I walked down it by myself

and brought up a detail from the aid station and set them to work carrying bodies down the unused trail. During the day they moved five bodies, leaving four of them on an exposed spot two hundred yards short
of the battalion aid. Shells fell close to the detail, but I was unable to
contact them; none of them were hit. I helped to remove two bodies
from the crest of a hill, a dangerous spot for anyone to be exposed in
the daylight.

While I was with the medics in their building, a frantic call came over
the field telephone; the CO of A Company wanted to know if anyone
had seen the chaplain. "They've been shelling the trail I told him to use,"
bewailed the officer, "and I'm afraid the chaplain is out there by himself." The medic on the phone assured him that I was right there, safe
and sound. It does a man's heart good to know that others are concerned
about him.

I tramped back to the CP in Colli and from there phoned my assistant Kent, instructing him to take care of any KIAs in his area. Next I
rode back to the BSO to get additional mattress covers and my typewriter. As night fell, I got back to the rear aid station. Alone in a drizzle
I slogged up the donkey path in the dark, stopping for a few minutes at
a local home where a girl of fifteen lay sick; we had sent her some aspirin
and canned milk earlier in the day. By the time I arrived at the medics
quarters, the weather had cleared and there was some moonlight. That
night the phone rang often, and the wire to the forward CP was cut several times by shellfire. In the early morning I lay awake worrying about
the evacuation of the growing number of dead buddies on the hills.

On Saturday the rain had returned; I decided that nothing could be
accomplished that day because of the bad weather. I went out to investigate the four dead lying in the exposed area, but I was turned back by
exploding shells. After supper I trudged down to the rear aid, crossing
swollen creeks and slipping on the wet path and getting wet feet. I finished most of the November "Report of Chaplains" and then returned
to the forward aid station before darkness set in. The rain had stopped.

Most of Sunday morning I stayed in the medics quarters because of
an intensive enemy barrage in the area; during this time I held two brief
services for those at the aid post. Eventually I was able to go to the forward CP and the areas of A and B Companies for quick services with
small groups. In the forward area of B, I passed several riflemen in their
slit trenches, jumped down into one not in use, and turned to face several GIs on the slope of the hill. As I began to read loudly so that all

could hear, one of the men hissed, "Shhhh! Chaplain, not so loud! The Jerries are right beyond you." I soft-pedaled my voice and cut short my devotional message, somewhat upset that no one had warned me how close I was to the enemy positions.

Late in the day I went all the way back to the BSO and conducted worship in the moonlight for the rear echelon. Later at the rear CP, twenty-five turned out for a short service. After stopping for a few minutes at the rear aid and the ration dump, I retraced my steps to the forward aid. I was thinking of the men on the line, too long in their foxholes, most of them cold and wet, and all of them shelled again and again. My objective this Sunday had been to try to cheer them up by my presence.

During this action the medics had to man three aid stations. At the one least used and most remote from the fighting, actually along the first route taken in the advance, my assistant and one other medic were assigned to take care of any wounded who might stray rearward on the old route. One night they closed the doors and windows of the small farmhouse they were using, tightened them securely as a security measure, and then fell asleep near the glowing fireplace. Early the next morning one of them got awake, feeling groggy and very weak; he staggered to the nearest door and with much effort got it open. The cool air revived him enough so that he was able to drag his companion out into the open air. Only then did the two of them realize how close they had come to asphyxiation.

The following are my diary entries for the next three days.

> Monday, Dec. 6. In a.m. after breakfast at forward aid went with guide to D Company's new position and was shown where three bodies were. Also went to F. In both areas I held brief devotions for the men of the companies. While I was thus engaged my squad moved four bodies to the forward aid station. In p.m. made trip to forward CP and spoke with the new major now CO. [This was probably Alex E. McKenzie, Island born and in the 100th since its formation. If not it was William H. Blytt of the 133rd. Both of these men commanded the battalion briefly after Gillespie took sick.] After dark, call came for the litter squad for Company C. As I alone in aid station knew the trails near there, I guided squad in moonlight to C ration dump. Met patient and he was put astride a mule and taken down. I returned to the forward aid station.
>
> Tuesday, Dec. 7. After breakfast took new squad up to get bodies in D area. Got one out, when met wounded from C. Pointed way to aid station. He told of two litter cases in company so I took litter we were

using for dead and followed telephone wire to C; found they had taken patients to rear and I had come over exposed trail. Rested and returned, running fast over exposed area; whew! Made contact with aid men coming up and explained situation and they returned. Sent my squad to rear aid to rest. At 4 p.m. met them and brought one body to mule trail and sacked it. Decided against going for other two D men as in area being shelled. Slept at rear battalion aid, on litter close to fire, elevated—heavy cold.

Wednesday, Dec. 8. Tagged two of those dead brought down last night; fourteen bodies gotten down from hills in this action. Will let twenty-some others lie until troops move forward. Last night French officers came into our position. Went to forward aid in a.m. Spent most of day in forward aid station.

During these early days of December, the proper evacuation of our KIAs was my major problem. The physical removal of dead bodies over steep trails under battle conditions was nerve-racking, especially for one convinced (as I was) that it was illogical to risk lives in performing a task that could be conducted in safety later on. However, there was also a morale problem; the living were seeing many of their buddies lying dead, and the men assigned to me were handling corpses that were often horribly mangled, especially if killed by mortar fire.

Army planners had arranged for all men coming from the States to carry mattress covers. These were collected overseas and deposited in supply depots to be used by GROs in the sacking of the corpses. Under ideal conditions, KIAs were to be enshrouded and moved as quickly as possible for proper burial in a military cemetery. Our BSO ran out of these covers. It was my custom to inspect each KIA before allowing the detail to come close. If the body had been badly torn apart, I would wrap it in a shelter half, binding it securely with a cord. Any not badly mutilated were carried to a building near the battalion aid station and put out of sight until I could find mattress covers.

One evening I stepped inside the medics building and asked for volunteers to assist me in getting the corpses into sacks so that we could carry them farther down the trail to a point where trucks could be used. Not a single person responded to my call for help. I left the aid station and began to do the job the best I could by myself; I sympathized with anyone who did not want to get involved in so gruesome a task. Soon Staff Sergeant Goto of the medics appeared and began to help me. Goto could be extremely gruff when he wanted to, and he never minced words in bawling out one of his men who didn't do a job right. But on this occasion, Goto was as sad as he was mad. He spoke to me in a low voice, "Chaplain, we ought to take them out and shoot them!" He certainly did not mean that any of his crew should be harmed; he was simply venting a heartfelt disappointment with his brothers. The two of us managed to complete the dreary work.

✪   ✪   ✪

On Thursday, December 9, French Moroccan troops[4] came into our positions to relieve us from the fighting. One of their mortar squads got lost, and I used my college French in trying to help the adjutant's orderly locate the North African men. Neither their soldiers nor their medics appeared proficient by our standards. One of the tribesmen (all enlisted men were from tribes from the mountains south of the Mediterranean Sea) wounded his hand on a booby trap. The troops seemed uncouth, and we feared that they would not treat the native folks very kindly. None of us, nor any of the Italians, were able to communicate with these "Goums." Late in the afternoon the medics and I followed the last of our troops down the trail off the hills. At the road head I climbed into the cab of a troop truck to return to our kitchen area. I shaved off a ten-days' beard.

In the dark of predawn I ate and then slept on until noon of the following day. I was physically and mentally exhausted, as were most of the men; in addition, most of them had badly swollen feet from the long, cold stay in wet slit trenches.

Friday, during our preparations to move farther to the rear into a rest area, I met the new chaplain of the 1st Battalion and realized that during our days in the hills I had been the only chaplain in the regiment. We all ate an early supper, but our column of vehicles did not move out until late afternoon. Since Kent did the driving, I sat in the jeep and dozed off and on in the moonlight. Often the chaplain's jeep was the next-to-last vehicle in the battalion convoy. The last was the small truck whose men were responsible for fixing any repairs necessary on the move. When the repair truck stopped to assist a broken-down vehicle, Kent and I brought up the rear of the line. Poor Kent was always kept busy on such a trip, speeding to catch up and then breaking hard to avoid ramming the vehicle ahead as the whole column telescoped in and out hour after hour.

About two a.m., we arrived in the vicinity of Alife, but no one knew precisely where our units were to set up camp. We milled about until the companies were assigned areas. I felt miserable and cold and expressed my discomfort by reprimanding any of those I felt were responsible for the lack of planning. Finding nothing better, I placed my shelter half on the ground, piled a bit of straw on top, and bundled up in four blankets. I did not awaken until noon.

After lunch on Saturday I felt almost normal again. When the GRO phoned about the corpses still lying back in the hills, I explained that removal of the bodies was impossible so long as dangerous battle conditions prevailed up front; he seemed to understand. I pitched a pup tent and put my bedding roll and personal equipment in it. After looking over the lessons for the morrow, I tried, unsuccessfully, to arrange for a Catholic Mass.

Again I spoke with the new chaplain, who I assumed was the regimental chaplain responsible for assigning me to some of the smaller units in addition to my responsibilities to the 100th. I retired early, but twice was called to the phone in the battalion headquarters tent, once with regard to worship for some regimental units.

After shaving on Sunday morning, I put on a clean shirt and clean trousers. Near the medics tent I preached in the open to the men of the battalion. Then I conducted worship in the rain for twenty GIs at the regimental antitank company bivouac. At 11:30, Col. Carley L. Marshall, CO of the 133rd Regiment, called me to his tent and informed me that I was being promoted to regimental chaplain and would become a captain! Our battalion officers had predicted that when I reported to Marshall, no matter for what reason, the CO would quickly turn the conversation to J. E. B. Stuart, the rebel leader of Civil War fame. They were right; the colonel lauded his hero and nothing more was said about me or my job as chaplain. Marshall had a DSC for bravery at Fondouk, Tunisia (Fondouk became "Von Duke," the colonel's nickname among the troops), but I was not impressed by the man and decided to stay out of his sight as much as possible.[5]

Sunday afternoon I put up a tent fly to replace the too-small pup tent, but I found it was just as unsatisfactory. I went to headquarters and requisitioned a wall tent in accordance with army regulations; up to this time I had not needed one.

At 3:30, four came to communion. After supper Lt. Rocco Marzano, our Italian-speaking officer, who after attending my battalion service had gone to a civilian Mass in Alife, reported to me that the priest's sermon had been similar in content to mine. This was no surprise to me, for the Gospel for the Third Sunday in Advent was the same for both Lutherans and Roman Catholics.[6]

Up to this date, December 12, because of diary notes, the story has included many little details to make realistic the life of a chaplain with combat troops. Most of the time the days were filled with activities; most of the activities depended on the decisions of the chaplain, made without direction from any superior officer. No one instructed me to assist in getting the wounded to the aid station, or to hold services for small groups virtually under enemy fire, or to circulate among the men up front and in the rear. Indeed, upon occasion, officers and men expressed surprise when the chaplain greeted them in dangerous situations with a cheery word. I was not asked to carry medical supplies and extra blankets or a litter. Most surprising of all, I was not appointed GRO of the battalion until December 23, 1943 (effective January 1, 1944), more than two weeks after the last of the combat events recounted thus far. (This assignment of the chaplain as GRO lasted only until February 25, 1944, when army policy absolutely forbade the appointment of any chaplain as a GRO.)

Nor was the activity of this one chaplain extraordinary. In 1945, a booklet of eighty-six pages, titled *Chaplains of the Fifth Army,* was printed at Milan, Italy. It recorded the actual activities of numerous combat chaplains during the war in Italy, giving examples of chaplains who, observing a particular need with no one near to perform it, promptly assumed responsibility: establishing a collecting point for the wounded, selecting an area on the Salerno beachhead for a military cemetery at a time when it was not certain the Americans could hold the area, acting as aid men and litter bearers, conducting worship under fire, visiting the men on the front line. Some of these men of the cloth were awarded decorations, others were not.

On page 17 of the booklet, the writer, after concluding the account of a chaplain with the words, "His tireless energy and sincerity in his work have endeared him in the hearts of all with whom he was associated," continued with this paragraph.

> In a like vein is the tribute paid in simple sincerity by the soldier who during these days and later, had observed the ministry of Chaplain Israel Yost. "Chaplain Yost," he said, "gave the impression not of a hero, shining with bravery in the midst of threatening danger, nor of the coward cringing with fear as the enemy fire ranged about over his head. Rather, he seemed a faithful minister among his flock, moving with loving uncon-

cern, as though there were no more danger than in a parish in peace-time."

Like many aspects of this war, the role of the chaplain in combat had to be established by those actually performing a padre's duties. Technical Circular No. 4 from the Office of the Chief of Chaplains, dated March 1, 1942, with the title *The Regimental or Unit Chaplain,* contains eleven pages of good advice for chaplains in general but has not a word about chaplains in combat. The booklet *The Chaplain Serves: Chaplain Activities, 1943,* from the Office of the Chief of Chaplains, March 1, 1944, includes a section on "The Chaplain in the Combat Area" describing not what a chaplain is required to do, but what some chaplains actually do.

It was not until *Technical Manual, TM 16-205: The Chaplain* was issued in July of 1944 that the combat chaplain's duties were spelled out, apparently on the basis of what chaplains in 1943 had established as the procedures to be followed. Conscientious chaplains in World War II were already following to the letter and beyond what the Army of the United States suggested should be their standard of conduct under fire.

Notes

1. Kent Nakamura (1918–1994), a graduate of the University of Hawaii, was a librarian at the Hawaii State Library prior to joining the 100th. After the war, he resumed his career there.

2. The world was not kept from war. Yost's oldest son, Christian Michael Yost, who was born during World War II, was drafted into the army to serve in the Vietnam War. After several years of teaching in New York, he moved to New Hampshire, where he is a builder and construction consultant.

3. The Apostles' Creed is a statement of Christian belief in one God known as Father, Son (Jesus), and Holy Spirit. The Confession of Sins is a statement of penitence for one's wrongdoings followed by the pastor's pronouncement of God's forgiveness. The Offertory is a reading or song through which the worshipers offer themselves and their resources to God. Collects are short prayers.

4. This refers to the Moroccan troops known as "Goums." The Goumier, ethnic Berber tribesmen from the Atlas Mountains, were mercenaries who formed the nucleus of the Free French troops in North Africa. They wore bathrobe-like outer garments known as *djellaba,* turbans, and GI shoes and were armed primarily with American military weapons and their own traditional steel knives. In the tough, mountainous terrain of southern Italy, under the command of Free French officers, they were formidable fighters who are given credit for a daring attack of thirteen thousand men across high mountain peaks, which defeated the Germans from behind at Monte Cassino. Unfortunately, their bravery was offset by a reputation for stealing from American troops and raping and murdering Italian citizens and pillaging their towns. The tension described by the

author between the men of the 100th and the Goumiers was typical of U.S. troops of the 34th Division. The 100th felt particularly protective of the Italian peasant farmers and villagers who had no protection other than themselves and other GIs (Bimberg, 63).

5. In April 1943, the 34th Division attacked the Germans at Fondouk Pass in Tunisia. The German army was defending itself in a high mountain pass. The U.S. attack was repulsed with heavy losses as the valley was defended with mines, tanks, mortars, and artillery. British and U.S. forces ultimately took the position, but only with heavy losses.

6. Despite differences between the Lutheran and Roman Catholic Churches, the two denominations follow the same Christian calendar and usually read the same Gospel passage on a given Sunday. Advent is the four-week season prior to Christmas.

Gen. Mark Clark, Commanding General of the Fifth Army, reviews the 100th Bn, Leghorn, Italy, August 23, 1944.

100th Bn in combat, France, October 24, 1944.

100th Bn soldier writes a letter home.

100th Bn aid station, France, October 29, 1944.

Chaplain Yost in combat uniform with the netting of his helmet cut away to expose the small, white cross painted on it.

Chaplain Israel Yost's altar kit (with his first name misspelled) and his chaplain's flag. (Courtesy of Homer Yost.)

Kent Nakamura, Chaplain Yost's assistant, with the chaplain's jeep.

Chaplain Yost leads a service at the Franco-Italian border, 1945.

Richard "Dick" Hirano and Chaplain Yost in front of battalion aid station.

Chaplain Yost places a temporary marker on a military grave in Italy.

V-Mail letter Chaplain Yost sent home to his wife, Peggy, showing Italian artist's sketch of him.

Family photo Chaplain Yost carried with him during combat showing daughter Monica, wife Peggy, and son Christian, early 1944.

Chaplain Yost's tent at Ghedi Airfield near Brescia in northern Italy at the end of the war in Europe, May 1945.

Capt. Katsumi Kometani, dentist and morale officer, with Chaplain Yost in front of the chaplain's tent, Ghedi Airfield, May 1945.

Chaplain Yost leads a prayer service at the end of the war in Europe, May 1945.

SIX

A Reprieve before Cassino

WHAT A relief to be away from the front and not even in reserve but actually assigned to an area for a period of rest, the first such experience since the 100th came ashore at Salerno! The men who had survived were entitled to these days of relaxation beyond the reach of enemy shells and bombs. There was a bit of a program to harden the men physically and some instruction of a military nature, but most of the time was for resting and catching up with life.

The men were housed in pyramidal tents, several squads under each canvas, with their blankets spread over straw on the ground. Company mess tents adjoined the soldiers' quarters, and the whole battalion became a reunited family. Most evenings, just after dark, movies were shown out in the open; upon occasion USO groups entertained. Once, Red Cross girls—real American women—visited, bringing doughnuts and coffee and laughter. Genuine bathing was possible; I took a shower on December 16, the first such comfort since I had disembarked from the *Rajula* in mid-September.

Mail accumulated during the combat days was distributed, along with packages; doughboys leisurely wrote long letters to folks back home. Winter uniforms, overshoes, and extra blankets cheered the weary GIs. The beer ration loosened their tongues, for they needed the catharsis of expressing their gripes and telling their war stories to buddies who understood what words were inadequate to express. Meals were tasty, ample, hot, and served at regular intervals. Card games lasted for hours, gambling for followers of Lady Luck and cribbage for the others. Once again Hawaiian music, both vocal and instrumental, echoed throughout the One Puka Puka.

Not all the free time was devoted to pleasure. Minds turned to somber reflection. As soon as the remnants of the 100th had stumbled off the hills, questions were asked about buddies in other companies. Who had been killed, who wounded, and how seriously? Then thoughts about the future surfaced. Will they put us back into combat? Are we getting replacements for the empty slots in our units? Do you think the war will end very soon?

Many were thankful as they compared these days of luxury with the eternity of discomfort from which they had just escaped.

"No got water anymore; we spread out shelter halves and raincoats to catch rain."

"Me, I put out helmet, upside down, to catch the drops."

"One buddhahead, he suck on frozen ground, he so thirsty."

"Good t'ing it rain; but sometimes it rain too much, two days, two nights."

"Hey, you forget the time it snow?"

"One time in morning, I pull out canteen to drink, no can, water all frozen."

"You one lucky guy. You got one Coleman stove. Me, I burn strips of K ration box to heat water to warm coffee."

"No can lie down. Stand up all night. Too much water in hole. Good t'ing sun come out in day so I can dry socks and shoes."

"Me, I sit all night with back against side of trench and no can catch much sleep."

"One guy, he took off shoes and no can put 'em back on. He try fo' crawl back to medics. Trench feet, bad t'ing!"

"Boy, my feet still hurt. Wet and cold too much."

"Good t'ing scrub grow some places. Some days I hide and make fire fo' cook."

"Good t'ing that scrub. It no hide smoke. I no can smoke."

"How come we got winter underwear, but summer uniforms? Oh, da cold up dere!"

They recalled how much better the Jerries were living in their reinforced dugouts and how effectively they had used their mortars to make life miserable for the AJAs. They talked about how American artillery shells fell right on them so that they had to phone back not to have our guns fire; our guns could not come up far enough and our men were too close to the Germans for effective use of shelling. They praised the mortar fire of the heavy weapons company; it could not destroy the German positions, but it kept the enemy from moving around very much.

Men shook their heads when someone had to tell how this private and that officer died. They wondered what they should write home about friends who would not return to Hawaii. They spoke of their own chances of survival, a lucky wound to prevent future soldiering, or a wound to disable one for life, or death. Talking helped to get the agony out of the souls of the veterans.

During a period of battalion rest, the chaplain cannot take things easy. On three days, December 14, 15, and 17, I made all-day trips back to our hospitals to visit a total of seventy-six of our casualties. I considered the hospital visitation a top priority for me at this time. December 19 was a Sunday and therefore devoted to religious services. I was so busy that on two days I missed writing the daily letters to my wife and did not get around to scheduling any instruction classes for those who had been baptized. And all the time I could not forget that a big task remained unfinished: the removal of the bodies still lying up in the hills. I had put it off until the pressing spiritual duties had been cared for.

Early on Monday, December 20, I procured a truck and driver to take Sergeant Shimogaki and a detail of men back to the road head from which the donkey path led up into the area where lay our uncared-for KIAs. The Goums had not been able to push the Germans off the hills, but by this time the region was reasonably safe. We spent the day carrying bodies by litter from the least exposed positions back to the truck.

The next day our group trucked back again and hiked up the five-mile trail, prepared to carry back more corpses. Shimogaki, of course, was with us to take care of any mined areas. This day we ran into a new situation: one body was in a partially buried condition and one was completely buried because a shell had burst directly on this foxhole, killing the soldier and also filling dirt into his deep position. After the men had cleared away the ground from one of these corpses, I tried to pull the body out but in the attempt sensed that decomposition had set in and the remains would not stay intact. We all agreed that without a solid container we could not remove this one or the other one. We therefore completely buried both, piled stones on the graves, and placed a rudely constructed cross on each mound. I read the burial service.

Later in the day we buried a third in similar fashion. One of the three thus interred was a lieutenant of artillery who had died trying to set up an OP from which to direct howitzer fire against the Germans and thereby assist our advance. We labored busily all day but were unable to complete our task. Late in the afternoon we returned to the truck, loaded the bodies at the road head, and went back to Alife. The truck continued on back to the American cemetery.

Wednesday I again supervised my GRS (Graves Registration Service) team. Again we found that one corpse could not be removed. As on the day before, I conducted the service of committal for our honored dead. These four interments were recorded in my December report to the Office of the Chief of Chaplains. On these days I was carrying an operational map, and after taking sightings I noted the coordinates and the hill designation. Here is the entry for the fourth man buried.

> 4. [man's name], Pvt., Co. B, 100th Inf. Bn. (Sep.)
>
> Funeral: December 22, 1943, Southwest of Scapoli, Italy
>
> Hill #900, Coordinates 02.80-31.85 on Map Italy 1/50,000 Sheet 161-IV Castel S. Vincenzo (Donkey trail leads from mass of rock which rises above last house in Mass Fonte Costanza, along north side of hill #801 up to hill #900; where this trail hits first clearing on #900 turn right, i.e., west, fifteen feet to grave.)

(At the end of the war in Italy, with my CO's permission, I inquired of the GRS unit in Italy about all the isolated burials of our KIAs because I intended to request permission to assist in the evacuation of any not yet removed. We were appreciative of their reply that all such bodies had been removed to military cemeteries.)

While Shimogaki and the detail carried down other bodies, I went scouting by myself on another hill to find the shortest route for transporting other KIAs out. The few Goums I had seen, though not friendly, recognized me as an American. As I was walking along with my head down, carefully picking out each step, I was thinking moodily of the stupidity of the army making the chaplain into an undertaker and pulling him away from his really important business of dealing with the living. All of a sudden I became aware of danger. Here is how I wrote about it to my wife a week later.

> Did I tell you about a close call I had recently? I was walking by myself from the direction of the frontline (toward the rear) in a sector not then occupied by troops. As I rounded a corner in the path I just happened to look up and ahead of me. I saw on the trail (coming from the opposite direction) a man dropping to one knee and taking aim at me with his rifle; also two others behind him were taking cover. My instinct was to drop down behind a big log right beside me; but I checked my instinct, for I knew that if I took cover the rifleman would surely begin firing and I'd really get it! So instead I stretched out my hands a little sidewards (to show that I was unarmed, and incidentally I was not wearing my Red Cross brassard that day) and yelled, "Je suis Americain" (I am an American) and stood still. After a pause he stood up and motioned for me to advance; I did, speaking to him in his lingo all the while. He was finally convinced

that I was an ally and asked about the enemy ahead. I answered; so he and his two friends passed by going to the front, and I with relief continued rearward. Whew! My scanty knowledge of languages saved my life that time. Don't worry; hereafter I travel in such places with a group. Experience teaches one.

Although I could not write all the details of the experience to my wife, this was indeed a close call. The Frenchman involved (the others were colonial recruits) told me that at a distance I looked armed because the field shovel hanging at my side resembled a weapon and that my helmet looked like a German's. (His helmet was much different from both the German style and the American.) He explained that this was his first trip to the front and that he did not know exactly where his troops were. Apparently my words in French had delayed the action long enough for the three to take a second look and decide that I might be an American. Since none of our men were supposed to be in the area, he had not considered at first that I was an ally. This encounter convinced me further that my complaint about ordering chaplains to substitute for GROs was quite justified. Of course, when I told my story to my friend Shimogaki, he lectured me for ambling about in dangerous zones by myself.

Since for security reasons I did not dare write of up-front experiences on the same day they occurred, I did occasionally relate them to my wife a few days later. The December 29th letter quoted above continued,

> Want to hear another tale? One day a sergeant and I were going forward to get out some dead. The enemy were supposedly several miles ahead. As we approached the area where the dead lay, a few shells fell way ahead of us but near the area we wanted to enter. We thought nothing of it and continued on. A very few minutes later we heard the screaming sound of another volley on the way. He and I hit the ground together; the shells fell some distance ahead but in the area to which we were en route. We looked at each other; I said, "Let's try again," so we kept going. Just as we got in the area near the destination we heard the screaming warning again. The sergeant flopped into an old slit trench and I dropped behind some rocks. One shell hit ahead of us and one to our left. "Come on, Sergeant," I said, "we're getting out of here," and we turned and double-quicked rearward. I figured it wasn't worth the risk to move the bodies that day; and we didn't. Oh me! But don't think such things happen every day; both of these are quite unusual experiences. And you and I both know that God has both our lives in His keeping; if He wills I return, I shall, regardless. So I feel free to write of such experiences knowing you want to share them and knowing you will not worry over them. Right?

We did not complete the grisly task by the end of the third day, and I was becoming concerned about the approach of Christmas. I wanted it to be a morale-building celebration for the battalion. I decided that further work as the GRO would have to wait until after December 25. Therefore, Thursday was to be reserved for religious duties including preparation of the sermon for the Nativity. As a rule I made only a few notes in planning my message for a given Sunday or holy day, but for Christmas I took the time to make a longer-than-usual outline and I sent a copy of it to my wife.

Like most others I had received Christmas packages and opened them on the day of arrival. From Peg came the promised muffler, tissues (for my sniffles), washrag, soap, nuts, money belt (mine was about worn out); from brother Bob [Robert L. Yost], two pairs of socks, handkerchiefs, sardines, peanut brittle, fruitcake; from the president of my alma mater, stationery imprinted with the statue of Gen. Peter Muhlenberg of Revolutionary War fame.[1] Even though I had little time for relaxation, I was enjoying my wall tent, pitched a short distance from the Headquarters Company tent. I felt more like myself now that I had a whole day to use the way I planned it. On the next day I planned to rehearse a caroling group and perhaps train a trio to sing "We Three Kings of Orient Are." By my calculation no more than five corpses remained up in the hills for us to remove; we could easily attend to that right after the holiday.

What was going on in the regiment I did not know. After my brief interview with Colonel Marshall, nothing more was said about my regimental duties if I were indeed the larger unit's padre now. The only time I had seen Von Duke again was on the day he ordered all commissioned officers to attend a special session on preparing trucks for unit moves. I could not see how the matter concerned me, but, as commanded, I joined the assembly of all the lesser brass not on duty at the time.

First, the dapper colonel lectured us on the importance of proper military appearance of all our vehicles, all the while twisting the ends of his waxed moustache. Then he directed several squads of enlisted men to climb into the truck in proper fashion. Then he circled the truck with the officer group following him, pointing at this and that and insisting that every trifle be inspected. The whole procedure was so ridiculous that some of the junior officers tried to get behind others so that the colonel would not see their smiles or hear their snickering. The last point of reference was the way in which two tools were attached to the cab; Von Duke pulled at one of them and both fell to the ground with a clatter as he jumped out of the way. Above the poorly controlled laughter of most of us, the colonel called out in effect, "You see what I have been talking about. If you don't do things right, somebody can get hurt."

Content within the 100th, I had no ambitions of becoming the regimental chaplain or of serving any unit larger than a battalion. Thus far I had gotten along well with the majors who had succeeded Colonel Turner, and I was not eager to have to deal with any COs of higher rank on close terms. We had been assigned our fourth top officer, Maj. Caspar Clough, Jr., of the 1st Infantry Division, winner of a Silver Star. As yet I had not gotten to know him.

Officers and enlisted men worked together well in the 100th, in part because the officers treated the men as buddies and were not sticklers about military trivia. However, during these nineteen days near Alife, one case of hatred of an officer surfaced, brought on by one man getting more than his share of the beer ration; it was only when this particular soldier got drunk that he became angry and wanted to kill "the gentleman" he despised.

One evening Kometani brought this drunk to my tent and asked me to "talk with him for an hour or so" after he had taken me aside and explained the situation. Kome had already kept the fellow talking for an hour, always steering the conversation away from the man's obsession. I took my turn with the buddhahead and learned a lot about him but not why he hated the officer. When I exhausted my resources I took him to another understanding member of our battalion, and the poor inebriate finally fell asleep. In the morning, as a sober person, he had no consuming hatred and remembered little of the night before. As far as I know, the officer (a haole kamaaina) never learned of the incident.

Early on December 24, I was summoned to battalion headquarters and informed that Colonel Marshall had phoned orders for me to spend the day completing the evacuation of the dead. I considered this another crazy idea of "Hard-labor Hank" [a second nickname the men used for Colonel Marshall]. This was the last straw. Others might have considered him a qualified commander, and no doubt he was, but this was an order I did not intend to obey. Exactly what I said I do not remember, for I became very angry, but it must have been much as I remember it.

"I'm not going out on such a detail today!" I snapped at our battalion brass, all of them junior officers, for I don't think I would have spoken in this fashion to Major Clough. "The dead will not get any deader until after Christmas, and in this cold weather the bodies won't decompose any further, either. Today I have much more important work to do.

I must prepare for the services we have tomorrow." I saluted, about-faced, and stomped out.

Back at my tent, as the enormity of my brashness in refusing the order of a colonel cut through my anger, I became apprehensive as to what might happen to me because of my action. During the next hour I tried to collect my thoughts and to work out plans for Christmas Eve and Christmas Day activities. My concentration was broken as I became aware of increased activity around headquarters: men assembling, tools rattling, and then a truck pulling out. I waited in suspense to see what would be done about me. At length an officer stepped into my tent.

"Chaplain Yost," said the officer. He paused, cleared his throat, assumed an official stance, and proceeded in an official tone. "Orders have been cut for you to go to rest camp in Naples on the day after Christmas. We figure that you have been working too hard and need a good rest. Just as soon as you have finished with the battalion's Christmas activities, you will be on leave for five days."

"But, but," I stammered, "what about the detail I was ordered to take out?"

The officer laughed. "We put Sergeant Shimogaki in charge and they have left. It's not your worry any more."

"But what about the colonel?" I asked.

He laughed again. "Don't worry about him either. The One Puka Puka has taken care of the whole matter. Now, you just get to work with whatever you have to get done here in camp today for the men."

The 100th Battalion always seemed to have a way of taking care of its own, whether it was a drunken dogface or an angry padre. When I joined the 100th I was very much an outsider: a Pennsylvanian of German ancestry who knew nothing about Hawaiians or Nisei or the battalion, and a Lutheran, the kind of Protestant few of the unit's men knew anything about. Now in less than three months I was accepted as a "real" buddhahead. What a Christmas present the outfit gave me that year!

During the day some of the medics got together in the chaplain's tent to practice carols. Others got tin snips and cut tree ornaments out of tin cans from the mess tents: by twisting a long strip with the inside shiny surface exposed, glittering icicles were formed. Two evergreens were decorated with these and sparkling stars and red berries picked locally. One volunteer disappeared for several hours and returned with a wooden cross he had painted white; he planted it in a place of honor in front of one of the trees.

When it got dark, the carolers, after singing first at the officers' party, made the rounds of all the companies. In front of one tent their singing was drowned out at first by the loud noise of a card game in progress under the canvas. Then a voice sounded from inside the pyramidal (tent). "Shh, you hear that? The chaplain has some men outside singing Christmas carols." In the silence that followed, "Silent Night" and "Joy to the World" rang out.

It was getting late when the singers reached the last tent. As the final carol died away on the cold winter's night, the tent flap was flung back and out came a sleepy, half-dressed mess sergeant. "You men ought to have something for your Christmas spirit," he muttered. He ushered the group into his mess tent and made hot cocoa for everyone.

During this holiday season, two hundred copies of the *Spiritual Almanac* were distributed, and all who wanted New Testaments, Gospel portions, and tracts were given them. As the men received gifts of books from home, some of them gave me their copies so that I began to build up a lending library in my tent. From time to time Peggy sent me books; during this rest period the *Book of Concord* I requested of her came.[2]

I anticipated that days of inactivity might be in the offing, and I wanted some serious volumes on hand for study. I had room for such extras in the small trailer assigned to me for carrying such chaplain's gear as the organ and service hymnals.

On Christmas Day two services were held, attended by 225. I also attended the all-musical worship at the regiment and conducted a Lutheran communion service for the 1st Battalion at the request of the unit's chaplain. One of the companies invited me to their Christmas dinner: turkey, stuffing, rice, a fresh vegetable, wine, oranges, walnuts, and a freshly baked cake with icing and nuts on top.

The day after the Nativity was a Sunday; not responsible for any duties at all, I was on my way to Naples, traveling by truck with many of our men also off on leave. When I checked in at the rest facilities I was received with open arms and assigned to a room by myself. Not long afterwards I was called to the front desk and asked what suggestions I had for a worship schedule for the men. When I explained I was also on leave, the officer of the day expressed both surprise and disappointment, for he had assumed that I was their new chaplain; that's why my welcome had been so warm! This center was primarily for enlisted men; he suggested I would want to go to an officers' hotel. I declined with a smile; I told him I liked my accommodations and would use them for five days.

The mistake in lodging turned out to be a blessing for me, for one of our medics, T/3 Kiyoshi James Shiramizu,[3] was also billeted here. Because we found that we had similar tastes, he and I buddied-up during our stay in Naples. He was married and thought the world of his wife and little son; he was a gentleman in speech and conduct; he lived each day by moral principles and ideals. He was from the Mainland, one of the few kotonks in the battalion, and therefore like me. Together we toured the city on foot, went to the opera, shopped for gifts, and enjoyed the sights. Most of all we enjoyed each other's company.

This important Italian seaport had felt the scourge of war physically and otherwise.[4] Here is my description of conditions as I wrote of them to my wife.

> Had opportunity to visit large Italian city recently; the morals are terrible. Little boys and girls are agents for prostitution, approaching soldiers on the streets and saying, "Want a Signorina?" or "Nice girl of seventeen?" or talking more vulgarly. When not in too much of a rush, I stop and pointing to the cross on my collar say, "Sono uno cappellano, uno prete" (I am a chaplain, a priest). Immediately the agent is embarrassed and hastens to excuse himself. One little boy said, "No good!" and scooted away. The situation is deplorable.
>
> A sergeant (Jimmie Shiramizu) and I came in after dark one night and missed supper at our barracks. So we searched for a civilian place; finally a boy showed us a good printed menu so we followed him into a semi-private home and ordered spaghetti. A young lady appeared from the next room, in a long gown (perhaps a dressing gown). I began to wonder what sort of a place we were in. The food was good but I was nervous, wanting to get out of the place. A soldier appeared and I asked him about the place; he assured me it was all right, but I was glad to finish and leave. When I got to quarters, I recounted the experience to some officers and they remarked, "That's nothing unusual. You must remember that this is _____ [Naples; censorship prohibited naming the city]." But such experiences make me feel unclean and ill at ease. There is so much smut and vice in these abnormal situations of war as soon as soldiers and civilians mingle together.

At the rest camp there were movies. One night I went to see the picture; I wrote about it to my wife.

> A community sing preceded the feature; at one place it was indicated that the girls sing. Without hesitation all the men sang falsetto; it was a scream! Also, when "Don't Sit Under the Apple Tree" flashed on, the soldiers

roared; no doubt they were thinking of girls back home who have forgotten them and married exempted young men. Some of them have
been away from home well over two years.

December 28, Sergeant Jimmie and I went downtown to the San
Carlo Opera House where Gounod's *Faust* was playing. As we were
standing in line before the ticket booth, along comes Lt. Sparky Matsunaga[5] with two extra tickets, which he insisted we use as his guests. Thus,
for my first and only experience of real opera, I sat with Jimmie and
Sparky in a box on the audience's left at the front of the first gallery. The
orchestra, mostly of strings, was composed primarily of women. We did
not understand the Italian, but we followed the story on the stage with
interest. Afterwards, like good opera fans, we hounded the actor-singers,
and I came away with the autographs of five of the seven stars.

December 29, I sent a package of gifts to Peggy including some photos of myself taken in Naples. Also included was a small oil painting of
an Italian street scene and a bronze corpus of Christ to be mounted
sometime to make a crucifix on my study wall.[6] Jimmie and I visited the
ruins at Pompeii, but I was more impressed with the detailed Nativity
display in the modern church in the Pompei of today. By the evening
of December 30, I was back "home" with my "parishioners" near Alife.

On December 31, in preparation for another push against the enemy,
all of us Red Bulls moved to Presenzano, marching to assembly areas in
a New Year's Eve blizzard. The year 1944 began with a wet, cold day,
and I was struggling to catch up with paperwork. On December 24, my
November report had been returned by a chaplain-supervisor in a higher
echelon, primarily for minor details not in accordance with the latest regulations about form and punctuation. It had to be redone, and the one
for December was due, and we were getting ready to go into combat
again!

Our kitchens were still with us; therefore the chow continued to be
excellent. Nevertheless, in my daily letter home I suggested my wife send
me more Hershey bars. When my wife some weeks later took a package
including this request to the post office in Nazareth, Pennsylvania, for
mailing to me overseas, the postal official demanded to see the request
I had sent. When Peggy produced the letter, the official stamped over
the words I had written: "Nazareth, Pa., Parcel Post, Feb. 26, 1944."
Apparently this was to prevent her from cheating and using one request
several times. A number of my letters home were thus stamped so that
packages could be sent to me. Bureaucratic trifling at home to limit pack-

ages going to our soldiers and bureaucratic trifling overseas to produce letter-perfect typing in reports! Could we have won the war without the paperwork?

Sunday open-air services were held under beautiful cloud formations following a storm. Kometani remarked that the beauty of the land must be one reason Italy has produced artists and musicians. Monday the incoming mail proved that air mail traveled more swiftly than V-Mail; the arrival of Butterfingers, Tootsie Rolls, and Baby Ruths assured us that the PX system of the army still worked; and in the evening Doc Kome once and for all illustrated that no one could fall asleep quicker than he, or anyone snore louder than he. Tuesday was payday; I sent $120 home. Wednesday marked the completion of my December report, but, alas, the November corrections were not yet taken care of. Thursday I caught up on three-days' Bible reading. Friday the water in my canteen froze and I was accused of being able to fly because I ran a hilly stretch of path in just fifty-five minutes. Saturday everyone was in good spirits, but there was no special news to write home. All this indicates that the battalion was gradually moving into position in the hills guarding the approach to Cassino. From Sunday, January 2, to Saturday, January 8, there was activity leading up to a confrontation with the enemy, but no major skirmishes were fought and no casualties were treated.

By January 8, units of the 100th were in contact with the Germans in the vicinity of Hill 1190 on Mt. Majo. On the evening of this Saturday I walked with Sergeant Jimmie Shiramizu on the long hike to the forward aid station. We noticed a GI from another unit sitting just off the trail, apparently resting. When we hailed him and received no answer, we approached him—he was dead, probably frozen to death.

We were two soldiers slowly hiking up the stony trail, shivering in the cold of an Italian night. Both were helmeted, carried a full pack, and each had two canteens fastened to his web belt in addition to a trenching shovel. Neither carried any kind of weapon, but instead had two blankets apiece across the shoulders, and each carried a folded litter on his right shoulder. One had the marking of a technical sergeant on his sleeve and the other captain's bars on his collar. As we climbed higher up the steep trail, Jimmie shared with me what he called his "one gripe" against the U.S. Army.

"Chaplain," he said in a confidential tone, "I still can't forget that when I entered the army they wouldn't put a 'B' on my dog tags."

"Jimmie, are you a Buddhist?" I responded.

"Yes, Chaplain, I am, and I can't see why the military did not give me the right to believe what I want."

"Jimmie, I had no idea you were not a Christian. You always attend my services, and you conduct yourself like I think a Christian would."

"I like your services," he replied, "and I can understand what you preach. But I am still a Buddhist."

"I agree with you that you should be allowed to believe what you want. Only once has someone asked me to hold a Buddhist service, and I think he was joking. I told him I could not do that since I was a Christian. But I think he understood—and I think the rest of the Buddhists understand, too—that I have made no attempt to belittle those who worship in ways different from mine."

As we talked of other things I inwardly rebuked myself for never having opened a discussion about faith with him. I had simply assumed by his good life that he must be a believer in Jesus.

We plodded wearily upward until we reached the battalion aid, this time a small tent pitched on the side of the mountain under the protection of an outcropping of rocks; there were no buildings this high on the range. I set up my sleeping space in a cleft of a rock a short distance forward of the medics. Doc Kometani had been assigned to man an aid station several relay points to the rear; this was one of the few times he was not able to be up front with me.

Sunday continued cold with patches of snow on the ground. I put a canteen cup of the snow out in the sun to melt. During the day some medics asked me to conduct worship; the best I dared do was read some scripture to them, for forward of us our men had contacted the enemy, and I felt that our area was not safe enough for a group to assemble. Indeed, on this day two of B Company were killed and a third so badly wounded that he died of his wounds the next day.[7]

Monday, January 10, was so cold and with so little sun that when I removed my gloves, my fingers became cold in a short time. Inside the aid tent, a single candle burned feebly against the increasing gloom of the night.

"Jimmie," said the battalion surgeon,[8] "we are short of aid men and we are short of litter bearers. . . ." His voice trailed off, making his message match the question his glance at the sergeant seemed to be asking.

"Gotcha, doc," replied Jimmie. "You can pick up litter bearers easier than aid men. Which company do you want me to report to?"

This was not the first time that Sergeant Jimmie had volunteered to fill in a needed position with a platoon up front. With his rank of tech sergeant his normal place during combat was with the forward battalion surgeon, a relatively safe spot when the action got dangerous. But both he and the battalion surgeon knew he could be of more real use to the wounded if he went farther front. It was not that the doc was asking him to do something he himself would not do. The medical captain outranked the other battalion surgeon, and protocol indicated the junior officer should man the forward aid station rather than the senior surgeon—but our doc knew he was of more service forward than at the rear. The captain and the sergeant understood and respected each other. Sergeant Jimmie took a medical officer's kit and disappeared forward in the dark.

Soon the hell of war broke out in earnest somewhere over the top of the mountain. A steady stream of wounded paused at the aid station for treatment and then continued, limping or carried by four men on litters, down the path in the dark to a medical clearing station somewhere down and to the rear.

All the litter squads were busy. The chaplain's assistant volunteered to help with the evacuation forward. When a wounded soldier brought the report that all eight men of two litter squads had been hit, I stuffed my shirt with extra dressings and took off for the front. Here are the notes I wrote shortly after the tragic events occurred.

> In the p.m. two litter squads went out on call from B Company. About three quarters of an hour later one man stumbled into the battalion aid saying all were hit, that several had started back, but only he had made it. I was about the only man free to leave the battalion aid, so I stuffed some small carlisle bandages and sulfa powder packets in pocket and started off. Found way to B Company area (they and C Company had made an advance earlier in the p.m.) without seeing any of the squads. Rufus (Company B aid man) said he had seen four of the litter squad on the skyline [to the rear of where he and I were squatting] before shell hit; also pointed to a badly wounded B Company man nearby; I spoke to him and told him we'd get him out as soon as possible but that our litter squads had just been hit. Also prayed for him. Then started back uphill through some snow; met Jun Enomoto (Company C aid man). Explained situation to him and asked him to come with me. As I neared the crest of the hill I heard someone calling for help—Kengo.[9] Nakano[10] also spoke to me. Kengo told me [two private messages in case he did not survive]. I asked Jun to treat Kengo and I put carlisle on N's head (leg also bad). Felt pulses of three others lying close—no pulse. Turned Hayashida[11] (Dental Assistant) over and called him by name: eyes glazed. Told Jun to also check pulses. B Company messenger approached so he and I put Kengo

on litter (two which the squads were carrying were lying nearby) and started back, telling Jun to tend to Nakano. Got Kengo over skyline. Discovered my assistant (Kent Nakamura) had walked half [way] back and was lying wounded with some men resting by rock. Spoke to him and then set off to get carrying party. Missed battalion aid in darkness and went little out of way; arrived and found group had set off; followed them and finally got Kengo and Nakano back; several helped Kent walk rest of way. I assisted Doc Dahl in dressing wounds (opened bandages and sulfa packets and held light). Also got some of the Ammunition and Pioneer Platoon to go after Second Lieutenant Miyamoto[12] in C Company. Meanwhile the badly wounded man in B Company died.[13] Worked till about 3:30 a.m. Short two litters, so two men lay on blankets and shelter halves on ground. Sergeant Jimmie Shiramizu had gotten half way back though badly wounded, hit in abdominal region; Doc gave him plasma. Last man (Kent) could not be evacuated till about 10:00 a.m. Slept 2½ hours and then got up to help with sick call. Made eight EMTs out before the technicians were up.

Previous to the above an aid man, "Chicken,"[14] came over the hill calling, "Chaplain, Chaplain." He had been hit in the rump and elsewhere and was calling me to help him down to the aid station.

(At the end of these notes I wrote the names of eight of the nine who made up these two litter squads, listing three as KIAs[15] and indicating how the others were injured, stating that the unnamed one suffered from concussion; the wounds of four were serious; Kent's wounds were all superficial.)

My assistant did not normally serve as a member of a litter crew. On this particular night he had come to me saying that he had been asked to assist the litter bearers because the medics were shorthanded. I had explained to him that I would not order him to go any farther forward than the aid station where he was helping out but that if he decided on his own to volunteer he had my permission. Thus it was that he was involved in this tragic event.

Hayashida, one of the KIAs, was Doc Kometani's helper as Kent was mine. I do not know why he was with the litter crew this night; perhaps he, too, had volunteered. Doc heard of the death of his assistant some hours later from one of the wounded who had passed through his relay point on a litter.

Among the casualties was Sergeant Jimmie, badly wounded in the abdomen but quite aware of the situation.

"Doc," said Jimmie, "I see we're short of litter bearers. You know I'd walk to the rear if I could. I can't. But I have a suggestion."

"Speak up, Jimmie."

"Since I'm a medic I want to be the last of the litter cases to be carried down the hill. I can take it. Let the others get back first."

The battalion surgeon opened his mouth to reply, but he read the look on Jimmie's face and said nothing. The sergeant was the last of the critically injured men carried out of the forward aid for the long transport to the hospital. When his litter was finally picked up he waved a cheery good-bye to the surgeon and the chaplain as he left the battalion aid tent.

We had no helicopters in World War II; the wounded were carried to the rear on stretchers—to a road where ambulances were waiting. Here is the way the situation near Mt. Majo is described by Murphy (1954).

> It sometimes took hours to move litter cases back to the battalion aid station. From that point the injured were carried down to the nearest ambulance by six-man teams, stationed at twelve relay points, each about an hour's haul from the next. The first two stages in a wounded man's journey to the hospital often took twelve to fifteen hours. Three stations along the route supplied blood plasma or other aid, and provided hot drinks and a rest place for the walking wounded. (164)

Sergeant Jimmie died of his wounds four days later at an army hospital somewhere in Italy. When I saw him last I had no idea that he would not pull through. Our five days together at Naples had made us close friends; the memory of his personality has never left me. (Historical note: Jimmie's widow instituted proceedings against the federal government for restricting her right as an American citizen to return to her home on the West Coast, one of the earliest of such actions after movement out of relocation centers became government policy. I was not aware of this until after my retirement in 1981, when I began an indepth study of the history of the Japanese in America.)

Hindsight raises the question: why did these nine men bunch up on the skyline, apparently as they were deliberating which way to go? If they had been carefully keeping proper distance as is normal under combat conditions, a single shell would probably not have done so much damage. At the most only five men should ever be in close contact with each other: four litter bearers and a casualty on the litter; sometimes we got along with just three carriers, and sometimes just two, at least over exposed spots. For me this was one of the most sobering experiences of the war, for most of those hit were personal friends. No doubt that's why I look back to see how it could have been prevented. This catastrophe made me even more a member of the One Puka Puka; now I felt exactly as these AJAs felt, for so many of the casualties were close friends of those who survived.

On Tuesday censorship prevented me from writing to my wife about the tragedy of the night before. "Last night was an extremely busy one for me; later I'll tell you about it. I didn't know whether I was coming or going. But every day has an ending." The next day, however, I had good news to share with her. "The fellow who was hurt back in November by the mine I tripped is back with us. He still has a partial paralysis of the arm, but looks fine. I'm glad he was not seriously hurt." Men returning from the hospitals were the only replacements we were getting; without them the ranks would have been slim indeed. Many returned before they were fully recovered; they knew how badly they were needed by their buddies.

On Thursday the good word home was this: "It's so good when I visit the men to hear them say, 'Chaplain, we wondered where you were since we didn't see you for a few days—thought perhaps you were hurt.' They are so solicitous about my well-being. I can't do much sermonizing under these conditions, but I hope my life is witnessing for our Lord." As the official GRO I directed the evacuation of KIAs; our men were now able to use mules for the long descent. On this day I buried an unnamed German, and the next day three known and one unknown, recording the place of interment just as carefully as I did for American KIAs.

Friday, the brief note home read, "I'm gloriously dirty at the moment . . . but I'm not bothered about that too much. When I get the chance I'll wash till I sparkle." Saturday, instead of writing a letter, I took the time to visit an Italian family, sharing with them some bouillon soup and instant coffee in exchange for a seat near their fireplace. Sunday there was no time for services, but as I saw men I reminded them of the day and gave them tracts if they expressed interest in them. Monday we played an old army game: first we marched forward, and then we marched back again over the same route; then we retraced our steps to the place to which we were first ordered. This was no fun at all; we were carrying all our equipment and each march covered several miles. I complained to our officers in the name of the troops and was told that the nonmarching colonels were the ones who could not decide just where our jumping-off place was.

On January 18, I had time for an informative letter to Nazareth.

One night two girls, about eight and thirteen, came to our group look-ing for two soldiers to take home for a meal. A sergeant and I went. The folks were refugees from a nearby city, living now in a large house in a village. We had finely chopped pieces of mutton first, tender and good; then a heaping dish of *bianca farina* [white meal], and then cooked beef. Bread was also served—yellow and salt-less like cornmeal bread—and of course wine. Wine is drunk like water, but I explained that I took wine only at communion.

The night before I had some real macaroni with (somewhat flat) tomato sauce—with another family. Also slept on a good bed; this fam-ily was afraid to use upper floor due to artillery shelling, so they offered it to us and we used it. I've done some rugged hiking lately and upon occasion have melted snow for drinking water. But no snow has been very deep, and the sun's rays are warm, and we have sufficient clothing. . . . I carry so much material that I look like a mule when I'm en route; but I always get there.

These Italians have terraced fields right up the mountainsides, and live in remote spots far from roads; only by donkey can such spots be reached. I've often wondered how often a priest gets up to them—almost wish I could stay and be pastor to such, for there is so much to be done for them.

Again and again we are surprised at how young the German soldiers are against whom we are now fighting. Most of the prisoners are very glad to be taken by us; I've talked with quite a few. Many are not from Ger-many proper but from Austria, etc.

It's too bad I got behind in keeping a daily account; now it's hard to begin again. Lately I've been helping the battalion surgeon [Dahl] a lot, and he is glad to have me assist. . . . Sometimes I can even suggest sub-stitutes—recommended soap in water as a good antidote for swallowed gasoline and the doc agreed.

At the beginning of the January advance I started carrying a surgeon's medical kit. I wrote the brief instructions on the top of the few pill bot-tles, but I did not intend to give out medicine—I carried the kit so that our doc would have extra supplies in the aid station. At this time, too, I began carrying EMT tags in order to label the KIAs without having a medic coming with me. When he signed a batch of the tags for me, Dahl said, "You can see where a man has been hit, Chaplain. Just fill out the tag the best you can and that will be all right with me."

On January 19, while the battalion was inactive near San Michele, I wrote Peggy some philosophy and observations.

I just asked the officer next to me what he was writing about, and he replied, "I'm telling my wife that I haven't taken a bath in 1944 yet." That goes for me, too. I sure am dirty. My hands have black grit ground into them. But who cares! The sun is shining, and I'm resting, and right now everything is peaceful—don't know for how long, though. There's been one good thing about this campaign in Italy: we hit the easiest battles first and then worked up to the tougher and tougher ones. Now I have some experience and know how to get things done, more or less. Some things that at first work on you, you eventually get used to, more or less. About the worst job is being the mortician, but I can do even that work all right.

The Italians are quick to come over the battle areas as soon as troops move on. They pick up blankets, overcoats, biscuits, food, straps, wood—just about everything but ammunition and guns. And I've seen kids up in the hills in snowy areas without shoes, helping parents salvage things.

At this time the 100th was "on hold" in front of Cassino, waiting for the generals to decide just how the doughboys should be thrown against the Gustav Line. Patrols of the 100th were probing the German defenses, and some shelling occurred daily. Most of the soldiers were making themselves as comfortable as possible and fraternizing with the local peasants. So far as I knew, all KIAs had been removed to our cemeteries. I felt that I had caught up on all my responsibilities, but actually I had not. Without an assistant, for no one as yet had replaced Kent, I let some of the paperwork go for the time being.

On Saturday, January 22, when a shell exploded rather close to me, I ran to see if anyone had been hit. I found a thirty-one-year-old Italian male gasping for breath. As I took his pulse but found no beat, I saw that he was bleeding from wounds near his heart. Since I could do nothing for him, I took cover to protect myself. Sunday no groups could gather for worship, but I conducted brief devotionals here and there. Monday I washed out my "long johns" but could not bathe properly because of the cold and the lack of a towel—I had left mine somewhere—and someone with dull scissors cut my hair. I also spent some time censoring letters for enlisted men, a task I often assumed during the lulls between battles; the ways the Hawaiians expressed themselves were often humorous, making this an enjoyable chore. All of us were aware that dangerous fighting lay ahead. A long letter home on January 24 recorded my faith in God.

> Sometimes when shells fall close I tremble, but I'm always sure that He is taking care of me (us). If He wants me to return to you and ours and parish work in the U.S.A., He'll bring me back safe and sound. I take all necessary precautions but my safety rests in His will. How can we be otherwise than thankful to Him Who has proved Himself so good to us thus far!

Notes

1. John Peter Gabriel Muhlenberg, a clergyman, left his parish to raise and lead a regiment in the American Revolution and became a general in Washington's army. He later served three terms in the U.S. House of Representatives. A statue of him sits on the campus of Muhlenberg College, Yost's alma mater.

2. The *Book of Concord* is the collected documents of the confessions of faith of the Lutheran Church, published in 1580.

3. In the army of World War II, "T" designated a technician; the number following the "T" indicated the pay grade. In today's army, such a position is called a "specialist," designated by "E."

4. Naples was captured one week ahead of schedule. "The Germans had demolished sewer lines, power plants, reservoirs, aqueducts and large public buildings. They had left delayed fuse bombs in public buildings and barracks that would take more than 100 American and Italian lives. The port machinery was broken, the railroads ripped up and the important harbor clogged with sunken ships" (Blumenson, 146).

5. Spark M. Matsunaga (1916–1990), a lieutenant in World War II, was wounded twice. A graduate of Harvard University Law School, he was an assistant prosecutor in Honolulu. Following a private law practice, he became a highly respected legislator, serving fourteen years in the U.S. House of Representatives and thirteen years in the U.S. Senate.

6. The painting still hangs in the home of one of the Yost family. The bronze body of Christ was mounted on a wooden cross after the war and hung on the study wall of every parish Pastor Yost served; it now hangs in his wife's dining room.

7. The editors think these were Toshio Kawamoto, Kiyoshi Masunaga, and Yutaka Nezu.

8. Capt. John J. Dahl.

9. Kenneth Kengo Otagaki lost a leg, two fingers, and the sight in one eye that night. Despite his injuries, Dr. Otagaki had a distinguished career on the faculty of the University of Hawaii College of Tropical Agriculture and Human Resources (CTAHR) and was named CTAHR alumnus of the year in 2005. In addition to teaching, he was chair of the State Department of Agriculture, international consultant on agricultural technology with the U.S. State Department, and a private consultant for agricultural enterprises in Hawaii.

10. Haruo Nakano.

11. Hideyuki Hayashida.

12. The editors think this was Harry I. Miyamoto.

13. The editors think this was Hachiro Ito.

14. "Chicken" was usually a nickname for the Japanese first name "Chikara."

15. The three KIAs were Hideyuki Hayashida, Isamu Ikeda, and Masaichi Katsuda.

SEVEN

Failure at Cassino

L IKE MOST ordinary GIs, I knew nothing of the overall plans of the 34th Division, the II Corps, and the Fifth Army, and very little of the objectives of neighboring battalions. Once an engagement began I was concerned only with what went on in the 100th. When the forward aid moved, I went with it unless I was busy elsewhere and not free to leave the immediate task. I understood little of the scope of the Battle of Cassino until years later, when I looked up the facts in history books. I was aware at the time that this was a great conflict, that the enemy was firmly entrenched, and that American troops were suffering heavy losses as the days of the attack mounted.

To engage the enemy our AJAs had to cross a wide, flooded plain sown with mines, then the dry bed of the Rapido River with high walls on both banks, and, last of all, an open road bounded on the east by the river and on the west by a steeply rising hill. Enemy machine-gun fire effectively covered all the approaches except four irrigation ditches in the flooded fields and the eastern sides of the river walls, but mortar fire could reach some of these sheltered zones. Barbed-wire fences topped the western bank of the Rapido; all brush and trees had been cleared from the plain; German guns, mortars, and artillery were installed within bastions of cement in the city and in the surrounding hills. Gen. Mark Clark (1950) describes the Gustav Line thus.

> It was a line built by the famous Nazi Todt Organization on terrain that the Italian War College had used for many years to illustrate to students an area that was ideal for defense against almost anything. (261)

On the evening of January 24, the battalion was at the line of departure, poised to move out after dark. During the half hour before midnight American artillery steadily blasted the German positions. The

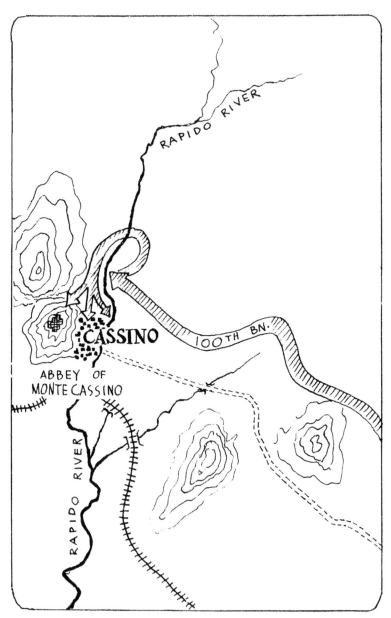

From the beginning of January 1944, the 100th moved into position on the outskirts of Cassino, where they faced the German Gustav Line. Yost wrote, "To engage the enemy our AJAs had to cross a wide, flooded plain sown with mines, then the dry bed of the Rapido River with high walls on both banks, and, last of all, an open road bounded on the east by the river and on the west by a steeply rising hill." By February 22, only 521 of the original 1,300 men of the 100th Bn who had landed at Salerno were left.

advance began with Sergeant Shimogaki and his platoon clearing a path-way through the minefield; when rifle fire broke the sergeant's sweeper, he crawled through the mud locating trip wires with his hands. By five a.m., A and C Companies were secure along the seven-to-twelve-foot-high stone wall on the east side of the river. During the night the for-ward aid had been set up in a small, stone farm building in a field inside the eastern edge of the muddy flatland; its sole doorway faced the enemy. Even though it must have been under observation by the Jerries, it was not shelled by them.

The next day B Company tried to join the other two companies by the wall, but the wind blew away the smoke screen under which the advance was made, and most of the boys of B were pinned down in the mud. Major Clough was wounded in the arm, and Maj. George L. Dewey of the 133rd Regiment was put in command of the 100th tem-porarily. That night B Company was pulled back out of danger. Later, under cover of darkness, Capt. Mitsuyoshi Fukuda of A Company led Majors Dewey and Jack Johnson along with a small group across the flats to set up a new command post for an attack in the morning.

Random machine-gun fire hit Dewey and Johnson, and Johnson was also hit by fragments of an exploding mine. Both were carried to our forward aid, Dewey first. I do not know why one preceded the other, whether the decision was made by the circumstances, the litter bearers, or others. Dewey was hurried through our station, carried to the rear aid, and transported by ambulance to a hospital. When I heard that by the time Johnson arrived at the rear no transportation was available, I walked by myself to the rear aid and then stumbled along the dirt road to the 100th's rear CP. In the blacked-out building I found our officers in con-fusion; my pleas for a vehicle went unheeded. No one knew what to do or where I could get help for Jack. Saddened and disappointed, I shuf-fled back to the rear aid. Just a few yards from it, I heard the sound of a guard, whom I could not see, changing the position of his rifle. "It's the chaplain," I called out. "If you shoot me, I'll come back from heaven and haunt you." There was a laugh, and the sentry replied, "Advance, Chap-lain; I know who you are."

Johnson's life ebbed away during the night. Officially he was reported KIA on January 25, but when I made a record of the personal effects I took from his clothing for safekeeping, I listed his death as January 26. His dying affected me as had the losses on January 10. The planned advance was never made, for it was an order impossible to execute, and our men were withdrawn from the river wall. Dewey and Johnson should not have gone forward, but as after the event of January 10, this is hindsight.

As the official GRO, I set about moving as many of the dead as could be reached with reasonable safety. As we extricated the body of a sergeant from the ruins of a small building, I remarked to my crew that the explosion that had killed him must have been severe, for the telephone receivers he carried stuffed in his jacket had been shattered. That evening I entered the CP and asked if anyone had seen my friend, the communications sergeant. When I received no response but only stares, I left the headquarters. One of the men followed me and outside said, "Chaplain, what's the matter with you? Don't you know where Sergeant Komatsu[1] is?" As I looked at him blankly, he continued, "You picked him up today yourself. You even said how badly he had been hit. He was the one with the smashed phones in his jacket."

I stared at the soldier. To think that I had helped to prepare my buddy for burial without recognizing him! Part of the trouble was that I was not always familiar with Japanese names and remembered faces better; part was the fact that violent death can change features so that they are no longer recognizable.

On January 28 I wrote to Peggy.

> We've had some hectic days lately. As you say, it's tragic to lose so many lives when the ultimate end is certain. We've lost some good men on some of these pushes. One day lately one of the men turned up at the aid station in his bare feet. I asked him what the trouble was and he explained that he was getting a wounded soldier out of a muddy place and the mud stuck, so he finally took off his shoes and overshoes so he could work better. His feet certainly must have been cold, but he didn't complain at all. These men of mine have dandy spirits, much better than many of the others around us. But they have taken terrific beatings from the weather and the enemy.
>
> The Italian folks nearby have been asking me for a Mass; I explain I am Protestant. Every night a group of them gathers in a nearby house to say the rosary. We can hear the melodic, chanting-like mumble and the solo voice of the one who recites the leader's part—impressive.

About the same time I also wrote the following.

> I've seen American barrages of shells so thick and continuing, the air filled with noise, and the sky lighted, and sparks flying on the distant hills; and I've pitied the poor Germans caught in all that sizzling mass of fast-flying, sharp-cutting metal. (God have mercy on man's treatment of man.) And

yet as soon as the shelling stopped, up started the burp of German machine guns, and soon we were patching up legs and arms and bodies. Yet few men break under it all. Cold weather must help to deaden pain in lacerated bodies, and nature must somehow take care of pain. Not only enlisted men fall in battle; officers are in the thick of things, too. The company aid men are heroes. They follow troops into the battle lines and render first aid under fire. We have one who time and again has improvised litters and personally seen to it that wounded are brought back to the aid station. In fact, usually he has been way up forward when I've visited the men in their holes on the line. He's a Mormon who takes his religion seriously.

I think our battalion has won for itself a good name; the men have never once broken ranks, but they've stayed and taken beatings. So what's left of "us" (the 100th Battalion) may bear ourselves with pride, if there is any consolation to having a good name. Some good friends are gone— one was a Buddhist. It's worried me since that he died a Buddhist and not a Christian. I visited the men prior to a recent action; I knew many would not live through it. I asked many, "Are you all set to go?" hoping they would take the opportunity to speak of religion if they cared to. None did, but maybe they knew what I meant.

On Saturday, January 29, I held brief services for all the companies; I knew that we were moving forward again, this time into a defensive position. I preached directly about why God spares some of us: it is for our conversion to his way or to do his work. I also read to them a favorite hymn of mine, "Fierce Was the Wild Billow," [2] appointed for the Fourth Sunday after the Epiphany. [3]

On this Saturday the battalion's morale soared high: Maj. James Lovell rejoined the outfit. In October, between Caiazzo and Alife, Lovell had been hit by a fragment of a "screaming-meemie" in the right leg, so seriously wounding him that at the Caserta hospital there was danger of gangrene setting in. For recuperation he was sent to Bizerte, North Africa, where he was warned not to do a lot of walking lest paralysis set in. Before his leg was completely healed—it was still bleeding— Jim went AWOL and hitched a plane ride to Naples, taking with him others who wanted to get back into the fighting. There he was interrogated by two lieutenant colonels who accused him of bringing to Italy men without orders.

Directly after the confrontation and before anyone could follow up on the accusation, the major sought out a truck heading for Cassino; he and some of his "without-orders" guys rode on it back to the 100th. This was a typical One Puka Puka kind of stunt. Major Lovell promptly relieved Major Clough since he was senior to him and became our CO for the second assault on the Gustav Line. Apparently Lovell's hospital records never caught up with him.

On Sunday the only worship I could conduct safely was in the evening for headquarters personnel; Major Lovell attended. By candle-light I read the Gospel for the Transfiguration[4] and then spoke of con-fessing Christ, then having a hilltop experience with him, and later feel-ing a lack of spiritual power in the plains of life. Three paragraphs of this day's letter home seemed important at the time.

> I wish I could carry more tracts and New Testaments with me, for men are always anxious for such literature.
>
> I received Rollin's [Pastor Rollin G. Shaffer[5]] letter of October say-ing he would assume guardianship in the event anything happened taking both of us away from our bairns.[6] That's good, for he and Ethel are fine persons. However, I don't think events will come to such a pass.
>
> Last night a group of our men stood and watched me load myself; they wanted to see if I could carry all the stuff I proposed to. I got it all on and our supply officer said, "We don't need mules; just let the chap-lain carry everything!" However, the load is beginning to get too heavy, so I'll begin to cut down on things. But I like to keep warm, eat well, read, and write letters; and also to have medical supplies and clean clothes on hand, so it mounts up. I always carry my Bible in my musette bag.

In my contacts with officers and men I tried hard to always show a cheerful spirit as well as be careful of my words and general conduct. Whenever I could, I joked about my own situation. In addition to always carrying extra equipment—often a litter and several blankets for use in the aid station—I made fun of myself by occasionally stopping to jump and click my heels together in the air. Once, after climbing an excep-tionally steep and long hill, when I had come to the top and was about to slip out from under my pack to rest, I found myself looking into the pointed finger of Major Johnson and heard him say, "Okay, Chaplain, let's see you click your heels now!" With a last reserve of strength I just barely did it, to the jeers and cheers of the soldiers nearby.

At the end of January I was informed that I had been promoted to captain on January 16, two days less than a year after being commissioned a lieutenant. The initial suggestion for the promotion came from the office of the division chaplain, was written up for Major Clough's sig-nature, and was approved by Colonel Marshall. Actually it did not come through the 133rd Regiment, and I was never appointed regimental chaplain as Von Duke had told me. Headquarters of the North African Theater of Operations issued the official order by command of Lt. Gen. Jacob L. Devers. The new rank increased my monthly pay by fifty dollars and upped the quarters allowance (rent) for my wife. Most important of all, I was still the chaplain of the 100th.

The events and thoughts of the next few days were written home; the battalion remained in defensive positions as other battalions probed the enemy's fortifications.

Monday, Jan. 31

This morning I caught up on some lost sleep, though I did get up and shave and eat breakfast before taking the nap. This afternoon I took a walk to see some of the men. Incidentally, while pushing through some briers, brush, and trees I found a little bird's nest stuck in a low bough. It reminded me of when as kids we went out along the creek to play.

I'm using those blanket pins and they work fine. I put five along the side and one at the foot and then crawl in the resultant sack. That way the covers are always fully around me. Thanks for sending them to me.

Tuesday, Feb. 1

I got thinking recently about how modern "civilized" war compares to ancient war. It's only in "modern" warfare that men live in holes dug in the earth; in "barbaric" times they could always put up in barns and houses—just an indication of how civilization "progresses." Of course, some of us get to stay in buildings. When these big guns go off they bounce even the solidest of stone structures—fairly bounce you around the place. The noise you get used to, unless shells hit close. There seems to be a different sound to German shells landing and exploding; at least it's easy to pick out which is which.

At night and often during the day, as we gather in small groups, the conversation drifts to old campaigns. We remember this and that incident and recount the details. I guess it's because we are now World War II "veterans"—an outsider hasn't a chance in such a group.

Thursday, Feb. 3

I spoke some time ago about experiencing just about everything except strafing; today we thought we were getting that, too, for a plane swooped low over the house and bullets splattered the wall. After it was all over we discovered that the plane was ours and the bullets were from nearby troops mistakenly firing at it. . . . I've a nasty job to do again; I've been putting it off, hoping conditions would change and make it easier, but it did not work that way. [This is a reference to my job as the GRO.]

Friday, Feb. 4

Had a few shells fall close to some of my squad today; I was with the squad, so I guess the shells fell close to me, too—no? But we all quickly jumped into ditches and holes and weathered out the "Dutchman's" volley. So we have another experience to write about. Oh, me! You see, Peggy, God is protecting me; we can depend on Him to work all for our good. Right now one of the noncoms has mixed some orangeade and it's real fine-tasting. We certainly eat well, except when out fighting where it's hard to get food to us.

Saturday, Feb. 5

Got my pants muddy yesterday, so our S-1 [adjutant] called and had a new outfit brought up to me; it's what is called "arctic" clothing and it's real warm stuff. Everyone seems to look out for the chaplain.

"Rotation" [will begin] to apply to us in March; a few men of those overseas six months or more are to be sent home on furlough. However, this will never apply to me since I stand near the bottom of the list in years of army service, and also since I would not feel right in taking a turn before others. Only a very, very few can go each month; by the time rotation reaches me I'll have grey hair—and let's hope that the war is over long before that.

After sleeping late on Sunday and realizing I could not hold group services, I began my rounds of the companies. Near A Company, a bomb fell about a hundred yards away, killing one soldier and wounding three. I was crouching in a hole behind a slight rise in the ground and therefore was not in danger. At other times I have been as close when bombs fell, but this was the first time I actually saw the projectile leave the plane. Then at B Company, the men showed me a German KIA. After lunch I visited C Company, and then also stopped by D Company, reminding all the men that it was the Lord's Day.

At the last company, several of us were sitting at one of the two entrances to an elaborate German dugout, which our men had taken over. Suddenly five mortar shells rained down and we all dived inside for safety. Tanks were drawn up nearby; in each of these, someone quickly pulled the hatch cover closed, and no one was hurt. At the other entrance to the dugout, one lone Nisei had been sitting, scraping wax off a K ration box for use in making a candle. He received a direct hit and was killed instantly. I wrapped up his body—his legs were badly mangled—in a shelter half for transport for burial. I completed my round of the battalion by walking to the CP and then returning to the battalion aid.

That night, sitting by a fireplace with boots and pants off, I wrote home by candlelight, informing Peggy that her March check would be three hundred dollars; that a medic had just handed me a piece of buttered toast; that outside the cars [jeeps and trucks] were passing with chains a-clanging through the thick mud, reminding me of pleasing wintry days back home in Pennsylvania; and that I was upset by all the contacts with death, but not afraid of dying since I trusted God's care.

The events of the next day are recorded, first in my diary notes and then in a letter to my wife.

Monday, Feb. 7

At house near Cairo that has roof blown off and a machine gun from a tank on the rafter. Buried unidentified German on hill; Company B boys dug place after several rocky tries. Went to CP and heard of coming move. Mortars fell close to aid station and also later when I went there—not so good. Toward dark three casualties from a mine were brought in—168th Infantry lieutenant had right foot blown off, Danish Lutheran from Elkhorn, Iowa; he said he was not worried since they were infantile paralysis legs anyway—just hoped his four brothers were better off. Enlisted man also had badly torn right leg; when I prayed he asked if he was going to die; held his hand while doctor dressed wounds—did not want me to leave him. Ate and lay down until 2:30 a.m.

Monday, Feb. 7

When I got up this morning one of the medics had coffee ready for me; also we had crullers to go with it—pretty good. Then I censored some mail for one of our soldiers, read some mail I received, and now am writing you.

Outside the view is scenic. A valley lies between high mountains. Two villages of white houses are visible nestling against the hillsides across the lowlands. All over the valley individual white houses speckle the brown of the winter earth. The hills are partially brown, partially green; behind them rise the snow-capped peaks. A few of the hills are slate gray of bare rock and thus add even more to the distant beauty. In the foreground the scene is a desolate one: burned tanks, cut trees, ground crisscrossed with tank tracks, litter of fighting men strewn all about. In fact, there is not too much left of the house we are in right now.

We moved toward the front in the moonlight toward a hill near the old castle outside Cassino, arriving in the vicinity just before daylight. The medics treated a wounded D Company officer as they took shelter behind a wall. The forward aid was set up in the basement of a ruined house in stalls for sheep or pigs. We had to stay under cover during the day. We were close enough to the abbey that I could count all the windows on two sides of it through binoculars. In the afternoon our refuge was shelled often. Litter squads went forward and brought back several casualties, one without his right eye.

On this day, February 8, Major Lovell, hit in the chest and three places in his legs, was pulled to safety by Sgt. Gary Hisaoka (Jim survived but could not return to combat),[7] and Masao Awakuni knocked out his second tank (the first was at Alife). During the night a shell exploded near the aid station, and two litter men got a few fragments in their hides. It looked like the end for all of us in the basement, but the rest of the shells fell just short or just beyond our sanctuary. We heard each missile on its way toward us—terrific! We treated several casualties by flashlight; for one I held the plasma up as it was being given. I slept for just one hour. In the morning I investigated a tear in my new pants and discovered that my pocketknife had stopped a piece of shrapnel.

Wednesday we breakfasted on K rations and hot coffee. Periodic shelling kept us under cover. Not far forward of us were enemy snipers, machine gunners, and OPs for mortars and artillery. Our morale was somewhat low, but no one went berserk. At one point I sang "The Star Spangled Banner" to cheer up the medics. Chattering with the litter men, I learned that one was from Easton, Pennsylvania (the address of my prewar parish was R.D. 3, Easton), and another was a Winnebago Indian from Nebraska (some of our litter squads were from the 34th Division's medics). I recall seeing a stray dog this day, the leanest hound ever; he reminded me of the starving children in eastern Europe.

During these days below the abbey of Monte Cassino near Castle Hill, two events spotlighting Doc Kometani took place. Both illustrate his unique place in the hearts of his fellow Nisei; the first displayed his understanding and compassion, the second his lack of concern for his own safety.

Kome and I and a medic returning from rest camp walked together toward the forward area to go to the forward aid there. When we came to a section of the trail under observation by the enemy, we decided to cross the open spot individually so that we would attract less attention and not be fired at. I went first, got to the rendezvous, and waited for Kome; after an interval of time, he arrived. Then the two of us sat in a sheltered place and waited for the enlisted man to join us. After some time I became alarmed because the medic did not catch up with us. Kome suggested that we wait a bit longer before checking to see if he might have been injured—we could not see far down the trail. After quite some time Kome said, "I don't think he's coming, Chaplain. I thought when we started out that he looked scared. I'm not surprised that he hasn't come."

"But that's bad for him," I replied. "He can be court-martialed for not obeying orders, for not coming back into combat."

"No, Chaplain, that won't happen. When we get to the aid station I'll phone back to the rear and have them reassign him to some duty back there. He's been in combat too long as a company aid man. He just can't take it any longer."

And that's just the way the matter was handled. No one was the wiser except the three of us involved. The soldier had already given all he could for the war effort; he no longer had the spirit to keep pushing himself. Those of us who were healthy and with high morale were able to carry on in his stead, just as he would have done for one of us had the circumstances been reversed.

Another day, when there was little activity at the aid station, Kome decided he would walk farther front to look over the situation. He invited me to go along, but for some reason I declined. Later on we had some wounded come through our aid post, and I was kept busy. But as the day wore on, I became concerned about Doc. No one had any news of him. Could it be that he was in trouble? Since he was in the area of our own troops, I reassured myself that someone would be available if he needed any help.

Shortly after dusk, Kome stumbled into the aid station, looking the most distressed I had ever seen him. He was covered with sweat and kept shaking his head in a manner peculiar to him. "No, I wasn't hit. I'm all right," he answered to our questions. "It's just that I got too far up front, ahead of one of our companies as I was going to another company of ours I could see. I got into an open spot, and Jerry began firing at me. I got down behind a rock. Every time I would move, either forward or to the rear, they fired at me. I had to wait until it got dark before I could move from that rock." We were glad to have our morale officer and dentist back; we hoped he had learned a lesson about roaming around by himself. In all his overseas service Captain Kometani never got a scratch in spite of all the hazardous situations he got into.

On February 12, most of the battalion was pulled out of its exposed position and placed in regimental reserve, but we were still within range of German guns.

My letters home record the events of the next two days.

Sunday, Feb. 13

Today was Sunday but all I could do was to read the lessons for the day to some men at the aid station—and a few hymns. I'm just fine, but how these men can stand the awful rigors of war is beyond me. As I look into their fine faces, begrimed and lined, I can hardly keep the tears from flowing. How man can thus treat man is beyond me. Loving you is so sweet that I almost feel guilty to enjoy it here amidst the sourness of decadent civilization.

Monday, Feb. 14

The sun is shining brightly now, but I have another nasty job hanging over my head as GRO so I can't appreciate the weather too much. But things always work out well. My assistant is fiddling around on his mouth organ—which reminds me: please send me one (ten cent one will do) in your next package. . . . Last night I stood outside looking at the stars and sang some of the good old hymns of the church. Doing that made me feel better.

The new assistant was T/5 Roger A. Kawasaki. When he reported to me he was aware that my former aide, Kent, had been wounded up front. I could read the question in his mind, so I assured him that he would not normally be in any extremely dangerous position up front; thus far he had served as a motor-pool driver. And here he was with me, under artillery fire and more!

Troops attacking the Cassino sector were convinced that the Nazis were using the Benedictine abbey towering high above the city as an OP and perhaps even as a fortress. The Allied forces, as a matter of policy, did not intend to assault this historic and sacrosanct monastery. Gen. Mark Clark (1950) insists that he tried his best to prevent its destruction.

> I say that the bombing of the Abbey, which sat high on the hill southwest of Cassino, was a mistake—and I say it with full knowledge of the controversy which has raged around the episode. The official position was best summed up, I suppose, in a State Department communication to the Vatican's Undersecretary of State on October 13, 1945, saying that "there was unquestionable evidence in the possession of the Allied commanders in the field that the Abbey of Monte Cassino formed part of the German defensive position."
>
> I was one of the Allied commanders in the field and the one in command at Cassino, and I said then that there was no evidence the Germans were using the Abbey for military purposes. I say now that there is irrefutable evidence that no German soldier, except emissaries, were ever inside

the Monastery for purposes other than to take care of the sick and to sightsee—and after the battle started, they didn't have a chance for sightseeing. Not only was the bombing of the Abbey an unnecessary psychological mistake in the propaganda field, but it was a tactical military mistake of the first magnitude. It only made our job more difficult, more costly in terms of men, machines and time. (312)

The blame for the obliteration of the landmark has been placed upon Lt. Gen. Bernard Freyberg, British hero of World Wars I and II, who insisted that he would not order his forces against Cassino until the abbey was bombed.

The aerial attack was an awesome sight as I watched it through my field glasses. The rows of planes coming unopposed over the target reminded me of freight cars coming into a railroad terminal to unload. At times a single flying fortress, passing over in formation without dropping its bombs, would circle round and come back the second time to unload its deadly cargo. I counted the bombs as they fell—or rather, tried to. Here is Clark's official report of what happened.

> A total of 255 Allied bombers participated in the attack, dropping some 576 tons of explosives. Most of the bombardment was accurate, but, naturally, where so many planes were involved, a few explosives fell within our own lines, causing some casualties.
>
> After the aerial bombardment, the entire area was shelled by our artillery. By nightfall, the whole sector was a mess of smoke and dust and ruins, through which an occasional figure could be seen in panicky flight through the artillery barrage. For the moment at least, the enemy was jarred off balance, and for the moment, there might have been a chance of a decisive success if Freyberg had hit quickly. (319)

In the next three days of fighting, the English, Indian, and New Zealand forces also failed to dislodge the Germans on Monastery Hill. (Indeed, it was not until the middle of May that the Allied forces finally broke through the Gustav Line.) The 100th remained in the vicinity of Cassino until February 22, subject to shelling all the time.

None of us had any knowledge of what happened to any persons in the abbey when it was destroyed. History now records that all the monks left beforehand but that a large number of refugees, from one to three hundred, were buried under the rubble. During the supposed carnage, the enemy was safe in their underground bunkers.

My letter to Peggy records my reflections at this time.

Tuesday, Feb. 15

Today I shaved off a week's growth of beard but left a moustache on. Next I need a good warm bath, but when that will be possible I don't know. Also I brushed my teeth for the first time in a long period.

The old One Puka Puka is still going though not as strong as before. We've been at it now for almost five months. The whole war is so crazy though so necessary if we would hold our American way of life.

It's funny how one gets sort of used to the unnatural things of war. When a blasted leg or arm is being bandaged I no longer think much of it. I've seen so many, and we usually are semi-tired, so our reactions and sympathies are dulled. But every so often the awfulness of it all overwhelms me, and I get tears in my eyes, and my heart faints. How low mankind can fall!

Until the 100th was relieved on February 22, German bombardment kept us all close to our havens of safety. The medics took over a captured pillbox, where I slept in a bunk with bedsprings—not soundly, since exploding shells awoke us intermittently. Because moving about outside was foolhardy, I did not even attempt to visit the companies on Sunday, February 20. That day a medic found some rations intended for the British troops from India, and we all enjoyed their dates. Two topics of discussion filled in some of the time: Hawaii and religion; one litter crew engaged in Bible study and asked my help with the archaic King James version.

On February 22, the remnant of the 100th, totaling 521, moved by truck convoy back to Alife for a rest; thirteen hundred was the battalion count upon landing at Salerno. I paid an Italian to shave me and to cut my hair, and I visited Italian friends, receiving from one wine for communion for the Ash Wednesday[8] Eucharist planned for the next day. I wrote my wife that I might let my moustache grow until I got back home.

Wednesday it rained so hard that worship could not be conducted, but I was able to get to the town's *stabilimento di bagni* (bathhouse), where I paid twenty-five cents to get myself clean. Thursday, sixty-five came to the Lenten service, and four communed with me afterwards in my tent, where I officiated in cassock and surplice before the opened altar kit with its lighted candles and small cross. Friday, my assistant, Roger, surprised me by shyly requesting that I baptize him; he said that he had already written home about it. (He had joined me during combat, and I had not questioned him about his religion.) He and I completed the January "Report of Chaplains" during the day.

The February 27 Sunday worship was poorly attended, in part because of the lack of energy of the men after spending days in combat, in part because of men on leave or at work on details. I felt that I myself prayed, sang, and preached in as lackadaisical a manner as the worshipers responded. I began my letter home with this doggerel.

Feeling sort of low, what better can I do
Than to sit down and write a line to you?

Monday, Feb. 28

It's almost tomorrow; I've just got back from visiting in the hospitals. . . . The fellows seemed genuinely glad to see me; most of them kidded me about my moustache and most of them noticed the two bars of a captain. One badly wounded fellow whom I had gone forward for and helped get back on a litter cried when he saw me. He was baptized by the hospital chaplain, but we had often talked about Christianity together and I think perhaps I prepared the way somewhat for the baptism.

Saw a Lutheran chaplain who was wounded in the knee and is probably out of the war for good.

On my monthly report I listed one hospital visited and a total of twenty of our men spoken to; that explains why Roger and I got back to Alife in the early hours of the next morning.

During the next few days I wrote the following letters to Peggy.

Tuesday, Feb. 29 9:00 a.m.

Funniest thing: I kept dreaming last night of being shelled, but I was with civilians and not in the army. I remember that I was almost frantic moving from place to place trying to get away from the shrapnel. And once I had just buried my face in mud when a fragment hit the spot I had just moved from! Wow! The dream was worse than the actual shelling we've taken at times.

It's now 2:00 p.m.; my monthly chaplain's report is finished and I've read an issue of *Life*. Right now a gang's singing hymns and songs at the organ; one of the medics back from the hospital is at the organ.

Part of the day it's been like spring outside. I joined in several innings of baseball, officers versus a company, and heartily enjoyed it.

Wednesday, March 1 Italy

We have a stove in our sleeping tent and are fairly comfortable. [I was sleeping in the medical officers' tent.] The weather is becoming milder right along. Soon I guess we'll be fighting mosquitoes and flies again.

Saturday, March 4

Last night each of us got three bottles of Coca-Cola, the first we've had in Italy! It tasted good, though I'm not a Coca-Cola enthusiast. We are finding out now why all Italians carry big umbrellas—it rains almost all the time; must be the rainy season.

Sunday afternoon, March 5

This morning I felt depressed, but after two services in the a.m. and a communion service at 1:00 p.m. I feel better now.

My sermon was on the Gospel for the Day and I spoke of "How to Pray." Not too many were out for services. Sometimes I wonder how much actual good chaplains do by service in the armed forces. You can't have any sort of instructive course for converts due to moving schedules, etc. Of course, you help morale, but that's not a preacher's purpose. Oh, well, the lucky ones are those who back home are working hard teaching catechumens, adults, Sunday School, etc.

After the excitement of combat, all of us found it hard to settle down to the ordinary way of living. Now we had time to think and that led to a lot of complaining. Officers in planning activities often forgot to include the chaplain's activities in making out their unit's schedules.

Tuesday, March 7

I had my teeth fixed. Kometani, my dentist friend, found two cavities and filled them. He advised me to have my silver fillings replaced with gold ones since gold wears better; at least he says some of my silver ones will have to be replaced soon.

Wednesday, March 8

This afternoon we had a fine show—all soldiers—with a juggler, a strong man, singers, tap-dancer, comedians, impersonators. I enjoyed it immensely. Some of the men have been tossing a football around in the evenings.

While at Alife the Red Cross served coffee and doughnuts one day in our area. The American girls of the organization wore the army's adaptation of ski pants and parkas. Of course the young women made a hit with the personnel.

By this time some of the publicity about the 100th, published in the American press, was getting back to our unit. An article in the *New York Times* reported that 50 percent of the AJAs were atheists. In my monthly reports I had listed our men who were neither Protestant nor Catholic under the category "No denomination." In October, I reported "forty-seven percent (some Buddhist)"; in November, "thirty percent (some Buddhist)"; in December, "fifty-two percent (Buddhist thirty percent included)."[9] At no time had I used the term "atheist" in anything I had written. Nor did I have as many preparing for baptism as the publicity indicated. Such reporting was quite unfair to the Nisei, but I knew of no way to correct the misinformation.

On March 10 (according to Murphy [1954]—I have no record of the exact date), the One Puka Puka trucked to San Giorgio near Benevento, where it became evident that we would soon be in combat again. Three (an officer, a noncom, and a private) went to the States on rotation, 151 men and 10 officers from the 442nd at Camp Shelby joined us, and many of our healed casualties returned from the hospitals.

At the evening mess on Saturday, March 11, a number of officers, both Caucasian and Nisei, in a joking manner asked about the "atheist" publicity. Their wives had sent them clippings, asking if they were among the atheists. I was already in very low spirits, and their banter added to my melancholy. By writing a long letter home that evening I was able to regain my composure. Writing out my complaints got them out of my system. Here's one paragraph of the letter as an illustration.

> The world's in an insane mess. Men on our side are only fighting because they have to (were drafted and went into combat). It'll be the same old mess when peace comes: men will seek pleasures, easy jobs, etc. They'll want our children for compulsory military training when peace does come. Politics will probably get worse. I've even heard of petty racketeering among rear echelon soldiers. I can see no peaceful place for a Christian. He ought to be out fighting sin with pen, word, life. Sometimes I think St. Paul was altogether right in advising against marriage since the last times are here. Energies ought all be put into preparation for meeting the Christ.

On Sunday I was no longer in the doldrums. The two morning services were poorly attended, but I blamed this on the rain. Whenever only a few attended, I felt I ought to ask for a transfer to another outfit, but on this occasion I simply told myself that I was going to stick with the 100th. I decided that I would have to force myself to read and study in my tent during rest periods and not waste time brooding. I reminded myself that I get low in morale only once in a while and I recover quickly.

Returning from the second service, I insisted that Roger take a shortcut down into a valley and then up a hill to the main road. Halfway up the hill the mud was so thick that when our four-wheel-drive jeep stopped, we could not move at all. Since none of our troops were in sight, I sent Roger up the hill to get help while I remained with the jeep. He returned with a driver and a larger vehicle with a winch on the front end. They played out the cable from the truck on the hard surface down to our jeep. With Roger using our jeep's power and the other driver operating his winch, the chaplain's vehicle inched up the hill. I had to face the jibes of the motor-pool personnel for several days.

Monday Night, March 13

Just came from seeing the picture *The Kansan* outdoors; it was a shootin' cowboy picture all right.

Had two shots, tetanus and typhoid, this a.m. and consequently my left arm aches from the typhoid shot. This afternoon I was so fatigued I had to lie down. Aside from helping a bit in giving the shots I didn't do much.

Sunday afternoon I read "The Hound of Heaven"[10] out loud to myself, and the last two days I've been reading now and then from that anthology of religious verse by Hill given to me by one of the AJAs when he received it in a package from home.

Tuesday Evening, March 14

Today I made out special notices for Sunday's church services and took them around to all the companies for posting on their bulletin boards. I hope thereby to get more out for services, come Sunday. At the bottom of each one I put this verse:

A great many men will pray in a pinch
When bullets and shells whistle near,
And then will forget to worship their God
When they're safe and there's nothing to fear.

Tomorrow I've planned to go and arrange some Lutheran communions for some units outside my own regiment. There are not many Lutheran chaplains in my vicinity, so I'll try to get around a bit more.

Two officers who have long been hospitalized because of wounds dropped in to see me today. It made me feel good. I've heard from one of them that a number of the men have been baptized in the hospitals, many of them Catholic, it looks like. Oh, well, that's up to them in the last analysis.

Tomorrow I intend to shave off my moustache; it's rather silly to have one anyway, I guess.

In the 1940s, a number of Lutherans did not feel comfortable about receiving the Eucharist from non-Lutheran clergymen. For this reason some of us Lutheran chaplains felt a responsibility for offering Lutheran communion services in units other than the ones to which we were assigned. However, some Protestant chaplains were weak in theological beliefs and could not understand why Christians such as Episcopalians and Lutherans preferred their own rites as much as Roman Catholics did. I never conducted a "Protestant" service of Holy Communion; I always used the ritual of my own church. On the other hand, I did not keep anyone away from communion. I always explained our essential beliefs about the sacrament and left each individual to choose to commune with me or not.

> Wednesday Night, March 15
>
> I spent the morning trying to schedule communion services and finally have one arranged. The other chaplain said the Lutherans communed with him—in other words, "Stay away," so! Tomorrow morning I'll spend time on Sunday's sermon, first time in months, for I hope to have a fair turnout at battalion services.

Each chaplain had to report each month how he had ministered to any not of his general religious group. Thus for March, I indicated that there were none of the Hebrew faith in the battalion and that my Catholic men were urged to attend Mass with the chaplain of the 1st Battalion of the 133rd Regiment and his Protestant men were invited to attend my battalion services.

Thursday, one of the boys brought me a fine wooden table he had made to set the altar kit on. I fixed up a display of leaflets with religious pictures on them. I tried to make my tent look like a chapel; normally the small altar was open and the cross and candlesticks in place. In the evening the Red Cross girls brought us doughnuts and coffee after working hours.

On Friday I visited some of the men fresh from the States, inviting them to attend worship. I heard from some of the old-timers that my verse on the church notices was stirring up the consciences of some. The medics practiced litter carrying with me as the victim; I had carried men on litters often—now I learned how it feels.

Saturday, some higher-up declared Sunday a workday for all troops, except for one hour of church. I canceled the special Lutheran service. To Peg I wrote,

From all appearances on the news front, there is many a battlefield between you and me. The easiest way would be to wish that I would get wounded severely enough to get out of it all but not enough to cripple me seriously for life. But I want to go through all of it with the men, the hard way. And that means staying in until the last round is fired. But that's as I wish, and as you wish, I'm sure. The days will be hardest for you, Peg.

On Sunday, a warm and clear day, 220 attended the battalion worship. For the first time since Christmas, I had a fellow play the organ. The sermon, "A Faith to Live and Die By," was based on Paul's motto, "For me to live is Christ, to die is gain." In the afternoon I joined the One Puka Puka on a road march and later played some volleyball. At six p.m., four Mormons and a Baptist joined me for Holy Communion.

On Tuesday I sent home my Gladstone suitcase full of military dress clothing, completely useless during combat. I had brought it all overseas because I had thought that my "limited service" might make me a hospital chaplain. I was happy to get rid of the blouse, "pinks," and "greens." New orders allowed us to write home that we had individually participated in the Battles of the Volturno River and Cassino; the press had long since broadcast the unit's involvement.

On Wednesday we enjoyed hot showers at a quartermaster bath and changed into clean clothes in preparation for our next engagement. Elements of the 34th had already shipped out to the Anzio beachhead. Although we were no longer a part of the 133rd Regiment, we were still attached to the division, and we, too, were Anzio bound. In addition to Kawasaki, four other Nisei were preparing for baptism; I explained to them the sections in the catechism about the Lord's Prayer and the Apostles' Creed.

On Saturday, March 25, while we were still in the Naples staging area, I spent an hour instructing the five catechumens in the remaining sections of the catechism, and then I baptized Roger Asaomi Kawasaki of Headquarters Company and four of A Company: Yoshio Kure, Seichi Wallace Higa, Horace Kango Sagara, and Yeikichi Arakaki.

During the rest periods in Alife and San Giorgio, I began fulfilling a newly assigned duty: the writing of letters to the families of those of the battalion who had died in Italy. Perhaps this new assignment was in place of that as GRO, for I was relieved of that position when we were withdrawn from the Cassino area. To me it made sense that a chaplain use his time corresponding with bereaved loved ones (a pastor's province) rather than supervising the removal of dead bodies (an undertaker's business).

I wrote twenty-five letters of condolence early in March, in long-hand on four-page leaflets, each with a religious picture such as "Christ the Good Shepherd" on the first page. Whenever possible, any specific details that might be comforting were included, such as "died instantly, no suffering," "brought to the battalion aid and treated," "gave plasma," "I checked with his friends." If I knew the soldier, I wrote of this. If I knew he was a Christian, I referred to his faith and added consolation from the scripture. If others had spoken highly of him, I mentioned the fact. Usually I reported that his body had been properly buried and that in time the location would be made known to the family. Occasionally, later on I received letters of thanks. Whenever a reply included questions, I answered as specifically as I was able. I kept typed copies of all these handwritten letters of sympathy. Here is an example.

Dear Friend,

The War Department has notified you of your husband's death on January 10. I want to express my sympathy for you in your time of sadness.

[Man's name] went forward with a group of litter bearers to bring back the wounded to the aid station; on the way a shell burst in their midst. As soon as I heard of it I went to the spot, but your husband had already passed away. I believe he died instantly, without any suffering. Later on I had his body taken to an American Cemetery; though I could not leave my post of duty to officiate at the burial, be assured that he had a decent burial.

My words of comfort seem so ineffective to help you in the long hours of sadness. Rather would I remind you of that Man of Sorrows who long ago gave His life for us mortals. May the Spirit of Jesus comfort you now in your hours of need.

Later on your loved one's personal things will come to you through army channels. And later on the Quartermaster General will tell you where your husband is buried.

God bless you.

CH ISRAEL A. S. YOST (Capt)
100th Inf. Bn. (Sep)
A.P.O. 34 c/o Postmaster
New York, N.Y.

Notes

1. Katsuto Komatsu.

2. The first verse of this hymn says, "Fierce was the wild billow, Dark was the night, Oars labored heavily, Foam glimmered white; Trembled the mariners, Peril was

nigh; Then said the God of God, 'Peace! It is I'" (Anatolius, ca. eighth century, trans. John Mason Neale, 1862).

3. The Epiphany season begins on January 6, the day that commemorates the revelation of Jesus as the Christ to the Magi (the wisemen).

4. Jesus' mountaintop experience with three of his disciples when he was visited by Elijah and Moses. His person shone with light, and a voice said, "This is my beloved Son . . . listen to him."

5. Yost's college roommate, also a Lutheran minister; each served as best man at the other's wedding, and they were lifelong friends.

6. Children.

7. See the appendix following for the letter Major Lovell wrote to Chaplain Yost before Lovell left the 100th.

8. The beginning of Lent, the forty-day period (excluding Sundays) of penitence and reflection prior to Easter.

9. At that time, the U.S. military had no "Buddhist" category; all persons who did not identify with the Christian or Jewish faiths were listed in the "no denomination" category. Many of the 100th who did not identify themselves as Buddhist were from Buddhist families.

10. Poem by English poet Francis Thompson (1859–1907) describing his futile attempt to flee from God.

Appendix

Major Lovell's Handwritten V-Mail Letter to Chaplain Yost Just before Lovell Left the War Due to Injuries

> To: Capt. I. Yost
> Hq 100th Inf. Bn.
> APO 34
> Local
>
> From: Maj. JW Lovell
> 2628 Hq Section
> APO 678 Local
> 1 April 1944
>
> Dear Chaplain,
>
> I have intended to give you an expression of my appreciation for some time but have put it off again and again. Your acquaintance has been one of the happiest experiences of my life and one that I cherish greatly. One cannot help but be moved to look with admiration and respect upon a person who moves into a strange organization and reaches the place you did in so short a time. Your untiring effort to bring spiritual guidance and religious training to the officers and boys can be measured by the num-

ber of followers you now have. I know the boys will never forget that medical team of Kometani and Yost who have carried litters, given first aid, words of encouragement and inspiration to so many. It seems that I have outrun my usefulness as an Infantryman and that I will be returned to the states. It is a great comfort to me to know that the boys have a man as fine as you among them. Aloha, Major

/s/ James W. Lovell

Anzio and Rome

O N JANUARY 22, 1944, two nights before the 100th began the attack against Cassino, American and British troops had landed without enemy opposition at Anzio some thirty miles south of Rome, and a beachhead extending seven miles inland and fifteen miles along the coast had been established. The purpose was to drive a wedge behind the German position and cut off the enemy in the Cassino area. The Wehrmacht, however, had rushed in troops to halt any further Allied advance, and both sides had dug into defensive locations.

To this battlefield the 34th Division was transported in LSTs (landing ship tanks), two such vessels making the hundred-and-twenty-mile voyage each night from Naples March 17 to 26. The 100th Battalion disembarked on March 26 and trucked to a reserve bivouac near Borgo Montello. For nine weeks the Allies and the Nazis had faced each other with little change in their front-line posts; the stalemate would continue for eight more weeks.

The movement from Naples to Anzio was a new experience for the Nisei. LSTs are metal vessels 327 feet long with hollow holds for transporting heavy equipment to a beach; in this case, our soldiers were the principal cargo. Dogfaces [infantrymen], long accustomed to digging into the dirt for protection, felt "naked" on an exposed steel deck and inside the metal bowels of the strange ship. As usual, cards and dice helped take minds off the sailing. Landing was a renewal experience, for the white sand of the Anzio-Nettuno coast reminded the Hawaiians of Waikiki, as did also the villas that lined the shore. From the times of the Caesars this was where the powerful of Italy vacationed; Emperor Nero had been born here. Of course, only the ruins of the city remained—just another wrecked Italian community.

The type of fighting would be a new experience for the buddhaheads. An open plain with only occasional patches of wooded cover and

On March 26, 1944, the 100th Bn shipped from Naples, disembarked at Anzio, and trucked to a reserve bivouac. Yost wrote, "The white sand of the Anzio-Nettuno coast reminded the Hawaiians of Waikiki, as did also the villas that lined the shore. From the times of the Caesars this was where the powerful of Italy vacationed . . . Of course, only the ruins of the city remained—just another wrecked Italian community." After fighting toward the outskirts of Rome during April and May, in June the 100th Bn was ordered to Tarquinia, where Yost received his Combat Infantry Badge.

crossed with irrigation canals lay under the searching eyes of the Germans established on the hills to the north. Farmhouses dotted the flat expanse, two-story buildings with stables attached. The Italians had been evacuated, but their green fields and white cattle remained. German artillery could reach any part of the beachhead, and Nazi planes could strike any Allied site. Both sides had settled down into something like trench warfare: troops in dugouts or wrecked buildings, men in foxholes at the front, barbed wire and minefields between opposing infantrymen, patrols on foot or in vehicles probing from either side.

Over most of the Anzio sector, night had become the season of activity and day the time of rest. In such a static situation much effort was spent in making dugouts and buildings as safe as possible, with more and more sandbags, and in not revealing by daytime movements just where men and equipment were concentrated. Some additional effort was expended in decorating the interior of living quarters to make them look a bit like home. During daylight hours Jerry observers pinpointed targets; at night they concentrated on the roads where they assumed traffic was heavy.

In this part of sunny Italy I used three homes, one after the other. The first night I set up my pup tent out in the open—we were not far from the coast—and fell asleep. The tent was a new issue; two walls, ground cloth, and end flaps all lightweight and sewn together, with netting over the airhole at the front—windproof and watertight and secure against insects and creeping creatures. In the morning beads of water from my breathing covered the inside walls, but this was only a slight fault as I realized that this canvas afforded absolutely no protection against shell fragments; I folded it up and stowed it away.

My second home was a narrow tunnel someone had burrowed into the side of a bank, with its opening facing the sea and not the enemy. For the next ten days I slept in it, with my typewriter, pack, and other gear close beside me. It was cozy but a bit crowded; for light I lit a candle. It was not really a dugout, for it had no reinforcement and was so low I had to back out of it on all fours, but it was comparatively safe.

When on April 6 the battalion went into defensive positions between Borgo Montello and the front, I joined the medics in using the cattle barn attached to the farmhouse where some of our headquarters men were living—my third home. Its thick cement walls made us feel safe even though we knew that a shell or two could easily demolish them. For some reason our sanctuary was never shelled, and we stayed there until a few days after the May 23 breakthrough.

For the first few days I visited around the area, meeting several chaplains who had come overseas with me on the *Hawaiian Clipper*. Roger and I, sitting on the ground near the entrance to my burrow, completed the March "Report of Chaplains." The occasional booming of an enemy cannon did not bother us, although the pesky gnats did. We thought they might be forerunners of mosquitoes; we had been issued mosquito bars and head nets. I wrote home, "About the prettiest night scene of the war is the firing of antiaircraft guns during an air raid. You can't see the shells go up, but they make a flash. The red tracer bullets from machine guns look like sparks; there are hundreds of them criss-crossing the sky. But it's deadly for any planes coming into range." On March 31 came orders forbidding any further roaming around.

I listened for the first time to "George and Sally," the German propaganda broadcast beamed at American soldiers. Good American recordings were played, interspersed with the reading of the names of prisoners of war taken by the Nazis, news from the Axis viewpoint, and admonition against believing all that the British and Americans tell their soldiers. George began in a crooning voice, "Easy, boys, there's danger ahead." The effort was intended to sap our morale; we considered the program a morale builder. I suggested that after the war Nazi George and Sally should be looked up and given government pensions. Someone else remarked that this was one program without advertising; I suggested that the reason might be that the sponsor, the German government, was going out of business soon anyway.

April 2 was Palm Sunday.[1] I circulated among the companies holding services for small groups, for our area had some tree cover. Instead of a sermon I related the events of Holy Week. We sang a verse or two from five of the hymns printed on the sheet "Hymns from Home," made available to chaplains: "Church in the Wildwood," "God Will Take Care of You," "O God, Our Help," "Faith of Our Fathers," and "Battle Hymn of the Republic." I reminded the men that we had been able to hold good services on Christmas so that they should not feel too upset about not having proper Easter worship. (Some outfits were on the line both Christmas and Easter.) I gave a catechism to an AJA who asked to prepare for baptism. One fellow reminded me that the insect repellent we carried was effective against the mosquitoes that were beginning to bother us.

I wrote home my objection to the hymn sheet the army issued; none of the hymns were strictly Christian and nowhere was the name of Jesus used. I argued that we ought to have three types of sheets: one for Protestants, another for Roman Catholics, and a third for Jews. On the positive side, I did express my appreciation for having such hymn sheets; I could carry enough in my pack for even a well-attended service.

This same day Lt. Col. Gordon Singles of the 69th Division became our CO, replacing Major Clough, who had been in command since Major Lovell was hit the second time; Clough again became our executive officer. Also, boxes of candy and cookies arrived from my brother and sister (and the next day a package from my wife). It amazed me how the postal service kept up with our troops.

On April 4, a second group of replacements from the 442nd at Camp Shelby joined us, 261 enlisted men and 18 officers, bringing our total strength up to 1,095, the highest since the end of November. Unfortunately, our veterans had little time to prepare them for combat, for on the evening of April 6, we moved into dugouts and farmhouses on the northeastern section of the front.

April 6 was Maundy Thursday;[2] I was able to assemble forty for worship and later to commune seven. I placed my pack board between two trees, spread my chaplain's flag over it, and on top opened up my private communion set; since it had only six small glasses, two soldiers had to use the same chalice. Another candidate for baptism asked for instruction and received a catechism for study. That night I hiked with a full pack as the 100th took over the positions of the 1st Battalion of the 133rd.

Good Friday[3] I stayed under cover with the medics in their converted stable. At noon I began privately to read "The History of the Passion"[4] in the *Common Service Book* of my denomination. I noticed that 1st Lt. Angelo A. Mastrella, our assistant battalion surgeon (and like Captain Dahl a Roman Catholic), was reading from the missal I had given him the day before. One of the enlisted men to whom I had recently given a New Testament was also engaged in private reading of scripture.

Saturday night I made a tour of all the companies in their dugouts and farmhouses, asking one person in each location to agree to read to his buddies the next day the Easter Story[5] from the Gospel of St. Mark. (Referring to this later in my monthly report to the Office of the Chief of Chaplains I wrote, "Cooperation was excellent, and every officer in the battalion is to be commended for aiding the chaplain, not only on this day but also throughout the whole of the present campaign.")

I was establishing a practice that would continue through the weeks ahead: beginning Sunday night I visited platoons from dusk until midnight, holding a service at each location and proceeding in like manner on Monday and Tuesday nights until I had contacted all those on the line. Normally someone would drive me to as many spots as could be approached by jeep, and then a platoon or squad guide would lead me to the next group. After the first week I objected to having a guide with me because that meant he had to return by himself through the dark; I felt that I could take care of myself between sites and not expose another to danger, but the men insisted I should always have a companion. If any of the unit were sleeping, others awoke them to participate in the worship.

For April I recorded fifty-seven such evening services with a total of 1,162 attending—these in addition to six morning services. On Sundays I led worship for those at the medics headquarters station and, by much walking, at two other places during daylight hours. Wednesday nights I jeeped to the rear to conduct Thursday services there, to visit the hospital, and to contact other chaplains. Repeating the same ritual so many times in a week created a personal problem: I found myself announcing the hymns, singing, praying, and sermonizing almost mechanically. On my visits I distributed religious literature including missals for the Catholics; I also had several Jewish *Service Books,* but at this time we had none of that faith among the officers.

Circuit riding by night I described to my wife as an eerie experience.

> As I ride at night under the starry sky over white-topped roads in a peep [small jeep] without lights, it is hard to realize that here men are throwing death at each other. Sometimes enemy planes come overhead, dropping flares that seem to hang in the sky and that light up the countryside for miles. Then we must stop and wait, lest our moving forms bring the planes down to strafe. Always on such tours there is the danger of a shell landing near, or a bomb falling close, or flak from the ackack [antiaircraft artillery] ripping down to hurt or kill. Even machine guns might send stray bullets zipping toward one. But the immanence of such man-made death seems unreal as does the odor of decaying cattle, an odor rising from the bloated carcasses lying near the road. On such trips I am nervous inside until once again we are back to our safer (?) place of sojourn. And yet I know that none of this can harm me personally since the heavenly Father has me in His keeping and rules over the length of our days on earth. But the feeling is an eerie one.

One night I had to lay low for a long time because of continuous enemy shelling. Up front huge shell craters pockmarked the ground every hundred yards or so in every direction. Railroad guns, hidden by day in tunnels, were rolled out at night and fired by the enemy; GIs dubbed these shells "the Anzio Express."

My letter of April 17 added to the story of my eerie night experiences.

> Last night I went out after dark and visited some of my men and had services with them. I did some walking alone along roads toward the battlefront. It's an eerie feeling on a pitch-black night, with ears cocked to be sure to hear the guard's challenge, "Halt!" and then the sign to which you must answer with the evening's countersign. And one begins to walk faster when tracers and ackack make their appearance, and especially when the ackack begins to burst overhead, for then there is danger of the flak falling down and wounding you. But the trip was worth any risks; the men voiced their appreciation and two more asked for baptism. I had extra catechisms along, so each received one, and I'll be back to instruct them later on.

The long days had to be spent inside the battalion aid, where the strongest temptation was to waste time by doing nothing. The same sort of life was also the ongoing experience of the infantrymen in their dugouts and houses closer to the front, with the big exception that they had to take turns manning foxhole outposts close to the Jerries and participating in patrols into enemy territory. Chow time and mail call were the two events that broke into the boring routine.

The kitchens remained in the rear near the coast, and only rarely was any cooked food sent up from them. Our basic diet consisted of 5-in-1 and 10-in-1 rations to be heated by the soldiers at their posts. At noon on Easter Day we ate frankfurters (Vienna sausages in army parlance), beets, carrots, bread and butter, and jam—I suspect that the bread had been sent up from the rear the night before. We ate in groups of five or ten, as the name of the rations indicate: enough for five men in one box, or for ten in the other. The enlisted men prepared the chow for the officers, and we all ate from the same tin cans and pots. Sometimes I drank tea, sometimes powdered coffee. There was not a great deal of variety in the menus provided.

The Hawaiians, however, were skillful in supplementing our food supply. Many an ox got in the way of either our fire or that of the enemy and graced our tables as American beefsteaks. On my night tour of April 18, a dugout buddhahead gave me greens he had picked in the fields. From time to time we dined on new onions, watercress, Chinese peas, artichokes (the first I had ever tasted), fresh lettuce, and a variety of greens—"greens" referred to anything edible that could not be identified.

There was plenty of time for experimental cooking. Masaichi Goto concocted doughnuts out of ration crackers, soy cereal, sugar, dehydrated fruit spread, and hot bacon grease. Someone made fudge that never hardened and tasted of caramel. Coarse Italian flour found on the premises was sifted through outstretched medical gauze, mixed with GI tooth powder (on the theory that the powder contained soda and salt), and served as pancakes. (A joker insisted that in this way we were brushing our teeth while we were eating!) Small minnows and crayfish were caught in a nearby irrigation ditch and fried whole in deep fat.

Treats from the rear surprised us from time to time. Once each of us received seven fresh eggs to be cooked as each individual preferred. Packages with cookies and candies kept arriving from the States. On May 2, each man received a ration of beer. On May 13, a PX ration of chocolate candy was distributed.

Mail call was looked forward to, and the answering of all the letters took up hours of our time on the beachhead. Not all the correspondence brought good news, as three excerpts from letters to my wife illustrate.

> Yesterday one of the men came and asked me to pray for his sick girl-friend; it appears that she has a bad case of arthritis and hadn't written for such a long time that he was beginning to wonder just what the matter was. And then he had a note from her, and being upset he wanted someone to turn to. This is the second or third time I've been asked to pray for some loved one.
>
> Another man showed me a newspaper clipping that announced the death of the wife of one of our men. As yet the husband is not aware of the death, so it is up to me to inform him. We had heard rumors of the death, but now it is confirmed. I know the man in question quite well; he's had a bad concussion and hasn't fully recovered from it.
>
> This morning I did write a letter for one of my men who just received word of his wife's death in the States. He is quite distraught and I've been trying to help him. He married a La Crosse (Wisconsin) girl and got along well with her folks. He is one of the men I know pretty well. It's hard to help share his grief.

Special events, the brainstorms of individuals, helped to relieve the listlessness of our inactive life. These included music (both vocal and instrumental), clowning, and "bright ideas." Just for the fun of it, I composed some doggerel to be sung to the tune of "Oh, Susanna."

> Oh, when the war is over and we all are home again,
> We'll freeze no more in wet foxholes when it begins to rain.

We'll sit in comfort all the time and tell about the way
We tried to take Cassino on a February day.

Chorus: We belonged to the 100th Infantry
Afighting with the Red Bulls there in Sunny Italy.

Doc Kome went up front too far and had to lie all day
Behind a rock awishing he were somewhere far away.
Said he when in the dark he came to where the medics stayed,
"I know now that my place is here at the battalion aid."

Chorus

When Captain King got to the road, imagine his surprise,
The cannon of a German tank was pointed at his eyes.
He hit the dirt in nothing flat, two shells whizzed overhead;
The muzzle couldn't come so low, so Captain King's not dead.

Chorus

Of course our minds have but one thought when there are tanks
     to hunt.
And so the cry went down the line, "Awakuni to the front!"
Masao came, bazooka-armed, a rocket set to go;
First shot he knocked that Mark IV out as all *kanaka*s know.

Chorus

Each night the ration crew came up with ammo, food, and drink;
Their job's no fun at such a time, no matter what you think.
When shells fell thick one of the crew thought something hit his back,
But luckily the fragments stopped in the webbing of his pack.

Chorus

The medics taught me songs of old Hawaii and had a lot of fun with
me for my poor pronunciation of the *kanaka* words, until I asked them
to translate the exact meaning of some of the words and found they
could not. I copied the words of several songs into the loose-leaf notebook I was preparing for use after the war. And, naturally, from time to
time fellows danced the hula for the benefit of admirers.

May 1, a Sunday in 1944, is Lei Day in Hawaii and was celebrated
by the Nisei stringing garlands of the colorful flowers in bloom near
their beach homes, but it was not until the Saturday following that the
festival caught up with me. Then I was presented with a box and told to
open it right away; inside was a lei made of hard candies tied together;

the neckpiece hung down to my waist. The donor explained that he had forgotten to give it to me on May Day.

A buddy sent me a tonette.[6] At first I had difficulty playing it, but within a week I had mastered a number of simple tunes on it. Peggy sent me my old mouth organ, and I often played it. We had fun singing "Old MacDonald Had a Farm" because Medic Teruo Goma always had trouble with the animal sounds.

One of the bright ideas for recreation turned out to be rather stupid. An officer set up a target against a haystack behind our quarters and invited me to join him in shooting some rounds with a carbine. I complimented myself when all my shots hit the target. Before long, rifle bullets came flying over our heads from somebody beyond the haystack. Apparently some of our shots had come close to men of another unit and they were warning us to stop the foolishness. We complied immediately. It was safer for all concerned to go inside and use the dart game someone had sent us.

Card games whiled away some of the time: cribbage, solitaire, and pinochle—I taught them the last one. The Special Service Division supplied us with pocket books for reading—not just novels, but also nonfiction works. In one two-week period I read eight full-length volumes and typed up notes on all of them. At one of the company CPs I noticed a biography of George Washington Carver and asked an officer how he liked it. He answered, "You feel clean when you've finished reading it." I carried a copy of the Lutheran Church's thick *Book of Concord* for occasional reading and a Bible for daily reading; of course, I had my own *Service Book* with its hymnal section. On Easter Day I read to myself all the hymns of the Resurrection.

The Wednesday night break in routine when I went to the rear and the more relaxed Thursday it made possible always refreshed me. Here's a description of one such day that I wrote to my wife.

> Last night I came to the rear and thus this morning enjoyed a good cooked breakfast. Then a shower and a shave—nice hot water; while taking the shower I also washed out underwear and socks so I'll have clean ones for the next time. (I always carry a change of underwear and socks in my pack.) Then one of the men cut my hair. What a change! If only the outside clothing were also clean. But all this certainly makes me feel good.
>
> By the time all this was over it was time for a service for the men in the rear, and it was a nicely attended one. We sang, had prayer, lessons for

the First Sunday after Easter, and a sermonette, "Overcoming the World" —the last the weak point in the service since I had not given much thought to it, unfortunately.

On April 17, I rode an Italian motorcycle to visit in the beachhead hospital. It was fun, but the reason for using it was a practical one: I could go by myself. Otherwise I had to use a jeep and driver and that would put two of us in jeopardy during our movement over roads that were often shelled. At the hospital area I saw a touch of home: nurses' clothing hung out to dry! (At times even this area came under enemy fire, and medical personnel, including nurses, were occasionally wounded or killed.)

A week later I helped myself to some real doughnuts, hot out of the Red Cross baking machine—four of them to make up for the noon meal I had missed. It was a beautiful day with apple trees in full bloom. On May 4, another Thursday, I watched some of the 100th practicing with weapons on the firing range. I shot an M-1 rifle twenty-four times but hit the bull's-eye only four times. I was invited to try firing a grenade from a rifle, but when I saw how the recoil knocked the user back against the side of the pit, I declined the offer. I also passed up a turn with a bazooka; there's no recoil from this weapon, but handling it did not appeal to me.

The following Thursday I spent most of the morning trying to locate a chaplain who had some Lutheran men who wanted to see me; I was unsuccessful. On May 18, the next Thursday, which was Ascension Day,[7] I attended Sergeant Shimogaki's lecture and demonstration on the use and defusing of mines. He stressed that if one is calm and takes his time, these infernal devices are not dangerous; but I had long since decided that I would let this particular military device stay in the hands of the experts. Often I looked in on a Roman Catholic chaplain, once to secure missals and another time to arrange for him to baptize two of the Nisei who had requested baptism by the Roman Catholic Church.

One Thursday night when returning by jeep to the forward aid, all of us saw the bright flashes of shells landing directly ahead on the road we were following. How relieved we were as we got closer to realize that the flashes were from our own guns firing!

To decorate the "rooms" of their "homes," soldiers put pinup girls on the walls. To offset the type some of the medics had posted, I hung up my chaplain's flag above the couch I was sleeping on. In one company CP the captain had a very special pinup girl displayed: a little girl lying in bed under a quilt, holding her soldier-daddy's picture and smiling at it. A medic's pinup was also one of a kind: a ten-year-old girl wearing a pink dress and with two pink ribbons in her hair, holding a white prayer book and standing framed in a church window. (I later was told the little girl was the new juvenile movie star Margaret O'Brien.)

It hardly needs saying that we did not have electricity, or running water, or toilet facilities up front. Most of the time candles were used for light, but some enterprising GIs manufactured canteen lamps for burning gasoline. For cooking we had Coleman stoves.

Four AJAs received instruction for baptism during our Anzio days. On April 30, Nikichi Iwai of the medics received the sacrament in the aid station with Captain Dahl and T/3 Etsuo Katano as witnesses. The ritual was interrupted for several minutes while a fire inside the building was put out; someone had been careless with a cigarette. Kenneth Hideo Koji of D Company, after a night catechetical session in his squad's dugout in the course of a weekly visit, was baptized on May 8. The L-shaped structure was not more than four feet high inside, probably the lowest-ceilinged "church" in the world. There, in the wee, small hours of a Monday morning, all of us participated in the sacrament on our knees: the convert, the chaplain, and the two witnesses, Capt. Robert J. McKelvy and 1st Sgt. Martin J. Tohara. On May 9, two others, both of A Company, became Christians: Masaru Fujimori, with Pfc. Richard K. Chinen and Sgt. Asao Tanaka as witnesses; and Asao Tanaka himself, with Richard Chinen and the newly baptized Fujimori as witnesses.

A constant topic of discussion during these lackluster days was: when will the war end? This question depended on another: when will the invasion of northern Europe begin? On May 6 I wrote home,

> Everyone is trying to predict the date of the invasion. I had spoken for May 4. The fellows started to kid me about being wrong, but I said I still felt the date was right, but I admitted that I might have been wrong about the year! That remark toned down their joshing.

On an earlier date I had written,

> This beachhead is so dull that there is even a dearth of rumors, which is something in the U.S. Army! We bolster our morale by building up our faith in rumors, and then when they don't materialize we get another rumor in its place, and so the time passes somewhat. As I read this aloud the doctor [Dahl] took issue; he says that things are so far gone here that it's no longer possible for anyone to even think.

Officers were still being sent to rest camp for a few days. I had mixed feelings about whether I should take my turn. On May 6 I wrote to Peggy,

> I've been debating in my mind whether or not I should take my turn at the rest camp when it comes—and it ought to be soon. I hate to leave the men for those several days, and yet I guess it's within my rights to take a short vacation. The place they have is well in the rear and is quiet and peaceful with good scenery all around and churches to visit. I'm weakening; I guess I'll go without ado when my turn comes.

However, I did not have to make a decision; such leaves were canceled until after we had pushed out of the beachhead.

In the middle of May, we learned of the War Department's announcement that no Japanese American troops, exclusive of a few specially trained interpreters, would be used in the Pacific because of the danger of infiltration by the enemy and possible retaliation by the Japanese against relatives of AJAs sent to that theater of war. One of our Nisei officers mentioned this to me as encouragement that we would get home before the war in the Far East ended. I reminded him that if the announced policy is adhered to, we might well be used as guards over here in Europe because we could not be assigned to the Asiatic theater.

Kome had taken care of my tooth problems during the early March rest period, but now I was troubled by the GI glasses I had begun wearing when we came to Anzio. The frames were inferior to my civilian ones, and after a few days' use, green marks appeared at my temples and over the bridge of my nose. They fitted too snugly, and I blamed my occasional headaches on them. Otherwise I felt hale and hearty. In spite of our fears, flies and mosquitoes never became a cause for concern while we lived in the lowland so close to the Pontine marshes. Even though I always got cleaned up on my weekly return to the rear echelon, I sometimes took a helmet bath at the forward aid. Part of the time I wore a green fatigue uniform. Usually I slept with all my clothing on. Some of my clothes were beginning to wear out, after nine months of roughing it.

Whenever I was on hand when casualties came into our stable, I helped the doc. I also accompanied him on his sick calls to the companies. Dahl was normally a taciturn person, but on occasion he could be scathing in his criticisms. One day a litter squad carried in a GI who was loudly complaining about his pain. After examining him, Captain Dahl barked at him to get off the litter because there was absolutely nothing the matter with him; the soldier meekly obeyed. Just then another dog-face hobbled in and apologetically requested the surgeon to take a look at his leg. To our amazement this second man had a broken leg and needed hospitalization. Our medic exploded. "See what I mean!" he scolded loudly. "Here's a guy you let walk in when you should have carried him. Instead you gave a goldbricker a ride." These were not his exact words; he usually salted his speech with numerous "damns." Once I suggested that he add a "p" to his curses so they would come out as "damps," but he replied that he was too old to change his ways.

My days during the long stalemate were spent comfortably enough, but I would much rather have been on the move, making some progress toward the concluding of the conflict. Often it was hard to realize that there was a war going on. For periods of time not a shot was fired; instead, one heard the birds singing. One day a flock of geese flew over-head, northbound, in their flapping, changing formation. Some days heavy oxen with immense horns wandered unattended along the roads. Receiving raisin bread from the kitchens was the highlight of one day; another day was made special by an issue of rice, and I was laughed at for eating it "spoiled" with sugar and canned milk. On Ascension Day (May 18) Kent Nakamura returned from the hospital; he would soon again become my assistant, replacing Roger Kawasaki, going back home to the Islands on a medical disability.

On May 22, the day before the Allied advance, an event occurred that was so interesting but also so absurd that I wrote down an account of it directly after it happened.

> In the late afternoon of a clear, warm day the medics got a call that we were to pick up eight wounded Americans which the Germans would leave at a designated bridge on the battle front. Two ambulances and a medical peep with two litter squads were made ready. I finally decided that I might just as well go along for the fun of it. So with Red Cross flags flying we set off across the flat and open land and drove almost to the blown-out bridge. We dismounted before a shell-hole in the road and walked on forward on foot with each squad carrying a Red Cross flag high. One of our riflemen met us and showed us where to go along a ditch leading into a large irrigation canal [the Mussolini Canal]. I rounded the mound and saw two young German soldiers speaking with one of our unarmed lieutenants and one or two enlisted Niseis. One German spoke fairly good English, and there on one bank of the ditch we talked. The Germans were dug in behind the mound across the canal bed (it looked dry to me), and one in an Italian uniform was busy digging away. I found

that there were no wounded to be evacuated but that they wanted to arrange for us to send a burial party on the morrow at noon to bury American dead behind their lines. When I heard the story I was not interested and shortly walked off, saying that it was not in my power to do anything about such a matter.

The Germans were both young, possibly no more than eighteen. They wore field caps and not helmets. The one spoke fairly good English. Once when talking to me (he understood that I was a chaplain) he turned to the American officer (who I suppose could speak German) questioning how to say *"vielleicht"* in English; I simply interrupted with "perhaps." He knew I understood German because I had addressed him in German when I approached him, but he wanted to use his English. When I spoke to him I used German, and then he finally broke into a long explanation in German about a dozen or so Americans to be buried, much of which I didn't understand—several of the dead were here, some there, and one at least near their house. After a few minutes I turned abruptly away, and as I did the German gave me a snappy military salute, which I returned. When I left, the American officer and the German soldiers were apparently still kibitzing in the canal that was No Man's Land. I had kept the litter men behind the mound, and so we all set off back to our vehicles. En route I picked up a Bible (not a New Testament, but a complete Bible) alongside a slit trench; it had shell fragments almost through it.

I went last in the return; I noticed that one of the medics had wandered off the road and was picking poppies about twenty feet away. I hailed him and reprimanded him—there was danger of mines and of attracting fire, though we were behind our own lines. He meekly offered me a poppy and when we got to the aid station volunteered that he'd never wander off again like that.

The front was very quiet all this time and had been all day. There was no danger in the above incident except the remote possibility of a shell falling short. But the whole matter was absurd—to go between the lines to discuss the burial of a few dead soldiers. I think the Germans had something up their sleeves at the time.[8]

I have always thought that the Germans were fishing for some indications of what our forces were planning. Since I was aware of the attack planned for the next day, I was very careful not to say more than simply that the battalion command had no power to make the agreement the Germans were requesting.

Tuesday, May 23, was a busy day at the battalion aid, with casualties coming in as the result of the breakthrough, although most of the 100th were still in reserve positions. One GI was in great pain because of a broken arm even though he did not have an open wound. He had set off a mine, and the explosion had thrown either a rock or a flat hunk of steel at him sideways, causing the fracture. Most of the time such an explosion resulted in wounds all over the body and instantaneous death. Often during the day the roar of Allied artillery was so deafening that a machine gun firing close by could scarcely be heard. Seven divisions had launched the drive and caught the enemy by surprise. By this date the Cassino line had been broken, and units of the Fifth Army were only some thirty miles away from the Mussolini Canal, which the 100th had crossed over to dislodge the Germans from its eastern bank.

Wednesday was a quieter day for the medics; the 100th was still in reserve and the fighting had moved away from us. We enjoyed French fries made of small, new potatoes; the kitchens had sent up the treat the night before. With the idea of having lamb for supper, some aid men ran after a flock of sheep, but all the animals escaped. Three officers and 112 enlisted men from Camp Shelby joined us as replacements.

Friday, I was summoned to the CP to interrogate a POW who claimed he was Russian. I could not understand his language, but since he spoke a mixture of Italian and German I translated his story of mistreatment at the hands of the Nazis. My letter home was newsy.

> You have heard by this time of the striking advance in this area. What a relief after such a long wait!
>
> Recently I witnessed a plane crash. The boys were yelling that they had seen a man parachute from a plane. I grabbed my [field] glasses and watched him glide down. His plane, pilotless, circled around us and then struck the earth some distance away, and pieces flew all over. The pilot was unhurt and no one was near the spot it crashed, fortunately. . . . Recently I saw a medium bomber come down in flames. Luckily four men were able to parachute out.
>
> Today I saw a family of Italians returning to their shelled lands and house. They had a wagon piled high with household wares and were pulling it themselves, chanting some sort of a hymn as they snailed along the dusty road. How pitiful so much of life is because men make it that way. *Esquire* magazine is said to have carried this sentence: "All the civilized nations are at war, and all the uncivilized are at peace!"
>
> I had a dandy bath at a farmhouse pump. It was cold water, but once you got under the spout it was refreshing; the sun was nice and warm in addition. I washed out the towel afterward; I like it to be fresh-smelling whenever I use it, so I wash it quite frequently. Having shaved and brushed my teeth before, and with clean underwear on, I feel real good.

On Saturday, May 27, the 100th, still in a reserve capacity, moved northwest fifteen miles by truck toward Lanuvio. Now we began fighting the dust of summer as we had fought the mud of winter. By conducting nineteen separate services I was able to reach most of the battalion for worship. Such multiple sessions were effective—the smaller the unit, the greater the percentage of men attending. Usually a platoon service brings out every available man; too often only the faithful few attend a battalion meeting.

Tuesday, I wrote home from a small but beautiful, modernistic rural church, heavily damaged by shell fire. In it the Stations of the Cross were painted on the white cement walls in black, gray, and brown. Across the road in the Scuola Rurale, Italian slogans written on the walls of two classrooms proclaimed, "The people who abandon the land are condemned to decadence" and "Of all work the noblest and most enlightening (or disciplining) is that of the land." The air was heavy with the noise of the battle being fought ahead of us. In a German newspaper issued on May 26 to the men on the Italian front, I read one article playing up the gap in America between civilians and those fighting and another stressing the growing sex immorality in the United States, especially by what the Nazis called "Victory Girls."

Wednesday, after finishing the May "Report of Chaplains" (exactly on time), I typed a long letter home.

> Recently a soldier came to the aid station saying that there was a badly wounded German nearby. I took a litter squad and set off. He was only a few hundred yards away and had been lying there for about four days, he said. He was badly wounded on arm and leg, and the flesh was already rotten, and putrefaction had set in. All we did on the field was to give him morphine. Then we put him on the litter as gently as possible and carried him in. As we cut open the clothing to which the flesh had rotted he was in intense pain, but he certainly had willpower. I helped to dress the wounds and it was all we could do to stand the odor. I gripped his good arm and hand while the doctor was putting on the splints. He will lose one arm and leg, but if the infection has not gone too far he does have a chance of living. He said he was *"evangelische"* [Lutheran] when I spoke to him, so I had a little prayer in German with him. He was thirty-five and has three sons and one daughter at home. I had seen that he was married since he wore a wedding ring. We all agreed that he deserved to pull through after lying in pain all that time. He had little to say, merely stating that his comrades had been forced to leave him behind when they were retreating from the enemy—that was to be expected in war, was his comment. The whole idea of war is so absurd.

Sometimes I wonder if it would not be better for men to suffer tyranny rather than go through all the agonies of war, especially since one war leads to another. But then I remember that under tyranny our wives and children are the ones who suffer. Therefore it is better for us men to go through the hell of war so that our wives and children may be kept pure.

When a battle is in full progress it sounds as though a thousand or so construction engineers were building a skyscraper (machine gun fire is somewhat like the noise of riveting) and another thousand furniture movers were dropping pianos and large plate glass windows from the tenth floor of a building. The din is terrific at times. Our tanks and guns fire out from near us, and the enemy shells explode near us, too, and all the while there is the staccato of the machine guns and the automatic rifles.

I'm getting hungry. I was after the boys a while ago to get something together and now they are finally stirring themselves. We'll have warm Nescafe and warmed up C rations, but they are not too bad since we haven't had them for quite some time. I think I told you before that my motto is: When in doubt, eat! It hasn't failed me yet.

As I look at wrecked buildings I wonder how in the world they will go about rebuilding them. About all that can be done with the worst, so far as I can see, is to place dynamite in them and blow down what little of them is still standing, and then rebuild from the ground up. But even worse is the cost in human life and limbs and faculties.

How can a man without faith in a personal God keep an even keel in days of battle? He really has no good reason for trying to hold himself in line and fulfill his duty. About all he can logically be concerned about is the saving of his own life. But to believe that there is a Father who has a purpose for one's life—then one keeps right on plugging away since the future lies in His hands and not ours.

Thursday, June 1, I wrote home at noon; our aid station was in a battered church.

While I'm writing this the Jerries are shelling us. Some have hit close but thus far the aid station has been spared. There's been too much movement around this area so I don't wonder that we're being shelled.

I was sitting drinking a cup of coffee when a shell hit close by. Plink! Something fell on my shoulder and bounced into my cup. It was a piece of metal, probably part of the rain spouting outside. Of course it did me no harm, and we all had a good laugh at it. When I saw it was metal I quickly looked at my shoulder, but, alas, I couldn't find a scratch so I can't get an oak leaf cluster (for wound after receiving the Purple Heart).

All this is just to show you must not worry about me. I'm fine and I'm not worrying about myself. Now it's quiet again.

Last night our PX rations came in and I've eaten all five candy bars already. . . . The day before I was to go to officers rest camp all leaves were canceled because of the coming (but now past) push. I don't know when I'll get to go now. It really doesn't make much difference.

On Friday an enemy shell hit the tower of the church we were using, but no one was hurt. I met a chaplain fresh from a noncombatant area; he was unable to distinguish between the sound of incoming shells exploding and the noise of our guns firing. I remembered back eight months when I was just as green as he was now.

Saturday, I investigated an Italian wine cellar. At its deepest spot it was about thirty feet below the ground, and it extended the distance of a city block with chambers branching out in several directions. The Germans had added a wing and also small recesses as sleeping quarters. Well-like vents supplied air; two of them had ladders, no doubt to serve as escape routes. Straw covered the floor. Apparently the enemy had not needed to use this safe facility.

I cannot describe firsthand how the 100th was smashing through German resistance at this time. As others tell the story,[9] on June 2, the AJAs stormed through heavy resistance west of Lanuvio and the next day, at 7:20 a.m., captured Pian Marano at the cost of fifteen KIA, three WIA, and one MIA; American artillery caused some of the casualties. In the afternoon (June 3), Colonel Singles was put in command of a task force including the 100th and by midnight controlled strategic Hill 435. On June 4, "Task Force Singles" led the 34th Division pursuing retreating Germans and expected to be the first Allied troops in Rome. However, on June 5, when the Nisei were only ten kilometers from the Eternal City, they were halted and motorized units sped through their ranks. At nine p.m., trucks picked up these forward units of our battalion; at 10:30, only a few Italians remained on the streets as the buddhaheads' convoy hurried through the outskirts of the city. On June 6, the whole contingent assembled a few miles north of Rome, and the kitchens served a hot meal. On June 7, the One Puka Puka trucked forty miles north to bivouac near Civitavecchia.

During this glorious advance I remained with the medical detachment, riding in an ambulance and taking in the beautiful scenery. During one rest en route I visited a Trappist monastery over which flew the yellow and white flag signifying the place belonged to the Vatican. A curious sight was that of an American motorcyclist bringing back a captured German cyclist who was still riding his own cycle; the American would point which turn his POW should take. The Nazi looked spick-and-span; he must have misread his map and thus got into our hands.

The next day I wrote this letter home.

Thursday, Dusk, June 8 From a rooftop in Italy

The weather is excellent. Everywhere the wheat is ripe for cutting, and here and there men and women are at work either with scythe or American-style reaper and binder. Fruit is beginning to ripen now. I've had a few peaches lately.

Today I was able to hold services for all the personnel and tonight I had a communion service for twelve of the men. We had the candles lit and I used the large communion kit. We had it in the room of a house. It was the first time in many months that I've been able to have first-rate worship services. One group met in a bombed church—only the back half was intact; it gave atmosphere to the service.

The invasion news[10] for some reason didn't bring too much jubilation, perhaps because we were too busy ourselves at the time and also because we have been expecting it for so long a time.

Today I was tired. I thought I'd never get myself going to arrange for services, let alone conduct them. But after I got started all went well. One of the officers played the organ for the service in his company. I played for some of the other services, but one key sticks so badly that I finally had to go ahead without the organ accompaniment.

I've been driving my peep lately. My driver did so much driving on another detail that I thought I'd better give him a little rest. That way I keep my hand in driving too. I got bawled out by an MP [military police] for cutting out of a stopped line—I thought that they were parking.

On June 10, the battalion moved by truck seven miles to the vicinity of Tarquinia, where the 34th Division had set up a rest and assembly area in a valley. Here I received the Combat Infantry Badge (CIB), as did all the members of the medical detachment. I was so proud of it that I was going to send it home immediately, but we were instructed to wear the decoration. A glance at it tells the other fellow that you have been in the thick of combat.

Officially on this date, the 442nd Combat Team, less the 1st Battalion, 442nd Infantry, was attached to the 34th Division. The same order attached the 100th Infantry Battalion (Separate) to the 442nd Infantry to take the place of the nonexistent 1st Battalion (or, technically, of the skeleton 1st Battalion back in the States). This was of concern to me because to my knowledge the Combat Team had three chaplains, two of them

AJAs and one of them Caucasian.[11] While we were near Anzio I had heard rumors that since I was a 34th Division chaplain, it was likely that if the 100th were detached from this division I would remain with the larger unit. When I was asked to express my preference, I said I chose to stay with the 100th. I was assured that my wishes would be followed.

Now, however, a different situation had arisen. I knew that the two AJA padres would have to serve with AJAs; I could not take the place of either of them. What if the third chaplain was the regimental chaplain and outranked me in time of service—would he be assigned to the 100th and displace me? I would have to wait and see, but I did not feel very good about the future. I was the chaplain of the 100th, and I hoped to continue in that capacity until the end of the war, God willing.

Notes

1. The day Jesus entered Jerusalem greeted by adoring crowds waving palm branches; the beginning of Holy Week, the week before Easter.

2. Jesus' celebration of the Passover meal with his twelve disciples when he told them to take the bread and wine as his body and blood; "the Last Supper," just before his arrest.

3. The day Jesus died hanging on a cross; the Crucifixion.

4. The entire account of Jesus' arrest, trial, suffering, and death, as recorded in the four Gospels.

5. The account of Jesus' resurrection from the dead on the third day after his crucifixion.

6. See the appendix following for a soldier's reminiscence of Yost playing his tonette.

7. The ascent of Jesus to heaven, following his appearances to his disciples during the forty days after his resurrection.

8. Murphy (1954) has an account of this incident. He records that Captain Dahl was present at the parley, which Yost thought was the case (184).

9. See Murphy, 188–191.

10. Refers to D-Day, June 6, 1944, the day of the invasion of western Europe by the Allies.

11. The AJA chaplains were Capts. Masao Yamada and Hiro Higuchi, both from Hawaii.

Appendix

Chaplain Yost's Tonette

On the occasion of a 100th Battalion anniversary celebration in 1983, a member of the battalion wrote this anonymous reminiscence of Chaplain Yost playing his tonette.

I think most of us remember his deeds more than his words. I think I can say that Chaplain Yost's sermon got to us in the way he saw to the needs of the men of the 100th Battalion, day in and day out, often in the thick of battle. His sermon got to us in the compassionate way he cared for the mentally and physically exhausted, the wounded, the dying, and the dead. So, his sermon was delivered more by way of action than by way of preaching.

I remember an incident which is just one small example of the way he worked. We were marching on a dusty road in Italy. . . . It was a hot, summer day, and we were sweaty, tired, and low in spirits.

Then, our ears picked up an unusual sound coming from somewhere up ahead. It had a snappy, catchy tune. It sounded like a wind instrument. I was thinking—who could be playing a flute or piccolo out here, practically in no-man's-land.

A short while later, we saw who it was—none other than Chaplain Yost, sitting on a tree trunk, or something, on the side of the road, playing a peppy tune on a small wind instrument. . . . After we passed him, we could hear him still playing on the instrument for the others marching behind us. It was just the kind of morale booster we needed at that time. I think Chaplain Yost, too, saw that we needed it, and that's why his version of a one-man marching band. How much more effective than mere words! . . .

I'm sure I speak for everyone in the 100th Battalion when I say that we're grateful that a man called Chaplain Israel Yost walked and worked among us during those trying days in Italy and France. (Published in the *Puka Puka Parade,* September 20, 1983.)

NINE

North to Pisa

THE 442ND Regimental Combat Team was composed of those Nisei from the Mainland and Hawaii who were inducted early in 1943 when the 100th Battalion was in the South training for overseas combat. Officially activated February 1, 1943, with Col. Charles W. Pence in command, the new unit's cadre assembled at Camp Shelby on February 15 to put into livable shape the rundown training area assigned to the Nisei. April 13, the Hawaiian contingent of 2,686 arrived; small Mainland groups arrived from time to time, some even after basic training began on May 10. The AJAs were assigned to the various units of the team: Regimental Headquarters, including Headquarters Company, Antitank Company, Service Company, and the Medical Detachment; three infantry battalions, each with five companies; the 232nd Engineer Company; the 522nd Field Artillery Battalion, with three gun batteries; and the 206th Army Ground Forces Band. Intensive training was begun and lasted into the following year.

On March 4, 1944, Gen. George C. Marshall reviewed the Combat Team, and on March 15, preparations for overseas movement began. By the time orders came to move to a port of embarkation, so many officers and men had been sent as replacements for the 100th Battalion in Italy that a skeleton 1st Battalion was left in the States, and the team sailed with only two rifle battalions, departing from Hampton Roads, Virginia, on May 2 in a convoy bound for Italy. The ships carrying most of the 2nd Battalion stopped at Oran as the rest of the 442nd continued on by way of Palermo to Naples, debarking after twenty-eight days on the Liberty ships. Equipment was uncrated and made ready for combat use. On June 6 all units, except E Company of the 2nd Battalion, rode bouncing LSTs and LCIs (landing craft infantry) for the one-day voyage to Anzio.

After a five-mile hike to an inland bivouac, the tired troops watched

German planes bomb the supply depots in the wrecked city through which they had just marched. The 442nd began their move by truck on June 9 through Rome to join the 34th north of Civitavecchia. On June 11 the last vehicles of the convoy rolled into the camp near Tarquinia to bivouac alongside the One Puka Puka. The 2nd Battalion caught up with the team on June 17, picking up its E Company on the way.

The arrival of the 442nd Regimental Combat Team was not a thrilling event for the men of the One Puka Puka. Jealousy surfaced among men and officers. Command was now in the hands of a regimental staff that had no combat experience. Just how well the veteran 100th would fit into the larger, untested unit was of concern to many of the old-timers. Until June 20, the regiment geared itself for battle, drilling, hiking, firing weapons, and getting advice. During this same period 10 percent of the 100th visited Rome on twenty-four-hour passes. Two officers and sixty men spent five-day leaves at the Fifth Army rest center in Porto Mussolini. Swimming at a nearby beach, movies, and band concerts filled in the time along with an award-giving ceremony. Fifty men and two officers joined the Fifth Army group at an audience with the pope at the Vatican.

Sunday, June 11, the battalion church call was answered by a respectable number of GIs even though rain postponed the assembly until the afternoon. I set up an altar with cross and candles, wore cassock and surplice, and led the singing while an officer assisted as organist. I explained the Lutheran liturgical order of worship as we participated in it. Two Nisei told me they wanted instruction for baptism.

Monday, I borrowed my chaplain's jeep from the motor pool and took my assistant along on the five-day leave that had been so long coming; our destination was Sorrento, the fashionable resort town on the Bay of Naples. To my knowledge I was the only battalion officer permitted the use of a vehicle for such an excursion; I never heard anyone express any objections to my being thus favored. We had a five-gallon can of gas strapped on the rear for emergencies, but with the orders I carried I could get fuel at any rear-echelon motor pool. Kent was a congenial though often silent companion, like me a college graduate. On the way south we saw many clean and nicely dressed children, in contrast to the ragamuffins who scoured the battlefields, for in the neighborhood of Rome, which had been largely bypassed by the conflict, conditions were returning to normal. That night at the officers' hotel I luxuriated in a tub of hot water (the first such in ten months as I remember), used a regular flush toilet, and slept between clean sheets.

Tuesday, I rented a kayak, paddled out into the rough water of the bay, was dumped by a wave on some rocks, swam to a beach with the boat in tow, let two Italian boys help me pour the water out, and paddled back to my home port. In a skiff with a guide I explored the Grotta Azzura (Blue Grotto) and alone walked about the Isle of Capri. Other days were spent sightseeing, relaxing, and shopping. I bought a number of objets d'art in Naples and sent them home at once. I wrote to Peggy that it was a good thing that I had increased the monthly allotment to three hundred dollars and therefore had only limited funds to squander on gifts.

On Friday, Kent and I toured the Amalfi coast. Intrigued by a monastery on a high point along the sea, I had my assistant park the jeep in an open spot so that we could keep it in view as we visited with the monks. I thought I was being overly cautious, for we were in a remote area and had not seen anyone else in the vicinity. Since we were not in a combat zone I was personally responsible for my vehicle; if it were stolen I would have to pay for it. We returned within twenty minutes and discovered that a thief had cut the straps securing the can of gas and had carried it off. I was furious—the jeep was plainly marked with crosses. Some Italian rascal made a small fortune on the black market, but I was glad he had not taken our transportation.

After returning to Tarquinia, like the others I visited Rome on day passes. Most impressive for me were the catacombs of St. Callisto, where I first heard the story of St. Cecilia,[1] the martyr who formed with the fingers of each hand the sign of the Trinity as she was beheaded. With effort I located both the British and American churches, but neither was open. Best of all, I met people on the streets, mostly children, parceling out to them the goodies I carried. I was much more interested in people than in buildings.

On June 20, I noted a change in my status: "I am more or less acting regimental chaplain at present; it really doesn't change my position or rank at all." I was not clear what my relationship to our CO, Colonel Pence, was; I stayed away from the staff of the regiment and kept busy in my own battalion.

By June 20, all units of the Combat Team had moved to Grosseto, thus making another big leap up the coast of Italy. Here in the evening I instructed a class of thirteen preparing for baptism. I sent a package of souvenirs home, including the prized CIB. I was busy all day, knowing that we would soon be in combat again: washed myself and my clothes, arranged my belongings in the jeep trailer, wrote some official letters, sewed a button and a unit patch on my shirt, mended a jacket cuff.

On June 24, the team arrived in the vicinity of Gravasanno and bivouacked overnight. Sunday, the next day, the infantry marched thirteen miles to an assembly area just behind other elements of the 34th Division that were closely pursuing the Germans. Here at dusk I held a well-attended service; I preached on the Gospel assigned for the week, the parable of the lost sheep. We were again supplementing our field rations—at this time K rations—with vegetables and fruits of the land, some, indeed, even with chickens and rabbits. The days were warm, and hiking through the dust was uncomfortable. I think others felt as I did: as long as this means a rapid finish of the fighting, I don't mind it.

Before dawn on June 26, the 2nd and 3rd Battalions moved into the front lines near Suvereto. At six a.m., the 100th hiked forward two miles and at 9:30 another four miles, held in reserve behind the advancing battalions. At eleven a.m., the leading battalions were stopped by enemy resistance, and General Ryder narrowly missed being killed or captured as he scouted too far forward in a command car. At noon our B Company pushed forward between the other two battalions in an attempt to outflank the Germans. While I waited with the medics I wrote a letter to my wife.

Elements of the 100th reached the high ground behind the Nazis above Belvedere without being detected and then surprised several enemy units within the town itself. The capture of this town forced the Germans to retreat from Suvereto toward the waiting men of the 100th.[2] This action is described in detail by Murphy; he lists the evidence of an outstanding military feat: 178 enemy KIAs, 20 enemy WIAs, and 73 POWs, compared to our losses of only 4 KIAs and 7 WIAs; captured equipment included 5 tanks, 3 cannons, 1 self-propelled howitzer, 2 anti-tank guns, and 46 assorted vehicles (Murphy, 204–210). For this outstanding performance, the 100th Battalion (Separate) was awarded a Presidential Unit Citation, which authorized every member of the One Puka Puka to wear the special blue ribbon over the right shirt pocket.

The medics followed the battalion's sortie and set up the aid station behind a hill in a farmhouse northeast of Belvedere. We heard the noise of the battle ahead, but no casualties were brought back for treatment. As I sat on a chair in the courtyard, several shells whizzed over the house and exploded just beyond us. I catapulted myself headfirst through the doorway into the shelter of the kitchen walls. I felt a sharp sting in my left arm; a shell fragment had nicked the flesh. Though it took only a small bandage to cover the wound, the medics wrote me up for a cluster to my Purple Heart.[3] The mother of an eight-year-old girl was also hit by fragments. While the mother was treated for her superficial wounds, I held her daughter to comfort her.

When the clamor of the battle ceased and no WIAs came to our station, I walked over the hill to see what was going on. Our AJAs were collecting POWs in groups. A junior Nazi officer was resisting being moved away from his amphibious car, and his Nisei captor was becoming angry. I interrogated the German; he wanted to get supplies out of his staff car and the American GI kept threatening him with his rifle. I quickly set the arrogant Jerry straight: if he did not move quickly in the direction the American soldier was pointing, he would probably be shot. He moved. This victory was especially remarkable since the Wehrmacht units defeated were first-rate troops.

A day or two later I received credit for bringing in a prisoner of war —not officially. I wrote about it to my wife.

> I was standing near our aid station and went toward some Italians who were leading some fine-looking mules down out of the hills. After they passed I looked up the trail and there comes a German slowly and without out a weapon. I yelled and asked if he were a German; he threw up his hands, and I told him to come forward. We searched him and sent him to the rear. Of course I didn't "capture" him; he was coming in to give himself up and I was the first one he met. But it makes a good story.

Sunday, July 2, while the 100th advanced against light resistance, I spent a lot of time talking with POWs. I felt that they should know that they were losing, for they were being hammered hard by our units.[4] We ate rabbit and chicken and ears of fresh corn. I was beginning to worry about having to stay in Europe with occupation troops. We thought the war was almost over! I held a service of sorts at the battalion aid in the dark; I spoke of the Heavenly Father as our example in mercifulness; like him we must not hate others because others hate us. I was preaching to myself as well as the men. I slept on a spring bed without a mattress, first sprinkling my blankets liberally with insect-repellent powder before crawling between them in my underwear.

Portions of my Monday epistle to my wife were not full of cheer.

> As I look back I can see how we have all subtly changed in the nine months of combat here in Italy. We no longer have too much consideration for the property of Italians, though actually we do give much of

our rations for what we take. Death makes little impression any longer. We eat, sleep, and fight.

Recently several of us went to get a badly wounded German. We pulled him out of a dugout. His left arm was pulpy and broken up high. It took one large and one small dressing to cover the exposed flesh, plus two compress bandages. As I dressed the wound two others padded two sticks with straw and wrapped gauze around them for splints. The man had been talking to us, but we gave him morphine to ease the pain. Just as we finished the bandaging and were about to take the litter to our peep, he passed away. Had we gotten to him sooner we might have saved him. So it goes.

Recently speaking to several prisoners [in German] I asked, "Are you Catholic or Evangelical (that is, Lutheran)?" One answered, "Neither." Said I, "You are Nazi then?"[5] "Yes." Another answered, "I was Lutheran." I countered, "Why can't you say, 'I am Lutheran'?" His reply was, "I believe in God," and the implication was that that was all he believed in. The others spoke up either for Catholicism or Lutheranism.

Germany must be in dire need of troops. The S.S. or Schutzstaffel (Storm Troopers) were formerly the most fanatical Nazi soldiers, good fighters and selected men. But now most any able-bodied soldier is in the S.S., whether willing or not—young teenagers and older married men, and even foreigners like Hungarians and Poles. I've helped to treat many of them in the aid station.

July 4, of no significance to us overseas, the 3rd Battalion relieved our men up front. I caught up on my correspondence—and also caught some rabbits for the cooks. July 5, I worried that I would not get my ballot in time to vote in the fall presidential election. July 6 (Thursday), I held several worship services during the morning. In the afternoon I wrote home about one of my co-workers.

> One of the new chaplains was terribly blue today. He's going through the first reaction upon seeing his boys killed in action. After a while his mind will become "dulled" to the whole thing, just as mine has. But it is a bit harder for him since he has known many of his men back home. I tried to help him adjust by talking with him.

On July 7, when the 100th took the place of the 2nd and pushed on toward Castellina, the medics set up the aid station in a stone garage. German shelling was heavy. When Fumi Sano parked the medics' jeep in front of our station, I suggested that he move it to a less conspicuous place. Before he could, a shell hit the front stone wall, throwing debris into our sanctuary. Dahl and I threw ourselves flat on the dirt floor toward the rear of the room. Someone began to moan. The dust was so thick, no one could see anything. "I'm hit, I'm hit," the voice wailed. "I can feel blood on my leg." After the dust settled Doc examined the casualty and found that sticky liquid from a broken bottle had splattered over one of our medics—that was the blood. The pain the man had felt was caused by rubble falling on his leg. No one had been hurt, but the jeep out front had been badly wrecked. Other shells fell close, but all were near misses.

Sunday, July 9, was another day of combat without time for worship. Indeed, it was not possible to hold services until we got to Orciano on Friday. Here the Army Signal Corps took pictures of my men worshiping. During these days I helped take care of the civilian wounded and wrote two letters of condolence. My jeep and trailer were following along with the medics' vehicles; from time to time the medics used my jeep since it was fitted with holders to carry men on litters. I complained that the field desk issued to me was too bulky and planned to trade it off for a smaller one. After sleeping in a house one night, I discovered in the morning that it had a bath with running water; I bathed in the cold water and changed clothing. We received mail on some of these combat days. Usually I hiked with the medics as we followed the advancing line companies.

> Saturday, July 15, Night
>
> Today was a really busy day: letter-writing, tending wounded (including house calls with the doc to sick and wounded civilians), and one worship service. One thankful father gave us three eggs in appreciation.
>
> An officer gave me an enemy gun today; I have in mind giving it to Mike [my wife's brother, John Michael Landon] since he asked for one, though it's a good enough revolver, or rather pistol, to keep for myself, if I am able to send or bring it home later on. We'll see.
>
> Lately the shells have been coming too close for comfort. Of course the *tedeschi* [Italian for "Germans"] have a worse time than we since we have much more artillery.

On July 19, the battalion moved into liberated Leghorn to guard important installations and to perform MP duties for a week. Here in a spacious second-story room in some sort of institution I fixed up a real chapel: organ in place, altar set up with a prie-dieu[6] in front of it, small (leaflet) pictures on the walls, and tracts and New Testaments on display. Saturday evening, five attended Vespers here.[7] I arranged with a Roman

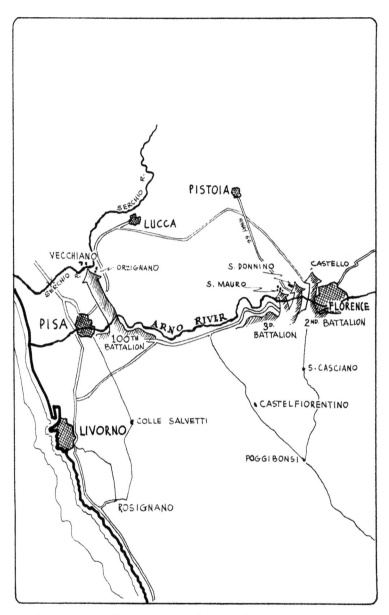

In July 1944, the 100th Bn, now part of the 442nd RCT, moved to Livorno (Leghorn). By August 16, they had moved south of the Arno River east of Pisa. On September 1, the 100th crossed the Arno River, moved across the plain, and dug in on the south bank of the Serchio River. The aid station was moved to a suburb of Pisa.

Catholic chaplain to have him say Masses both that evening and on Sunday, but an hour and a half later his assistant came to tell me their unit was moving out. For worship on Sunday we had flowers in borrowed altar vases.

Monday, nine attended catechetical classes;[8] Kent informed me that the other four who had started instruction had been wounded and hospitalized. Eighteen attended the Monday Vespers; four were from Caucasian units. The officers staged a dance, inviting local young women; I attended briefly as a matter of courtesy. Before leaving the port city, my men appropriated for me from an Italian house war souvenirs of the Italian invasion of Ethiopia: a curved sword, a leather shield, and a fancy cartridge belt.

One day during our stay in Livorno (Leghorn), a short Nisei private stood at his post on the main road into the city with orders to keep all unauthorized personnel out of the restricted area. A colonel with a convoy of trucks approached the lonely sentinel and the following conversation took place between the two.

"We are from the Engineers Corps," said the officer. "We are here to secure the port and make it ready for the ships to come in with supplies. Let us through."

"May I see your orders, sir?" replied the private.

"I don't have orders. I must get through."

"Colonel, nobody gets through without orders."

"I can kill you right here and take my convoy through."

The little Nisei drew a line across the roadway with his boot and said, "Colonel, you cross this line, you *make* [ma-keh]."[9]

"*Make?* What is *make?*"

"*Make* means you're dead."

"We can take you; you are only one."

"You think me stupid? I am a combat soldier. You are now covered by many machine guns. Cross the line and you *make!*"

The colonel turned his convoy around and went back to get his orders. Later on Gen. Mark Clark personally commended this 100th soldier for carrying out his assignment as ordered.

On July 25, the battalion joined the rest of the Combat Team at the 34th's rest center at Vada, a few miles north of Cecina. Here I set up my wall tent as a combination chapel and office and slept in the medics' quarters. The next day was a busy one: visits to companies, visits to two chaplains, catechetical instruction, shining combat boots, making and posting chapel notices. I borrowed a CIB from a soldier who had one extra, getting ready for the ceremony the next day. But I could not get a theatre ribbon, and my Purple Heart ribbon with its cluster had rust streaks on it.

On July 27, General Clark decorated our battalion colors and the company guidons[10] with the blue streamers of the Distinguished Unit Citation and authorized the use of the blue ribbon over the right front pocket of all of us. After the formation I had the honor of marching our Headquarters Company back to camp.

Friday, the noon meal was served at the beach and I went swimming before and after. In the evening we went Hawaiian, with a luau on the sands—the pig roasted in a pit with hot stones. An officers' party followed; Chaplain Higuchi engaged local entertainers for the evening's program.

On Sunday, I heard that one of our company commanders had scheduled a detail to blast out a latrine sump. I allowed myself the luxury of bawling out the offending captain. At ten a.m., eight men were baptized during the battalion service: Henry Yoshiki Nakasone of Medics, Fred Hisayuki Hosokawa and Kazuto Roy Izumi of Headquarters, Ralph Hitoshi Yoshioka and Keijiro Umebayashi of B Company, Mitsuo Furumoto and Masaichi Kotani of A Company, and Shigeru Tomita of D Company. All of these had received three hours' schooling in the catechism and one on the New Testament. Etsuo Katano (in charge of the medics since Goto went home on rotation) and my assistant, Kent Nakamura, were witnesses. Just after we had left Leghorn I baptized James Tsukasa Yamada of B Company because he was going off on a rest leave; Takegi Gushikuma of the medics joined Kent as his witnesses. These ceremonies of July 26 and 30 were important to me because I had been able to prepare the men more adequately for their vows than was normally the case overseas.

On July 31, I discovered Volterra, the alabaster town. In company with two other officers I visited the Cossio, the Mendici, and Italian Lieutenant Colonel Ricci's families, observing for the first time the living style of the aristocratic class. They, too, were suffering because of the war; the two sons of the *colonnello* and the son of Widow Mendici were among the young men of the town who were first held as hostages and then shot by the Nazis and Fascists as a reprisal for some partisan demolition. Signora Mendici spoke French, English, and German—all well.

Upon returning to Vada, I found lodging for a twenty-three-year-old woman and her chaperone. The young lady was on her way to a job with a Red Cross doughnut unit and had been visiting the mess crew in one of our companies where she had worked for a while in order to earn her food; she appreciated these men for treating her with respect.

On August 2, I shared with my wife the growing concern I was feeling about what I considered to be America's shaky ideals.

> After three years in the army some of the Hawaiians have relatives, some who are even citizens by birth, still in internment, and the soldiers here cannot even find out why they are still being held. Our wonderful America! We rave about Niemöller's imprisonment,[11] yet one fellow here has a stepfather who is a Shinto priest, citizen by birth, who has been imprisoned for three years, so far as the stepson knows solely because he is a Shinto (not state Shintoism). Yet some superpatriotic yell their heads off that God has a stake in this war, implying that he is only with our side. In South Africa, an Allied nation, colored men are classed on the level with animals—yet we fight for "freedom." In America, Japanese because they are Japs are imprisoned, yet we fight against the ideology of "blood makes a man different." Actually the philosophy of America seems to be pragmatism: what works is right. We used to condemn Russia for her policy of doing what at the moment works (e.g., her alignment with Germany and the partition of Poland)—only Americans always tag on some idealistic phrases and do them lip service. Christians ought to wake up to the absurdity of thinking that any nation is holy. There's no other land I'd rather live in, but there's lots of housecleaning to be done back home.

The next day I wrote the following letter to Colonel Turner in Honolulu.

> Dear Colonel Turner,
>
> Now that you are out of uniform the above title may be out of place, but to me you are "Colonel Turner."
>
> Perhaps you can help one of our boys in a matter concerning his stepfather and stepbrother. The soldier concerned is S/Sgt. Heiji Fukuda, Company B. He has been with the battalion all the way through the campaigning in Italy and has come through unscathed. Now he is worried about the internment of his stepfather, the Rev. Yoshio Akizaki, a Shinto priest, whose home address is . . . Honolulu. Yesterday I had Heiji speak with Chaplain Yamada about the matter, but we all felt that since you are at the home base you might be able to assist, if in nothing else than easing this soldier's mind that someone is fighting his fight for him back home. Yamada told Sgt. Fukuda that all Shinto priests have been held

thus, and that they are probably the last group to be granted freedom. But Fukuda is so convinced about his loved one's innocence that he thinks it unworthy of himself as a son not to do anything and everything for his stepfather. Also, he is fearful that should he die in action there will be no one to continue for him. We assured him that there are many interested persons in the Islands who are by their efforts helping loyal Japanese-Americans.

At the time he was apprehended (December 7, 1941), Rev. Akizaki had been a Shinto priest for twenty-five years. He was born in the Islands and educated himself entirely in the Islands. Later on he taught English in the Normal School in Honolulu. Two years before Pearl Harbor he took his first trip to the Orient to visit his parents, staying there for three months. In his conduct of his temple he was independent, not joining clubs and the like. His teaching concerned the God of Happiness, a branch of Shintoism. Sgt. Fukuda says that most of his time was spent with his stepfather, and he thinks he really knows him. (The priest is about forty-six years old.)

In January Sgt. Fukuda wrote to the War Department concerning his two relatives. On the 30th of April (all dates this year) he received the answer that his petition for re-investigation had been forwarded to the Commanding General, U.S. Army Forces, Central Pacific Area, for his action in the matter as the internees remain within his jurisdiction.

In October and November of 1943 there were two hearings of the case, but other than that so far as our soldier knows there was no trial. Has the internee in this case had all the consideration possible, or might something further be done? I am grossly ignorant in such a matter; therefore I am asking for your advice and help.

When Fukuda's name came up in the pre-war draft he possibly might have been deferred because of his work, but at the advice of his stepfather he freely entered the service. On the day of the sneak attack Fukuda was at home with his folks; as soon as he knew it was an enemy attack he reported back to his outfit. A month later was the first he knew that his father had been apprehended on the afternoon of December 7.

If Fukuda would learn that his father actually is guilty of some act against the nation he says that he would be the first to acknowledge the justice of this internment. He is so sure of his innocence that he would gladly take the responsibility of parole. If he were in the Islands he could make such inquiries himself, but he is at a loss what to do since he is over here.

The stepbrother, Takeo Akizaki, is also a citizen by birth. He graduated from high school with honors and was studying through the International Correspondence School. During 1941 he was assisting his father in the temple services. Takeo (aged 24) is married to a Southern California Japanese-American who was also born in the Islands and who at present is teaching at the Farrington High School, Honolulu; this brother, like his father, had no connection with Japanese clubs; he took two trips to Japan, one when young and once when about fifteen years old.

Possibly you will want to contact Mrs. Akizaki at the Farrington High School; she has been trying to help her husband and father-in-law.

I can appreciate how busy you are; but I also know of your concern for the men of the One Puka Puka. Thanks for any assistance you can give me and Fukuda.

On August 3, I made the long trip over dusty roads to visit the Cossio and Mendici families in Volterra. Upon arrival I learned that a Mass was scheduled for the young hostages who had been executed by the Germans. I attended and afterwards spoke with two of the mothers and the priest; the cleric took me to the place the atrocity was committed.

On Sunday, August 6, I conducted a Lutheran service for any in the 34th who were interested. Many who came to the upstairs grain room were of the Missouri Synod.[12] We sang "Beautiful Savior," "According to Thy Gracious Word," "Now Thank We All Our God," and one stanza of "A Mighty Fortress."

My August 7 letter reflected the empathy I felt for the poor, innocent victims of the war in Italy.

> Today I revisited some old scenes. One girl that Doc and I treated (she was wounded by shell fragments high on her leg and arm), I visited. She was upstairs and came to the window. At first she didn't recognize me, but when she did she came banging down the steps. She has only a slight limp. The arm is also healed though when I touched the scar, the metal could be felt inside. She is supposed to be fifteen though she looks twelve. Her mother offered me white wine; my driver drank, but I did not care to. But as I looked at the girl, a bit dirty in person and clothing but smilingly thankful, I could have cried. All too soon she'll be a drudge for some lazy Italian and in a few years will look aged. One feels helpless to be unable to give real help. Let's hope that my picture is more pessimistic than the future will prove.

August 10 was a morale-breaking day. The military had decided that medics and chaplains were not infantry and therefore under no circumstances could they be awarded CIBs; by official orders mine was taken away from me and the fact written on my permanent record (but I kept the one I had sent home as a souvenir). Furthermore, on this date the 100th lost its designation as "Separate" and became simply the 100th Battalion of the 442nd Infantry Regiment. This was a real blow to all those who had any part in writing the record of the One Puka Puka, including those who came in as replacements from the 442nd.

Worst of all for me personally, I received the written orders making me the regimental chaplain; I did not even know the assistant adjutant who signed Special Orders No. 125 for Colonel Pence. I could remain in the 100th as its chaplain, but I would now have to supervise the other padres and schedule the three of us to cover the smaller units. Three minor events were encouraging: I was preparing a soldier from another unit for Lutheran confirmation,[13] Red Cross ice cream was available for five cents, and the cantaloupe for dessert at one of the companies was excellent.

On Sunday, August 13, the regimental band played for worship even though they had supplied the music for a dance the night before. I got to thinking during the day that now I had little chance of getting home soon on rotation since I was brand-new in the regiment and might easily be passed over in favor of officers the Combat Team had brought overseas.

On August 15, the big news was the invasion of southern France. I ventured a guess that if this army in the South and the other one near Paris kept on rolling along, the borders of Germany would soon be reached and by October peace would be a reality!

On August 16, the 100th was detached from both the 442nd and the 34th to become a part of Task Force 45; we relieved another American unit in farmhouses on the flat land south of the Arno River, east of Pisa. For the next two weeks our infantrymen guarded a half-mile front and sent out patrols across the river. We medics occupied our own farmhouse toward the rear, and I practiced on the piano in it. Dahl and I ate off plates in the kitchen, and I slept in pajamas on a blanket-covered bedspring. I kept my fingers crossed, not wanting to be wounded or captured by the not-so-far-away Germans without my boots on. The men had a beer ration sent up to them; the nondrinkers did not get a substitute—no Coca-Cola for us. Saturday, August 19, Kent drove me back as far as Volterra, where we visited the Mendici family. My records show that I held a service for troops somewhere on this trip. Here's how I described the return trek to my wife.

> I was driving black-out, for a while following the "cat's eyes" of a peep ahead, and then alone in the starlight with eyes glued to the white road and alert for any posts with white engineers' tape (indicating a bypass or a narrow bridge or a dip in the road) and the looming hulk that means

another car is approaching. "Cat's eyes" are just that: two little dots of light showing at each lens. During the day Kent had been driving, so I was spelling him off.

On August 20, only one service was possible. Word came from the rear that the former chaplain of the 442nd had moved back and assumed his old position since his captaincy was a month or two older than mine. This meant that we had four chaplains instead of the three called for in the table of organization. I hoped that I was not about to be moved away from all the AJAs.

During the latter part of August our companies were not ordered to advance from their positions. Chaplains Higuchi and Yamada and I took turns at the officers' rest hotel in Rome. As I was entering the lobby there one evening a second lieutenant of the 100th was waiting for me.

"I have a favor to ask of you, Chaplain," he said. "You know that you captains have much better accommodations than junior officers like me—and more privileges. You can bring any guest you want into this fine hotel. I've met a real nice Italian young lady and I want her to have a good meal, but I can't take her to my officers' mess. Will you please take her to dinner with you and then to the dance afterwards? You'll enjoy her company." He must have suspected that I was about to reply in the negative, for he gave me no opportunity to interrupt him. "All I'm asking you, padre, is that she gets a good meal. She's a real nice girl, and I'd appreciate you doing this for me. Will you, please?"

"Lieutenant," I replied, "I'm a chaplain. What would the other officers think of me if I came into the dining room with a young lady on my arm? I do not like to say no to you, but this is something I cannot do."

"Please, Chaplain Yost."

"No, I'm very sorry, but I must refuse."

Moments later as I settled into my chair at a table by myself, I looked across the room and recognized Capt. Roy Fogel, a member of the parish I was serving when I entered the army. He looked up and saw me and came over immediately to shake my hand. "Pastor Yost, what a coincidence to meet you here," he said. For two hours we chatted about Hecktown, his family, mutual friends, my wife Peggy. I had often visited the Fogels on their farm. It was a joy to meet Roy—he was the only member of my parish I met overseas. I remember vividly one comment he made: "Pastor Yost, you have aged ten years since I first saw you in 1940."

That night in my reviewing of the day's events, I shuddered to think that I might easily have been influenced to do a favor for a friend and have compromised myself. Of course I wrote to my wife of this incident, just as I shared all my experiences with her; but if I had listened to the young officer, how would I have explained to anyone that wining and dining a Roman beauty was "doing a favor for a friend"?

The Rome visit was interesting and educational: St. Peter's, the Sistine Chapel, St.-Paul-beyond-the-Walls with its alabaster windows, St. John Lateran. After a long search I found the church that housed Michelangelo's sculpture *Moses,* but it was still covered with masonry as a protection against bombing. I enjoyed the entertainment the military had imported from the States, especially a troupe of three young women and a young man: pianist, cellist, violinist, and baritone. Hotel accommodations were excellent: lights, shower, bath, hot water, telephone, splendid bed—but the atmosphere of the hostelry was disgusting morally.

On September 1, the 100th advanced across the waist-deep Arno and on the next day across the plain beyond, digging in on the south bank of the Serchio River. The aid station was housed in a suburb of Pisa, and Captain Dahl acquired an Italian medical practice using me as his interpreter. He treated many cuts, boils, and infections resulting largely from lack of personal cleanliness. A mother brought in her strapping young son, who had scalded himself with hot water a few days before to avoid conscription by the Germans. Doc's clientele paid in fruit: grapes, pears, peaches, figs. During a brief period of shelling I rushed into the street and grabbed up a little girl and carried her into the safety of our building. The parents immediately became my benefactors; their little Franca claimed to be ten years old, but she was so small she looked like an eight-year-old to me.

One of our Nisei informed me that he wanted to marry an Italian girl. In such a case the chaplain had to investigate the situation, visiting the family and then writing a prognosis. I explained to the soldier how difficult it was to get the permission of the military authorities and how such a marriage would create many problems. Before any steps could be taken to pursue the matter, on September 5 we were ordered out of combat and moved to Castiglioncello, where the rest of the 442nd joined us the next day.

About this time the non-Nisei regimental chaplain suggested that I visit his unit while he visited the men of the 100th. I wrote him an official letter protesting such an arrangement. It looked like I would soon have to tangle with him to remind him that he was inexperienced overseas, "new" to the battalion, and lacking in any understanding of my position as the chaplain of the 100th.

As soon as we came off the line, Kent and I motored to the hospitals where our wounded were recovering. Since the action at Belvedere, the One Puka Puka had lost 3 officers and 33 men KIA and 11 officers and 158 men WIA. Two trips to talk with 11 of the WIAs resulted in us being soaked to the skin in pouring rain; the jeep had no protection against the weather so far as its passengers were concerned.

On September 8, in the rest area, I led a worship session at noon. It was a Friday and only a few attended. My record of the day noted, "Whenever the men have to walk some distance, not too many come." However, that was a simplistic explanation; morale was low and we did not know what the future held for the 100th and the 442nd. On September 9, I was informed that I was indeed the regimental chaplain, and this time the appointment stuck. I never did learn exactly what had been going on at the regimental level about my position.

On Sunday, September 10, the Combat Team moved in convoy forty miles south to the port of Piombino. Here at dusk I held two well-attended services before all our units boarded Liberty ships, the 100th on the *John Holmes,* headed for Naples. On the *Holmes* were one thousand passengers with but two latrines to use; we were so crowded that some men were forced to sleep on deck. Near midnight on September 11, all personnel debarked and set up bivouac in the dark in an olive grove several kilometers from Napoli. I wrote home, "The atmosphere is rather smelly this evening, perhaps because a pig stable is rather close nearby, and the dust hereabouts is most thick."

> Wednesday, before Supper, September 13
>
> Tonight I have a service for some of the smaller units in the regiment. I've arranged for a Catholic chaplain to come in—that is one of my jobs now as the regimental chaplain. We might have a few Jewish officers, so I've contacted a rabbi chaplain, too.
>
> This is the first time I've used the typewriter in several days. I thought that I might get at some reading today, but little things kept bobbing up and tending to them took up the day. I've made a rough but usable book-rack for the Special Service Edition books I've been accumulating, and all are now exposed so the boys can pick what they like.
>
> A while ago three little girls, begrimed and with bags denoting their trade as scavengers, came through the area, so I surprised them by calling

them over and giving them each a bar of GI chocolate. They said their thank-yous in English and got on their way.

Quite a number of the original 100th men are either en route to the States or are already there or in Hawaii—the wounded and reclassified. I'm glad for them, but of course all of them have some handicap now.

Thursday Morning, September 14 Italy

Please note the new APO number: 758.

Last night I went to see a movie, but with the adjusting of the screen, and the projector, and the sound track, and then finally the inability to get the power through the machine, there finally wasn't any movie—but it took an hour and a quarter to find that out. Maybe I'll get to see it tonight; it looked like an interesting one.

This morning we had fresh eggs for breakfast, sunny side up, with a link of pork sausage and a piece of toast, together with oatmeal and coffee—all in all not a bad beginning to the day. Looks like we might have fresh fish one meal today, too.

Today I'm staying right here and doing some reading and letter-writing, unless some GI comes in with a pressing problem of some kind. The evenings and mornings are getting to be quite cool; I thought last year that we would not need to spend another winter in tents and worse, but it looks like I erred in my judgment. At least the terrain cannot be as bad as last winter's, so that's a consolation.

Yesterday I discovered there is a Japanese-American in the Combat Team from Norristown, Pa. He had heard that I was from Pennsylvania so he introduced himself. He lives in Jeffersonville, between Norristown and Collegeville. [This was only a few miles from Phoenixville, where I had attended high school.] He is four years younger and we could not find any mutual acquaintances, but it was good to meet him.

The bookcases (rather rack) I made yesterday look real nice in the tent. Several men have been in to borrow books. Many of these paper editions . . . are good books. And some of the officers have given me their books after they've finished reading them.

I've got to get another blanket; one is no longer sufficient. And I wish they were just a bit bigger—no matter how you fold them they are always a few inches short and the head or feet of one's body sticks out!

The sermon for the services on Sunday, September 17, was based on the words of Jesus, "Take no thought for the morrow." It had three simple points: 1) Get a sane view of life; 2) Trust in God's care; and 3) Work for his principles. In the afternoon I attended a Lutheran service in another unit, but the celebrant of the communion was of the Missouri Synod, and, much as I wanted to commune, I did not feel free to do so.

On September 18, Colonel Turner's letter in reply to my appeal for help in the case of the interned Shinto priest arrived.

August 28, 1944

Dear Chaplain,

Your letter written on behalf of the stepfather of one of the boys arrived over a week ago. I decided that the best procedure was to turn the entire letter over to the proper authorities and that was done immediately. I called them a couple of days ago and learned (1) the decision as to release or non-release can be made locally (2) there is a *chance* of release. Probably nothing will be put into correspondence for a while at least. If anything further develops I will let you know at once.

1st Sgt. Nakamura, Staff Sgts. Goto and Kaizumi, and about 67 others got back the other day. That makes about 120 back here now.

The next morning I wrote to Peggy.

Wednesday Morning, September 20

Last night I had a real Italian dinner at a peasant home: spaghetti and sauce with cheese, then half a chicken stuffed with egg yolk, and fried rabbit with fried potatoes, and grapes as dessert. I couldn't eat all the food they put before me.

A twelve-year-old girl named Dolores comes to get my wash every few days. She never seems to have much pep; I suspect she works too hard to get much enjoyment out of life. She comes of the peasant class and there is a world of difference between her and Gella [Mendici of Volterra, who was also twelve years old]. I always give her a liberal gift of candy and chocolate because I pity her. She speaks broken English and most of the words are ones usable to ask if there is any wash to be done.

Lately I haven't taken off to visit any of the neighboring towns. Today I might have but now that it's raining I think I'll stay put in my tent. There's not much to see anyway. If I knew people somewhere near I'd enjoy visiting in a home, but just to shop (anyway I haven't any spare money for that) or to walk around is not much fun.

Dolores just came into my tent from out of the rain. And besides that, there are two of my 100th men here reading magazines. It looks like an all-day rain, so I guess my tent will be full of people all the day long, which is all right.

The longer I'm over here the more junk I'm throwing away, but whenever I go to load up the trailer it seems I nevertheless have even more. Of course as I go along I collect more and more books for the men to read, and they take up a lot of space, but it's worth it. I get a lot out of the books, too.

On Wednesday, September 20, I filled out my absentee ballot for the fall presidential election and sent it to Ward 1, Nazareth, Pennsylvania. Captain Dahl signed my form as a witness, and I signed his.

Late Afternoon, September 21

The rainy season has again struck us. No doubt this winter will be much like the last one, but now that I'm about to begin it again, I don't feel so badly. If I had known last year that I'd still be campaigning overseas this winter my morale would indeed have been low. But now, being some-what dulled (or toughened), the outlook does not demoralize me much. It's only a couple of months at the most and then spring will be here again and maybe a chance to come home. Hope springs eternal in the human breast.

I have just about decided that when and if the chance comes for rota-tion, I am going to ask not to come back to the 100th. Things have changed so much in the last year, and now that there are two American-Japanese chaplains here it would be better for one of them to be in charge, and since I am senior to both, it would be necessary for me to leave for that. Of course the chance might not come, and permission to leave this group might not be given, either. But I'll try to get a chance to get with another outfit after the furlough (which cometh next year sometime, I hope).

Overseas stripes for this war have now been authorized; they are bright yellow, straight bars worn on the left sleeve four inches above the edge of the cuff, one for each full six months overseas. I have two of them sewn on my shirt. Most of the 100th boys (original) have three since they spent seven or so months in Hawaii, which at that time was overseas so far as the army is concerned (though the year they spent in the States, which for them was definitely overseas, does not count as such). Doc Dahl will get his third one in a couple of weeks, too.

Saturday Night, September 23

Tonight I'm a bit dejected. How in the world some of these other chap-lains (as, for example, in station hospitals) have stood two years and more away from home is more than I can understand. With me the danger of so many hours has taken away the sting of waiting, for it meant concen-tration on the thing at hand. I guess I just don't have what it takes.

Today I drove out to Dolores' house to pick up my wash. Her family lives on a dirty street, but in a courtyard of it. I saw the living room with two big beds in it. She wouldn't take any money for the washing—only candy, chocolate, and soap. I pity such people with so little ahead for them in life. It's not that they don't have enough material things for happiness; it's rather that they have not learned what happiness is. I almost wish I could have a country parish in some such place and see if something might not be done for them. She's always worn the same nondescript gray dress —a tired, little girl of twelve. But she's always had a smile for me.

During this rest period, 181 replacements from Camp Shelby joined the 100th. Every day 10 percent of the men were given passes for Napoli. "Club 100"[14] was officially organized with Capt. Katsumi Kometani as president and Charles Hemenway[15] of Honolulu continuing as financial agent of the thirty thousand dollars already collected since the Camp McCoy days—now a clubhouse in the Islands was assured. The Combat Team became a part of the Seventh Army for service in France. On September 26, the battalion moved on LSTs from Staging Area No. 11 at Bagnoli to the USS *Samuel Chase;* at noon on September 27, all units of the 442nd Regimental Combat Team sailed for Marseille, France.

Notes

1. Yost's daughter, Maria, was given Cecilia as her middle name in honor of this saint.

2. The Battle of Belvedere took place in Tuscany and brought the men of the 100th Battalion international fame. A German SS Battalion used Belvedere as an observation post to send artillery and mortar fire down on the men of the 34th Division who were in the valley below. The men of the newly arrived 442nd were sent in to assault the German positions. The 442nd made an initial breakthrough, but a German counterattack sent them reeling back into an exposed position on a nearby wheat field. The 442nd was then pulled back and the 100th ordered to take the town. Capt. Sakae Takahashi of the 100th Bn B Company was then given the mission to infiltrate the German lines, encircle the town, and take it from behind. He broke B Company into three platoons: the first, under Sgt. Yeiki Kobashigawa, was to take the town; the second, under Lt. James Boodry, was to cut off German retreat on the main road that led to Florence; and the third, under Lt. Walter Johnston, was to cover the northern flank of the company against a German counterattack. The Germans were caught by surprise and the town taken. One of the German prisoners asked if the men of the 100th were Mongolians in the American army. Lieutenant Johnston replied, "Hasn't Hitler told you? These are Japanese. Japan has surrendered and is fighting on our side!" The Germans looked skeptical until the men of the 100th started shouting "Banzai!" (*Yank The Army Weekly* 1944)

3. At this point in the campaign, out of the 1,300 men in the battalion, 1,100 had earned Purple Hearts (*Yank* 1944).

4. The Germans were in retreat at this point to the defensive position known as the Gothic Line, which was located twenty-five miles north of the Arno River. During this

period only one German force, the Hermann Goering Panzer Parachute Division, offered resistance (Clark, 378).

5. Under Nazi belief, Adolf Hitler was sent by God and was therefore divine (Hillel and Henry, 26).

6. A narrow, upright frame with a lower ledge for kneeling on at prayer and an upper ledge for a book.

7. An evening worship service.

8. Instruction in the catechism, a handbook of basic Christian beliefs.

9. Word for "dead" in the Hawaiian language.

10. Identification flags of military units.

11. Martin Niemöller (1892–1984) was a former U-boat captain in World War I who became a Lutheran pastor and dissident in Hitler's Germany. Niemoller said he would rather "burn his church to the ground than to preach the Nazi Trinity of race, blood, and soil." He said this at a time when most people were afraid to speak out. Hitler was so enraged he sent him to the Dachau concentration camp.

12. Conservative branch of the U.S. Lutheran Church; different from Yost's.

13. Ritual in which a teenager or adult who was already baptized (usually as a child) professes his own beliefs and is accepted into full membership in a Christian church.

14. Club 100 was started by Captain Kometani with the idea that the men would have something to look forward to when they returned. Many of them, because of the racism prevalent at the time, felt unwelcome in the Hawaii Veterans of Foreign Wars and American Legion posts of the period. They wanted their own place. The club still exists and is located on Kamoku Street in Honolulu.

15. Prominent Honolulu businessman who was considered instrumental in protecting Japanese Americans in Hawaii from being interned during World War II.

TEN

La Belle France

T HE THREE-DAY voyage to southern France on choppy seas was uneventful. To help the men pass the time books were distributed from my lending library, including extra copies our executive officer had obtained from an air corps unit. An hour after our transport dropped anchor in the harbor of Marseille at noon on September 29, the battalion boarded landing craft. At 5:30 p.m., we all piled into "40 et 8s" (French boxcars for forty men and eight horses) for a four-mile, eight-hour ride to Septemes, followed by a mile hike to a bivouac where we tented for nine days, fighting first the wind and then the rain and all the nights the increasing cold.

On Sunday, October 2, our Catholic men attended Mass at a local church as arranged the day before. Doc Dahl attended and reported that most of the chanting was in French and only a bit in Latin. At services I told the story of Jesus as simply as possible; afterwards several Nisei asked for instruction in the Christian faith even though no classes were scheduled. (I had begun to feel that the other two Island padres should instruct any converts since it was unlikely that any of the Hawaiians would ever have an opportunity to join a Lutheran church.) In the evening I attended Vespers and the Benediction of the Blessed Sacrament at the Roman Catholic church.

On Monday the wind blew with such force that even letter writing was difficult; dust penetrated everything. I forced myself to speak French with local citizens and discovered that they understood passably well. We learned that the French looked down on Italians as a laboring class from a poor country and thought of themselves as more than laborers and from "la belle France." Many, however, spoke Italian.

Tuesday, the weather moderated, and several of us officers patronized a bathhouse for a delightfully warm soaking in a tub. Afterwards I sipped French lemonade while the others drank beer as we all sat on a sun porch on the main street, watching the world go by. Wednesday, the cold I had caught riding in the cattle cars began to clear up because of sucking ammonium chloride pills for two days. After the battalion surgeons had instructed some 650 men on proper prophylactic procedures against venereal disease, I presented a "sex morality lecture" emphasizing Christian principles concerning relations between men and women.

Thursday, I was still trying to find a way to use my mattress cover and three blankets to keep warm at night. Winter clothing was being issued to the men. Friday, a heavy rain dampened the spirits of all; my tent withstood the elements. I visited a neighboring town and located a Calvinist church founded in 1557 but did not meet the pastor. For seven francs (fourteen cents) I enjoyed a hot shower followed by a cold one. In the evening, by candlelight, I sorted my clothing and decided that several changes of underwear and a single change of shirt and pants would be adequate; several pairs of shoes and one of trousers would be returned to the supply sergeant. Saturday, I stumbled around in the mud and rain informing all units about the next day's Masses for Catholics.

Sunday worship centered on Joseph of the Old Testament, with special emphasis on his exemplary life and his recognition of God's purpose in his life. (On this Sunday and the previous one, combined attendance at the four services totaled only 758.) All day long quartermaster trucks from Epinal arrived in groups, sent by Seventh Army[1] headquarters to bring the Combat Team to the Vosges Mountains,[2] where it was desperately needed against the stiffened German resistance. (Because 25 percent of the vehicles dispatched broke down on the way south, the 3rd Battalion[3] had to move north in boxcars.)

October 9, 10, and 11, the One Puka Puka motored up the Rhone-Saone Valley, passing Avignon, Vienne, Lyon, and Vesoul. On the 430-mile ride I sat in the jeep waving to the people: schoolchildren, peasants wearing sabots, little girls with bobbed hair, curés[4] in cassock and beret, a black-gowned nun on a bicycle. We passed gas stations with Esso and Shell pumps, signs advertising Singer sewing machines, fields of potatoes, herds of dairy cattle, stone crosses at crossroads, steepled churches, town halls with tower clocks, vineyards turned brown, plowed fields, green pastures, beautiful rivers with smooth meadows running down to them so that meadow and river seemed to run together (like sea and sky without horizon), trees regimented in rows, orchards, hills where cultivated fields ran into the woodlands. Where grapes were being mashed, the presence of a press was announced by the odor before the eye caught sight of it. Roads were well surfaced though in need of repair. Farmhouses were supplied with electric power. Often gates bore signs with *"chien méchant"* (bad dog) on them. Towns were in valleys, not on hilltops as in Italy. We were touring through "la belle France" the Germans did not have the time to destroy; it was truly beautiful, as the rains of fall had washed it clean.

On Monday night, after the troops were bedded down in a pasture, I walked to a farmhouse and invited myself in by saying that I was a chaplain and wanted to write a letter and needed electric light to do it. On Tuesday night when the convoy stopped to bivouac, I was not so fortunate; I wrote no letter because there was no light, too much rain, and lack of cover. By Wednesday afternoon we arrived in an assembly area in an evergreen forest near Charmois devant Bruyères, about ten miles from the front lines. I warmed myself by taking a cold helmet bath in my tent and then hired a local woman to wash my clothes. We were now attached to the Texan 36th Infantry Division[5] and scheduled for combat very soon.

Thursday, I had planned to catch up on correspondence, but instead I spent the morning contacting personnel, including chaplains of other outfits. By evening I tackled the typing, including a letter to Peggy.

> Please try to find somewhere the manila folder on the cover of which is written in pencil the information concerning the Yost family. It may be that sometime in the future I'll be getting into Germany and I'd like to check old church records and trace the family a bit further back.
>
> I still have many a letter to write but at least I've finally gotten at it. I'd rather be reading tonight, but I've made up my mind not to take the easier way for a change. Then, too, I'm getting tired of carrying around all these unanswered letters in my dispatch case on my back.
>
> Have I asked you lately for a box of chocolate candy? Please send me a box of Whitman's or the like when you can. Is it difficult to get back there? I'm terribly out of touch with the civilian world. I didn't know Wilkie and Evangelist Macpherson had died until I saw accounts of their funerals a day or so ago. While helping to make history, I'm getting behind with other history. Such is *la guerre* [the war].
>
> Since I've been with this outfit for over a year now I've been thinking that I'll discontinue the lessons for the church year (for I might repeat too much, not having kept a record of sermon topics) and begin preaching on great words of the Christian faith: hope, faith, love, praise, and the like. We'll see.
>
> Today a chaplain gave me a long talk on how a battalion chaplain ought to be forward, at the aid station at least, and not in the rear areas. I let him finish and then told him I have two wounds already and that he

needn't worry about me leaving the front. He looked at me somewhat startled, and I explained that I was of the 100th (previously I had said the 442nd). He immediately became apologetic and said that he thought I was new to combat, had he known he would never have ventured to give advice, that he realized now that I knew as much as he did in the matter, that I should forget what he had said. I had a good laugh at his expense and assured him that the other two chaplains of the 442nd knew combat and were always up front where they should be. To say you belong to the 100th works a miracle, for it is a well-known and respected battalion.

More and more I know that everything is going to work out for the best in this matter of getting home; don't expect me for many a month. Once we spent a month together, how could we again be apart? God knows what He is doing in all these matters—patience is the virtue we need to strengthen by exercise.

Before we got into combat many of us were writing long letters home; like the others I took this opportunity before the days became busy with just staying alive.

Friday Evening, October 13 La France

It has become chilly in the tent, and the candle gives little warmth. I've been trying to outline a sermon on the subject "Faith in God" and have arrived at a poor outline that will have to do. Also I have picked the hymns and the selective reading out of the Hymnal for the service. Thus I may say I am somewhat prepared.

Today I was again busy at this and that; this being regimental chaplain involves a lot of running around, contacting attached units, finding a Catholic chaplain, and arranging times and places for services.

I met a fellow Lutheran chaplain this afternoon; he was on the same boat on the trans-Atlantic run and helped me spend the anxious hours when I was thinking of you and the baby-to-come. Said he today: "Say, Yost, what was it, a boy or a girl?" So I showed him the group picture of the three of you. He had some news of some of the others who were with us on that trip. Some have been called to their eternal home in the past year.

All is still well with me, except that the mail situation is still unfruitful. But I always console myself with the thought, "maybe tomorrow."

The one who did my laundry even darned some holes in my underwear; one pair is just about worn out. Her teenage daughter gave me the clothes since her mother was away at the time. I want to drop back tomorrow and thank the mother for the fine job she did, for I appreciate the thoughtfulness of the darning. Had I time I would have visited there tonight.

I have some steady customers for my lending library and more men are hearing of it and coming for books—this is as I want it.

Today I met the local curé and he surprised me by offering me a classroom for services. I explained that I was Protestant, but he said he knew that and wanted me to have a decent place for service. It was most considerate of him. I arranged to use the church itself for the Catholic Mass.

Today an older chaplain talking of the mail situation incidentally said, "I know my wife writes every week." Had he been looking at me he would have seen my eyebrows rising at the big interval between letters; but I can see how one overseas can easily drop into careless habits in letters to the loved one, and then she also with him. To receive only a letter a week from you would indeed be a privation for me.

As I was reading today of several of the kings of Judah who began right, but who in their later years of rule forsook the Lord Jehovah, I got to musing how common it was for persons as they grow older to lose their idealism and become so "realistic" that they turn to "workable" methods and forget the high idealism of their youth. I can see that this has been all too true with me in just the past few years of my aging. But with your help and more earnest attention to the Scripture I can still get back much of the needed spirit, and certainly we must for the sake of the Church and our children.

It is so comforting as I look ahead at the days of the war still to be endured to remember that our God still does overrule the things of earth for the good of His own. Often there rings through my mind the psalmist's phrase, "For His mercy endureth forever." It is counterpart of Romans 8:28.

At present I am wearing over my shoes the arctics I bought just before I left the States last year. They keep my feet warm and dry, and that is much needed during this season of the year.

If I were in a comfortable room with a blazing fire and a good reading lamp, I think I'd stay up for several more hours reading, but as the conditions are I think I'll go to sleep. Lately I've been sleeping well and long.

Saturday Dusk, October 14 France

At noon I realized for the first time that this week the U.L.C.A. [United Lutheran Church in America] was in session.[6] Some time ago I had noted the dates in my notebook so that I might pray for the convention, but today was the first time I looked at the book and so I forgot it.

My services went well today. For the one in the classroom the local priest put at my service, I put up the [field] altar, lit candles, and wore vestments. Quite a number attended my battalion service. The Jewish doctor said he liked my presentation on "Faith."

Today was a busy one, and almost I didn't get to writing you. Though Saturday, it was a Sunday for me.

The reason for the "Sunday" services on Saturday was the common knowledge that later in the day the rifle companies would be moving up to the line of departure at the front. Murphy (1954) gives a charming account of a Sunday church service in which the 100th supposedly participated on the eve of battle.

> On Sunday there was a simple church service in an open glade among the towering pines. The congregation sang "The Church in the Wildwood" and "Sweet Hour of Prayer" and recited the Twenty-Third Psalm, "Yea, though I walk through the valley of the shadow of Death, I will fear no evil. . . ." The padre gave a brief sermon on that real brotherhood of man which he hoped might follow the war, and the meeting ended with singing "America the Beautiful," "The Battle Hymn of the Republic," and "The Lord's Prayer." (226)

However, we arrived in bivouac on October 11, a Wednesday, and moved to the vicinity of Bruyères on October 14, a Saturday. (Murphy indicates that this move took place on October 14, but he does not include the day of the week [227].) As my notes attest, I held services on the Saturday morning of the unit's commitment to the front line, but the service was not at all of the sort related in the book. Murphy's account is spurious but not completely false; I believe his description is misplaced, that it in part recounts a worship program in Italy months before our arrival in France. Perhaps some soldier saved material from an earlier Sunday and gave it to the author, who dressed up the report a bit and fitted it incorrectly into the record at this point.

On Sunday, October 15, the Battle of Bruyères[7] began at eight a.m. and lasted for twenty-five days. Vivid accounts may be read in Murphy's *Ambassadors in Arms* and Shirey's *Americans: The Story of the 442nd Combat Team*. During these days I helped at the forward aid station, making occasional visits to rear units and one Sunday a tour of the 100th in defensive positions. This campaign differed from any we had encountered: a heavily wooded area in which shells bursting in the tree tops showered steel on all below who were not in covered dugouts, uncomfortable days of rain and mist, maps often useless because German troop movements had obliterated the trails, an enemy determined to hold its positions no matter what the cost, an American divisional general overanxious for a quick victory.[8] The rain, mist, and thick forests combined to confuse anyone walking in these mountains.[9] Only occasionally did

On September 27, 1944, the 442nd RCT, including the 100th Bn, sailed to France. On Sunday, October 15, the Battle of Bruyères began at eight a.m. and lasted for twenty-five days. The battle to rescue the "Lost Battalion" took place at Biffontaine. Yost described the area this way: "This campaign differed from any we had encountered: a heavily wooded area in which shells bursting in the tree tops showered steel on all below who were not in covered dugouts. . . . The rain, mist, and thick forests combined to confuse anyone walking in these mountains."

my letters home reflect the battle conditions. Our forward aid could not be located as close to our forward companies as it had been in former campaigns.

On October 18, when the town of Bruyères was liberated, the 100th was in the wooded hills. That Wednesday morning I wrote home.

> If the scribbling is somewhat worse than usual today, you must blame it on the position I am in, for I am sitting in a spruce-lined slit trench with a covering of logs and spruce. For light in this hole I have a candle on a piece of wood stuck into the side of the trench. It is a cozy arrangement but not too roomy. And occasionally a few drops of rain seep through; but I'm warm in clothing and blankets. We are having a variety of Indian summer these days. Last night I slept well in this "apartment" of mine. It is scouting with a vengeance.

The next day the battalion was in reserve on a hill northwest of the captured town, and the aid station was in a building. The mess crew sent up hot pork-chop sandwiches with gravy between the slabs of bread. On October 20, the 100th advanced against slight resistance; I wrote home about social rather than battle conditions.

> You have no doubt seen pictures of Frenchwomen who received hair-cuts (shaves, in fact) for consorting with the Germans. I have actually seen such. I can't see much justice or reason to it. In fact, in one case they wanted to cut the hair of a fifteen-year-old girl—hardly an affair for grown-up Frenchmen who ought to be fighting the Boche instead of taking vengeance on women, be they good or bad.[10] Of course, we must keep our hands off since it does not concern us. But to me it's a revolting business, whether the women deserve it or not. Personally I'd like to kick a few of the gendarmes in the full of their pants! For a while my blood boiled about the matter, but now I'm looking at it objectively again. So it goes! The whole system of European morals seems pretty low anyway. In fact, one does not see very much of idealism anywhere nowadays.
>
> In the last two days I've caught up on much of my correspondence and, since no mail has been coming in, my dispatch case is beginning to feel empty. I don't say much in a letter perhaps, but at least the one I am writing to knows I am thinking of him.

The next day our unit continued in reserve. We had C rations and coffee for breakfast, but for supper Kent made soup out of stew and cabbage to go with the fresh bread and butter sent up from the kitchens.

Saturday Night, October 21

Tonight a nineteen-year-old French[man] who helped us a bit today went to leave us. He leaned over as if to whisper to me but instead kissed me on both cheeks and told me to say good night to all the rest. Was I surprised!

Snow is soon expected over here. I think it will be better for us than rain and mud. I'm not dreading the winter much; one always manages to come through, and fairly well at that, too.

The next chance I get for a sermon I'll preach on "Hope." I've been thinking of that subject off and on today, though concentrated thought is often difficult in such situations as the present.

The new doctor [Capt. Joseph Shapiro] discovered a notice in French in one of these towns forbidding Jews to use the public telephone; he is saving it as a memento of the war. The notice was dated 1942.

That night I spent in a small farmhouse, sitting close to the *poel* (stove) and adding wood from time to time. Around me lay some of our aid men, snoring away. At a late hour I, too, stretched out on the wooden floor. It was a jolly, comfortable night.

Sunday, October 22, the 100th held a semicircular position overlooking Biffontaine; its support route to the rear lay in danger of being cut off by the enemy. A Jerry patrol intercepted a column of Nisei and captured Germans carrying our wounded to the aid station. Eighteen AJAs were taken prisoners by the enemy, but in the confusion Capt. Young Kim[11] and medic Richard Chinen escaped and found their way to us. Private Chinen was furiously angry because at the start he had tried to convince the buddhahead lieutenant in charge that the column was headed in the wrong direction. Captain Kim, very sick because his wounds had been untended too long, later told how Captain Kometani and the chaplain had hugged him to keep him warm and had continued to encourage him that he would pull through. (Note: I have no recollection of this; Kim told his story to my wife in 1983.)

On October 24, the One Puka Puka was relieved and pulled back to Belmont. On this day the 1st Battalion of the 141st Infantry Regiment pushed ahead too far in the hills north of Biffontaine and was surrounded by the enemy. On October 27, the 442nd was ordered to fight through to the beleaguered Texans. Not until October 30 were the Nisei successful. The 100th and the 3rd Battalions received the Distinguished Unit Citation for this rescue.[12] (In 1963 the state of Texas commissioned the Combat Team honorary Texas citizens in appreciation for saving its soldiers from capture by the Nazis.)

During this action I was busy at the aid station, except for hurried trips to the rear, especially to hold services for the Cannon Company and 232nd Engineer Company of our Combat Team.

Wednesday Night, October 25

My sermon for the past services has been on "Hope." Next I think I'll take "Love," thus completing the trilogy of 1 Corinthians 13. After that I'll take words like "grace," "peace," "holiness." The last services were well attended.

Saturday Dusk, October 28

I'm somewhat crummy and dirty, but just fine mentally and physically. If the paper shows spots of dirt it's because of very dirty hands.

At present I'm wearing a pair of heavy German socks over my own; thus my feet are warm and dry.

You ought to see me fell and trim trees—for covered slit trenches, of course. A hole lined with evergreen boughs is surprisingly warm, with two blankets and an overcoat to help. Rain of course complicates matters, but with a little extra work the huts can be waterproofed reasonably well.

The zipper of my combat jacket broke, so I had a French woman make tabs to keep it closed. Then inside she also sewed some clasps. She did a good job. We stayed in her home several days and I got to know the children. I'll write to them after the war. [Note: Alas, I never did.]

Monday

Just a while ago a French lady was in to see the doctor. She complained of kidney pains. I acted as the doc's interpreter—and most of the words were not in my little dictionary. Several times the doc said, "I don't know if you can ask her this, but try." The woman didn't seem embarrassed and certainly I was not. She has blood in her urine and pain and has always been irregular in her monthly time. Her husband has been dead some years. So it goes—another interesting experience.

The war is still in progress—very much so. Today I'm taking it a bit easy. I'm not holding any church services. They will come in a couple of days perhaps.

The doctor has finished the examination and now I'll be trying to give the diagnosis to the woman in my poor French. Such is life in the army.

On October 31, what was left of the 100th moved closer to the Biffontaine-St. Die road and occupied this defensive position until November 7; during this period additional men had to be evacuated because of trench feet and fatigue. A new type of field jacket, a woolen sweater, and shoe pacs or waterproof shoes were provided the infantrymen. By November 8, all of battalion personnel were back at Bruyères.

My October "Report of Chaplains" covered my activities since landing in France: four Sunday morning worship services with 758 attending and one Sunday evening devotions with 18 present; six weekday morning services for 702 and four weekday evening services for 230; one hospital visit to see 40 WIAs; fifteen personal conferences; transportation provided twice for men to attend civilian Masses; once an arrangement for a military chaplain to hear confessions; two military Masses by (Maj.) Bernard F. Roemer of the 36th Division Headquarters; tracts, New Testaments, and prayer books distributed as requested by individual soldiers; Jewish prayer book and Scriptures given to a Jewish officer.

As long as our soldiers were on the line during the early days of November, the medics manned a dugout forward aid station. The excerpts following are from letters written during this interlude.

> Wednesday Morning, November 1, All Saints' Day
>
> Last night was Halloween, but I was in no position for observing it. Instead I crawled into my blankets after reading some back issues of several *Lutheran* magazines and slumbered away. The noise of shells does not bother me as a rule.
>
> Today the sun is shining brightly and is most welcome, naturally. Two days ago I had a chance for a helmet bath but didn't take it. Next chance I have I'll wash, for I need it all right.
>
> Capt. Dahl and I are getting along well. After a year together we have gotten used to each other.
>
> Afternoon, November 1
>
> At the moment all is quiet. . . . But even as I was writing our guns began barking, and I can hear the whir of shells overhead—that's become an almost natural noise after all these months.
>
> Before I began this letter I made some notes for the sermon on "Grace." While I had the quiet and leisure I thought it well to organize some thoughts on the matter.
>
> This a.m. I wrote Doc Seyfried [our family physician], recounting some few medical experiences and reminding him that we overseas appreciate the heavy load the few civilian doctors left must carry in caring for our families. Mostly it was just to let him know he is in my thoughts.
>
> For dinner [at noon] we had some Betty Crocker vegetable soup; Elva [my sister, Elva Yost Seip] sent some boxes of it. The medics and I enjoyed it. We had fresh bread to go with it.

Saturday Morning, November 4

Good morning, after a good night's rest, disturbed only once when I had to make room for another soldier to come into the dugout. Now with a clear sky above and a breakfast of French toast and Vienna sausages inside, I'm ready to start the day with "Oh, what a beautiful morning!" Capt. Kometani came in puffing and saying, "Oh, it's a cold morning!"

One of our officers who went home on thirty-day furlough wrote me of the difficulty he had in leave-taking to come overseas again. That's one reason I'd just as soon see the war out before coming home—but some days are so long, and the reunion sometimes seems so distant. But there will come a day!

Am I crummy after eight days without washing and shaving! My hands have some black marks in them that rinsing with cold water will not remove. But of course I am feeling fine in spite of all the dirt.

I am very thankful for the group I am with. There's a good esprit de corps, and the fellows keep right on cheerfully all the time, with little complaining. Thus there's many a smile or joke to ease the day's load. I'm most fortunate (the proper Christian word is "blessed").

My back is a bit sore for two reasons: chopping trees and bending to get in and out of low dugouts. As I stoop I think, "This is to make a man humble." The lower the dugout, the safer—as a rule—unless it's dug deep into the earth, and we don't have time for such elaborateness. Unfortunately Doc Dahl and I have trouble waterproofing the ones we make; during a rain ours drip, a not-too-comfortable situation. But we've never gotten too wet. Capt. Kometani has decided he'll put his sons in the Reserve Corps when they are old enough—then they can go through the next war as officers. Officers do have it much easier as a rule. Kome also wants his boys to be Scouts so they can get used to the rough life. Often we get into such conversations over a cup of hot coffee or cocoa on a cold and long winter's evening.

Sunday, November 5, since the situation was static, I hiked around the companies on the line, visiting members of several platoons right at the front. I squatted alongside the foxhole of a newly arrived officer who had never met me and introduced myself. He seemed a bit surprised to see me. "Do you do this often?" he asked, referring to my visiting the front line.

"Only occasionally, depending on the situation," I replied. "As long as a man is by himself and takes advantage of natural cover, he is not in too much danger." I looked down the hill toward the valley where the Jerries were. It was a peaceful Lord's Day, and as we chatted it was difficult to remember that there was a war going on. I discovered that he was of the Jewish faith and explained to him that chaplains were concerned about all the men regardless of creed or lack of creed. In the course of my tour I handed out three hundred religious tracts and some *Lutheran Service Prayer Books.* That night I wrote to my wife.

> I'm having some fine services with the Engineer Company of the Combat Team. In their set-up they usually have a building, so I come after supper when most of them are back from the day's work. The atmosphere is more worshipful indoors and with books.
>
> In the Cannon Company of the CT, I discovered today a Japanese-American who is married to a Lutheran girl, of Wisconsin, I think. He was baptized by a Lutheran chaplain and now I'll instruct him in the Catechism for confirmation.
>
> If there was mail today I missed it because of my peregrinations (how's the spelling; I ought to have a dictionary). But when I am busy lack of mail is not as painful as on the long, tedious days.
>
> I've been reading some of the Epistles [of the New Testament] lately; like you I've more or less bogged down in the Old Testament. I'm trying to read the whole epistle at one reading.
>
> It's rather late, probably 9:30 p.m., and I'd better be getting to bed. Tonight I've deserted the aid station and so I am sleeping in comfort. I came to the rear to hold services for rear echelon members of the 442nd, combining business and pleasure thereby.

November 7 was Election Day back in the States, and I was aware of that. I wrote home on this day that I thought FDR would win but that whoever won would have little effect on the conflict overseas. I also wrote as follows.

> I'm encouraged by the services I've been having with the attached units of the 442nd Combat Team: Engineers, Service Company, Cannon Company, Headquarters, for there are always a few who afterwards come to say "thank you" in appreciation. It helps. Of course, services have been held irregularly since we've been in combat.
>
> The Christmas package from St. John's, Nazareth, came yesterday. [This was the congregation to which we belonged while I was in the military.] It contained food, a novel, gum, a small fruitcake, two washcloths—all in all, an excellent selection. The fruitcake I've shared already, but I'm saving the canned meats for later.
>
> I've been carrying a copy of Asch's *The Apostle,* but I haven't started it yet. Perhaps today I shall, though first I want to write some letters. Also, I'd like to visit some of the men; but perhaps I won't, for they are pretty well forward.

With a bit of foresight and some work a fellow can fix himself rather comfortably in a hole in the ground. Lately I've been using Sgt. Katano's since he's elsewhere on business. His is watertight and warm and large enough for me. Of course when there's work to be done we must leave our comfortable shelters.

For breakfast I had cream of wheat, Vienna sausages, toast with jelly, and coffee. Thus the day had a fair beginning. We often have Vienna sausages, and most of the men are tired of them, but I still enjoy four or five each time. They are much like frankfurters.

Program sheets for a Christmas service have arrived from the National Lutheran Council. I hope we are out of the line for that day so that we can have a real service.

Saturday is Armistice Day. Did they celebrate it back home this year? Now everyone is more concerned with the coming Armistice Day for World War II than with that of November 11. That day will come in due time.

For some reason all rotation and furlough to the States has been temporarily suspended. I hope it will not be for long, for I'd like to see Doc Dahl get a chance to get home. He's been over much longer than the others in the One Puka Puka.

Sometime in early November, I wrote an account of a night spent in a dugout. Here it is just as I sent it home.

Let me assure you that I am none the worse from the experience I am about to relate. In fact, in three hours or so I'll be drying out in a warm building.

The story is "A Night in the Deep Woods." It rained all day. The boys' holes, in spite of coverings, began to drip, and in some cases streams ran through them. Mine, built by Sgt. Katano for himself but used by me in his absence, was the exception. So at dark, about 5:30, I crawled in and pulled the flap down at one end. Really, one jumps down into the hole and then pulls the flap down. It is long enough to stretch full length and high enough to sit up.

I brought along a can of condensed milk, opened it, and drank a little, and then mixed cocoa and sugar in the rest to make a more palatable drink. Then I munched on some ration crackers, caramels, and hard candy. (When I first entered I had pulled off my boots—shoe and arctic all in one.) Thus intestinally fortified, I lay down to sleep.

Sometime later I got awake; my feet felt wet. I lit the candle stuck on a board pressed into the dirt side of the hole. Water had come through at the entrance flap—it was the V end of the shelter half and didn't quite cover the entrance hole—and the lower end of my abode was under water. I pressed some of the water out of my socks and drew on my boots.

Then I got out of the hole. The night was pitch dark. Then back into my hole. I placed my helmet upside down and padded it with a dry blanket, and sat with my head bent and yet still touching the top of the "house."

Thus hunched I began to read *The Nazarene*—60 pages; then I and II Timothy, and Titus. Then I blew out the candle and dozed a while. Awoke, and was cold, so I got out of the hole. Heard Capt. Dahl phoning in the next dugout and talked with him. And then finally saw why all looked so white in the night—it had stopped raining and was snowing lightly. After walking about a bit to warm my feet, I came back to write this to you from my flooded hole. It will shortly be daylight, and I'll pack up with the others for a warmer and drier place.

Over the years attempts have been made to evaluate the Battle of Bruyères in terms of its success in relation to the losses sustained. Orville C. Shirey, in *Americans: The Story of the 442nd Combat Team,* makes no value judgment, but he does highlight the difficulties of the assignment given the Nisei by the commanding general and praises the men for their heroism.

It is a tribute to the courage of the men that they were able to move at all. Most of the companies had been whittled down to less than thirty men on the line, and the men who stayed and took it were sick. Some had trench foot so badly they could hardly walk, and most of the others were beginning to come down with flu from the constant exposure to rain and cold. . . . (71)

The Combat Team loaded on trucks again on November 19 and headed back over the long, weary miles they had traveled a little over a month ago. This time there was no truck shortage in spite of the fact that 383 replacements had come in on the 18th. With almost two thousand men in hospitals, the unit was at about half strength. (73)

Like Shirey, Murphy, in *Ambassadors in Arms,* emphasizes the hardships of the experience and lauds the AJAs but expresses no opinion about the way the troops were used.

On 1 November, the 100th was in defensive position . . . and the combined effective strength of the rifle companies was now 175 men. (243)

The boys' tails had probably never dragged so low as on the morning they reached the Texans, but, with that job finished pride in their unit reached new heights. Their gang had again come through when the chips were down. Shoulders were stiff, chins up, as what was left of the outfit moved into Bruyeres. But though the spirit was the same as that when the 100th had been mauled at Cassino and had pasted the Jerries at Belvedere, the flesh was not. Now, in each skeleton company, only eight or nine soldiers could say they had crossed the beach at Salerno, and half of these had carried the scars of previous battles into this last mission. The rest were men who had originally come in as replacements. When the 3d Platoon of Company A started out to rescue the trapped Texans, only two of its members were veterans of Camp McCoy, and neither of these reached the "lost battalion." (244)

In 1982, however, an evaluation of the Battle of Bruyères was made by Young O. Kim in his keynote address at the 40th Anniversary banquet of Club 100 on July 3 in Honolulu.[13]

> Of even greater concern for the 100th from a command point of view, a view shared by Colonel Pence, the Regimental Commander, were the totally wrong information and crazy orders issued by General Dahlquist, the 36th Division Commander. A condition made worse because he never believed anything we told him to the contrary. He was personally a brave man but a dangerously ambitious man who sought personal glory and who cared very little for subordinates' lives. Much of the tremendous losses suffered by the entire 442nd can be attributed to his poor leadership. He violated every principle of leadership and tactics.
>
> In making final preparations for the last successful assault on Hill "A," we cut off all communications to everyone at higher Headquarters to avoid talking to Dahlquist. Hill "A" had to fall before Bruyères could be liberated. General Dahlquist insisted there was only a token number of Germans defending Hill "A" and only our timid assaults prevented its capture. We knew better from previously ordered unsuccessful attempts. When the hill was taken over 100 Germans were captured and over 100 automatic taken. These weapons were delivered to the 36th Division Headquarters. A wasted gesture. We suffered only two wounded in attacking in our own way on our own time schedule.
>
> That night while sheltered in Bruyères after being promised two days' rest, we were ordered at midnight to attack Hill "C" at 9:00 the next morning. We planned and worked at a feverish pace till 0900. Five minutes before 9 o'clock the Germans attacked the 100th's positions from where our own attack was to be launched. This required major last-

minute changes, but the attack against Hill "C" began on time. Five minutes after 9:00 the enemy positions on Hill "C" were breached and 50 Germans were captured and the hill from where we launched the attack was abandoned to the Germans. The 100th completed the taking of Hill "C". All this brilliant effort was negated when we were ordered against our wishes to leave Hill "C" later that afternoon by Dahlquist. Hill "C" had to be retaken by the 3rd Division at great costs.

The capture of Biffontaine, 7 miles behind the German lines two days later, placed the 100th in an untenable position. The 100th was forced to abandon the commanding heights it captured 5 miles behind the German lines and capture Biffontaine over our vigorous objections. This put us beyond the range of friendly artillery support and also beyond range of all radio communications for a worthless tactical objective. The attack was finally made on Biffontaine after receiving several promises from Dahlquist. None of which materialized. We later had to fight our way back from Biffontaine. We took heavy casualties because in one day of fighting we were extremely low on ammunition and in 3 days of fighting were without food and desperately needed medical supplies. We went into Biffontaine as the best unit in Europe, and came out with only one officer per rifle company and very depleted ranks.

In my opinion, a Lost Battalion was inevitable from the way Dahlquist was operating, and of course it happened. The 100th/442nd had to rescue the 1st Battalion, 141st Regiment, while suffering four times the number of casualties than the number of men we rescued.

My memories of France still show the bitterness burnt deeply into my soul. Later, Gordon Singles, while filling a Brigadier General's position at Fort Bragg, refused to publicly shake General Dahlquist's hand at a full dress review in the presence of the entire III Corps. Dahlquist was then a visiting 4-star General. He preferred remaining a Colonel than to shake Dahlquist's hand even though he asked forgiveness. Years later after he retired, General Pence could not mention Dahlquist's name without his voice shaking in anger.

Young Kim, mentioned earlier in the chapter as one of two who escaped capture by the Germans, was a retired colonel at the time he made the above remarks. He served as a combat commander in Korea and as an instructor in the army's officer training system. As an officer involved personally in the events he evaluated, he must be considered knowledgeable; his subsequent service within the military gave him a perspective from which to review his experiences objectively. He also cites the judgments of Colonel Singles, who was CO of the 100th at Bruyères, and Colonel Pence, who was CO of the 442nd at the time.

By November 8, all of the 100th was out of the conflict in the

Vosges Mountains. Apparently Colonel Singles had convinced old West Point friends on the Seventh Army staff that his men had done their share and deserved a respite. From Bruyères we moved to Bains-les-Bains, a fashionable spa, for a few days and then south to Nice. My letters home do not reveal our timetable but do tell of relaxed days.

Thursday Night, November 9 France

There's not too much to write about tonight except that I'm fine and dandy, and warm and dry, and anticipating a comfortable night's sleep. Tonight I would have liked to visit some French family, but I've no good contacts.

Saturday Night, November 11

Last night I failed to write because of laziness; excuse, please!

Yesterday I had a steaming bath in a large French *bain*. Also I bought some wooden shoes. The ones for kiddies are worn with heavy socks; others are hollowed out deeper and one wears a felt slipper in each.

Last night I visited a French family; one daughter was Monie's age: Lili did a lot of talking. [Our daughter, Monica, was born September 16, 1942.] The second was 13½ and eager to learn English. I gave her a lesson. She tried so hard to remember to answer "How are you?" with "I am well." The boy was 19 and a member of the FFI [Free French troops].

Today I saw a Frenchman sowing grain by hand, rhythmically casting each handful as he strode across the ploughed field; naturally I thought of the Parable of the Sower.

The French celebrated Armistice Day—they call it Victory Day. There was much hullabaloo over the Day today, probably because it was the first time in four years they were allowed to celebrate it. Everyone put on his Sunday best and put up flags. To us it was just another day of war.

Tuesday Morning, November 14

Last night my pen was dry so I did not write, though I was in a warm, clean building with lights. Also, I saw an American movie with French dialogue, faked, of course. However, the songs were sung in English with the French translation below the scenes. So I saw Ginger Rogers and Fred Astaire speaking French; the ones who do the improvising do it well. It actually looks like the actors are using French. Also I had some ice cream, actually a cross between sherbet and cream. But the French must think we are millionaires, for everything is very expensive, even laundering.

I've had a bath—in cold water—and changed clothing. As soon as I get a haircut I'll be feeling fine all around.

An officer is lending me his Jerry watch until one comes from you. So now I can be on time again.

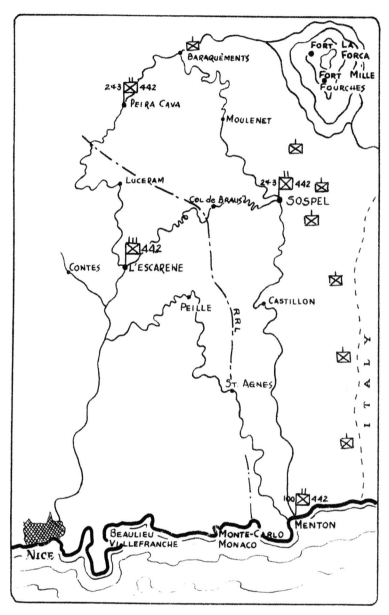

After the Battle of the Lost Battalion, the 442nd RCT moved to Nice, the French Riviera, and the Maritime Alps. The men of the 100th were assigned to dugouts on the French-Italian border at Menton.

It's been cold but not too bad. I'm writing this sitting out in the open so you can see it's not freezing weather yet.

I'm having a short church service in a few minutes. I'm going to say just a few words about "Love," ours toward God and men. For one thing it's too chilly to hold the men together for too long a service.

Wednesday Night, November 15

For five days I haven't heard any world news. I guess nothing startling has happened or else we would have gotten wind of it.

I've contacted some Protestants in a nearby city. When I get to visit it next time I'll have a meal with a young man who is preparing for the ministry. He belongs to a Pentecostal Church.

I went shopping for some Christmas presents, but the prices are sky-high, and I saw nothing I thought suitable. A little dress for Monica is priced at $20.00! The French are overcharging the American soldiers for most everything.

The move to Nice complied with orders attaching the Combat Team to the 44th Antiaircraft Artillery Brigade with the mission of patrolling the border between France and Italy from the sea north into the Maritime Alps. In this way the badly mauled AJA units could recuperate and at the same time prevent the German 34th Division from assaulting the Riviera from Italy.

One item of business related to the Battle of Bruyères remained for the chaplains to attend to: the writing of letters of condolence. On November 12, the CWO (chief warrant officer) of regimental headquarters sent me the new instructions, dated October 25, covering this task. The specifics included,

(1) Insofar as practicable, letters of condolence will contain: (a) Information relative to the circumstances surrounding the death, including specific cause (except in cases of battle casualties, when only "killed in action" or similar appropriate description will be given), and place (only general location and country will be stated). (b) Information about the burial service and approximate grave location (only general locality and country, such as "Normandy, France") will be furnished. In this connection, it will always be assumed that a Chaplain of the deceased's faith officiated at the burial and, after ascertaining the individual's religious preference from his Service Record . . . or Qualification Card . . . it will be stated in substance that a Catholic (Jewish, Protestant) Chaplain so officiated. It is important that the correct faith be specifically mentioned except when the deceased's records show his religious preference as "none" or when such records are incomplete in this respect, in which cases such statement will be appro-

priately modified. (c) Any other information of personal or sentimental nature which may be of comfort to the family.

(2) Letters of condolence will contain the same categorical description and date of casualty as does the official report and will state the subject's full name and serial number. They will be completely factual and accurate; however, no gruesome or distressing details will be given. Good taste and consideration of the addressees' feelings will be the guiding factors.

(3) Letters of condolence pertaining to casualties other than deceased are not required, but may be written. Where applicable, the provisions of paragraph 2 above will govern the preparation of letters of condolence pertaining to other than deceased personnel except that in no case will the specific place of casualty be indicated in case of missing or missing in action personnel. In case of sickness or injury, care will be taken not to magnify the patient's condition and not to indicate that there is or is not the possibility of return to duty.

(4) Security and censorship regulations will be strictly observed. Information concerning the location of graves (except as provided in . . . (1) (b) above), disposal of remains and effects, etc. will not be included, and photographs of graves will not be inclosed [sic].

(5) In order to insure that the letter of condolence does not precede the official War Department notification, it will be submitted through casualty report channels to this headquarters in triplicate, for review, accompanied by a franked official envelope addressed to the addressee. No letter of transmittal or indorsement [sic] is required in forwarding the letter to this headquarters.

Further, the orders reviewed restrictions applicable to everyone writing about casualties to the folks back home.

There will be *no* mention of casualties in private correspondence *at any time.*

(1) No casualty information in personal correspondence will be passed by unit censors. Disciplinary action will be taken against both the writer and the unit censor in any case where such information is found in correspondence which has been unit censored.

(2) No information concerning any casualty will be included in personal correspondence originated by any officer. Disciplinary action will be taken in all cases of violations. Under no condition will an officer reply direct to next of kin or other persons to any request for casualty information.

These guidelines altered my own procedure in writing sympathy letters to the families of our KIAs; to a great extent the process was depersonalized. Of course, I followed the military's commands, but I did not get to the task until much later in November.

Notes

1. The men of the 100th Bn and the 442nd RCT had been reassigned from the Fifth Army in Italy under Gen. Mark Clark to the Seventh Army in France under Lt. Gen. Alexander M. Patch.

2. The Vosges Mountains are made up of rolling hills heavily forested with pine trees. During both World War I and World War II they were strategically significant because important railroad junctions into the Rhine River industrial area of Germany are built through them. The German army had received orders to defend the Vosges Mountains at all costs.

3. At this time the 442nd was made up of the 100th Battalion and the 2nd and 3rd Battalions of the 442nd. The 1st Battalion of the 442nd was left at Camp Shelby. The 100th Battalion kept its identity distinct from the other battalions in the new unit.

4. Parish priests.

5. They were assigned to reinforce the 36th Division, which had suffered terrible casualties at the Rapido River during the attack on Cassino. The 36th Division, known as the Texas Division because it was made up of Texas National Guard units, had lost nearly a regiment.

6. The United Lutheran Church in America, the body of Lutherans to which Yost belonged, held a national convention every several years where clergy and lay delegates met to generate statements on social issues and set church policy.

7. This refers to the action in the Bruyères-Belmont-Biffontaine area. The main railway and road linking the two largest cities in the Vosges region, Epinal and St. Die, passed through the town of Bruyères. Opposition was intense. For the first three weeks after arriving in Bruyères, the 442nd was unable to advance (Duus 1987).

8. The 36th was now under the command of Maj. Gen. John Dahlquist, a general with little actual combat experience. His tactics, which consisted of orders for bayonet charges against German positions in broad daylight, were considered suicidal by the men of the 100th Bn and the 442nd RCT. They were openly disdainful of him and risked court martial by telling him to his face (Duus 1987).

9. Bruyères is located in a valley surrounded by three heavily wooded hills. German troops set up their fortifications in the woods, and heavy fighting took place in the thick pine forests. The men of the 442nd had to walk into the forests to attack them. It was extremely cold and wet and visibility in the forest was poor.

10. The public humiliation of young French girls for having gone out with Germans so sickened some of the men of the 100th Battalion that it affected them for years afterwards (Duus 1987).

11. Capt. Young Oak Kim, who was of Korean descent, became one of the decorated battle leaders of the 100th Battalion. He retired as a U.S. Army colonel.

12. A detailed description of the heroic actions of the 100th Battalion in France, October 15–30, 1944, is given in the citation awarded to the unit. See the appendix following for the full text.

13. Printed in *The Puka Puka Parade*.

Appendix

Official Army Account of the Performance of the 100th Battalion
in the Battles of Bruyères, Biffontaine, and in the Foret Domaniale
de Champ, France

Chaplain Yost received this official account of the action in France attached to
the communication that reached him shortly after his discharge, authorizing him
to wear an "Oak Leaf Cluster to the Distinguished Unit Badge," an award given
to all members of the 100th Battalion.

HEADQUARTERS SEVENTH ARMY
GENERAL ORDERS

3 August 1945

NUMBER 360

II—*BATTLE HONORS–CITATION OF UNIT.* By direction of
the President under the provisions of Section IV, Circular No. 333, War
Department, 1943, the following named organization is cited for outstanding performance of duty in action:

THE 100TH BATTALION, 442D REGIMENTAL TEAM is cited
for outstanding accomplishment in combat during the period 15 October
1944 to 30 October 1944, near Bruyères, Biffontaine, and in the Foret
Domaniale de Champ, France. During a series of actions that played a
telling part in the 442d Regimental Team's operation which spearheaded
a divisional attack on the Seventh Army front, this unit displayed extraordinary courage, endurance and soldierly skill. Jumping off in the attack on
the morning of 15 October 1944, the 100th Battalion fought an almost
continuous four-day firefight in freezing and rainy weather, through jun-
gle-like forests, to wrest the strongly fortified hill "A," dominating Bruyères, from a fanatically resisting enemy. When, during the course of the
attack, the progress of an assault company was delayed by a strongpoint
consisting of fifty enemy riflemen and an SP [self-propelled] gun, a second company of the battalion swept in on the enemy force from the flank
and completely routed it. To attack hill "A" proper, the battalion was
forced to cross one hundred and fifty yards of open terrain covered by
seven enemy machine guns and heavy automatic weapon fire. Following
an artillery barrage, limited because a draw lay between the two high
hills, the battalion, with one company acting as a base of fire, launched a
frontal attack. Covered by friendly tank fire, waves of platoon after platoon zig-zagged across the open field into a hail of hostile fire. So skill-
fully coordinated was the attack that the strongly fortified hostile positions were completely overrun, numerous casualties were inflicted on the
enemy, and the capture of the town was assured. During the three-day

operation, beginning on 21 October 1944, that resulted in the capture of Biffontaine, the 100th Battalion fought two miles into enemy territory as a self-contained task force. On the third day of the attack, the battalion launched an assault to capture the isolated town. In the first surprise onslaught the battalion captured large quantities of supplies and ammunition which it turned against the enemy. Counterattacking enemy troops and tanks approached and fired pointblank into their positions. Shouting defiance in the face of demands for surrender, the men of the 100th Battalion fired their rifles and threw captured hand grenades at the enemy tanks. Bitter fighting at close range resulted in the capture of the entire town. During this action the battalion captured forty prisoners, killed or wounded forty of the enemy and destroyed or captured large quantities of ammunition and enemy materiel. On 27 October 1944, the 100th Battalion was again committed to the attack. Going to the rescue of the "lost battalion," 141st Infantry Regiment, it fought without respite for four days against a fanatical enemy that was determined to keep the "lost battalion" isolated and force its surrender. Impelled by the urgency of its mission, the battalion fought forward, risking encirclement as slower moving units left its flanks exposed. Fighting yard by yard through a minefield the battalion was stopped by an enemy strongpoint on the high ground which he had made the key to his defense. As the terrain precluded a flanking movement, the battalion was forced to the only alternative of a frontal attack against a strongly entrenched enemy. Attacking in waves of squads and platoons, and firing from the hip as they closed in to grenade range, the valiant men of the 100th Battalion reduced the enemy defense lines within a few hours. Between fifty and sixty enemy dead were found at their automatic weapon emplacements and dugouts. On the fourth day, although exhausted and reduced through casualties to about half its normal strength, the battalion fought doggedly forward against strong enemy small arms and mortar fire until it contacted the isolated unit. The extraordinary heroism, daring determination and esprit de corps displayed by the men of the 100th Battalion during these actions live as an inspiration and add glory to the highest traditions of the Armed Forces of the United States.

BY COMMAND OF MAJOR GENERAL MILBURN:
PEARSON MENOHER
Brigadier General, GSC
Chief of Staff

ELEVEN

On the Border

F OR ELEVEN days in late November of 1944, the 100th guarded the snow-covered Franco-Italian border between St. Etienne de Tinée and St. Martin de Vésubie, patrolling on foot by day but returning by nightfall to warm billets and sharing village life with the friendly civilians.

Thursday Morning, November 16

I just went out into the snow to see if the Jell-o were solid—it is almost ready to eat. Please send some more of it in the next package—it's very easy to make in the canteen cup and goes well in this winter weather.

I am anxious to meet some of the children in the place I am at present. As long as I have some kiddie to talk to, give things to, and visit (and preferably a little girl), homesickness does not bother me too much.

Friday Morning

The winter air gives me a good appetite; I must have had at least six pieces of toast, with real butter and apple butter, for breakfast. Nothing is ever the matter with my stomach.

Saturday Morning, November 18

Yesterday one of the men told me of a place to buy cider; I got a quart. However, it is diluted and carbonated stuff and not nearly as good as the fresh apple cider. It cost six francs and a ten-franc deposit on the bottle; at present the franc is worth a shade over two cents. It is the only drinking stuff for me around here, so I'll be getting a few more bottles of it in the future. . . . We have steaks fairly often, but I'm not so fond of them; the others rave over them. Also we have much rice, which I doctor with cream and sugar. All in all, the chow is pretty good. . . . Looks like I'll have a room with a piano tomorrow, so I'll also set up the communion set and wear vestments.

Sunday Night, November 19

Tonight four of us officers spent an enjoyable evening together. Mostly our conversation concerned old battles, which is the usual case with comrades in arms. We tell the same stories over and over to each other but always with much zest.

Monday Night

Last night the conversation got on religion. We three discussed Christianity: I a Christian, one other a Jew, the third one raised a Buddhist.

Tonight I spent about a half hour visiting a family with a six-year-old daughter. She's quite advanced in school and writes very well. Over here they begin school when four years old. Free days are Thursday and Sunday instead of Saturday and Sunday.

Wednesday Night, November 22 La France

Tonight at 7 p.m. Anna came with the bottle of milk; you remember, she is 11 years old. I asked if she had asked at home if it were all right for me to visit the family. She replied affirmatively, so we set off through the town and down the steps. She lives in a house off a side street, like a narrow alley to us. I had a fine two hours talking with them, mostly the father. Her parents are poor. The mother gave me three eggs to bring back. We had a cup of coffee. I held out my finger for the 7-month-old to grasp. I'm always losing my heart to some kiddie I meet. Anna has now become in my mind a close friend, and always I wish I might do something for such a one to make her life fuller and happier. Actually such a feeling is a sublimation of homesickness, I guess.

At 9 p.m. I went and looked in for ¾ of an hour on a dance, our soldiers and French girls. Some few of our men were getting drunk, and one woman who has been with one of our officers for several days was beginning to dance suggestively when I left. Otherwise the affair was in order. A number of parents were in attendance as chaperones. I felt like cutting in on one couple. An attractive brunette with shoulder-length hair and a smiling face danced all the dances with the same soldier—she reminded me of Ruth [wife Peggy's sister, Ruth Landon Howard]—just to break up the combination I felt like asking for a dance, but since you were not there I did no dancing at all. I asked two of the medics to cut in, but they didn't. We finally decided it was his steady girl.

After the dance I sat talking with one of the medics in the aid station. He showed me how to handle chopsticks. They are actually easy to use.

November 24

I see that censorship allows me to say that some time ago I visited the city of Nice. I was wishing at the time that I had the address of Dr. Corbiere's folks—my French professor at Muhlenberg [College]. As it was, I hunted up some Protestants and spoke a bit with them. Nice is a wealthy place since it and Cannes and Monte Carlo draw the wealth of Europe. It didn't suffer much from the war, so far as destruction goes. Of course, the hotels have no tourist trade and haven't for the past four years, I guess.

I see in the paper that there is a lot of opposition to compulsory military training; I'm against it, too. But of course men in uniform have nothing to say about such things; we dare not try to influence any senator's vote!

Christmas packages are arriving all the time, so we always have candy here at the medics. I'm saving a few things for Christmas presents to some French. In fact, I'm also saving wrapping to make the gifts look like Christmas presents.

Upon the arrival of the rest of the Combat Team, the 100th was relieved from its sector and assigned to dugouts on the border from Menton (on the sea) north to Mt. Grammado, where we linked up with the rest of the 442nd now covering the line that our men had been patrolling. For sixteen weeks the One Puka Puka remained in this position, with its headquarters, supply and service units, and the medics comfortably established in pensions and small hotels in Menton. Once again I became a circuit preacher as I had been at Anzio, but this time I made my rounds during daylight hours. On Sundays I held services for units in the coastal area and on weekdays I conducted worship for the men in scattered groups close to the front.

In December, which included special Christmas services (the 25th fell on a Monday in 1944), I reported twenty-one Sunday services with 918 attending (21/918) and fifty-one weekday services with 825 attending (51/825); in January the corresponding totals were 20/407 and 63/1,202 —higher statistics even though December had five Sundays; in February, 24/650 and 69/1,360. I rode in a jeep as far as it could go, then followed the mule-pack trail to its end, and then climbed a narrow footpath to the first dugout. Beginning at the most northerly point, I proceeded southward toward the sea, worshiping with each dugout gang. Between positions I walked alone, carrying a burlap sack of GI *Service Books* (hymnals) over my shoulder. Letters home reflect this regularly repeated activity.

Monday Evening, December 4 Southern France

Today I did a fair day's work, and of a religious nature, too. In fact, I ought to be getting to bed, for it is late and I want to get an early start in the morning.

I've seen one Christmas tree—in a dugout on the front lines. It stands about two feet high and has cotton, red berries, and Christmas candy (cellophane wrapped) as decoration. It looks real nice. The same fellow has an evergreen wreath with red berries at the entrance to his spot. Not bad at all.

Wednesday Morning, December 6

The past three days I have been very busy, mostly walking. My leg muscles are now in fine shape. Today I intend to get some desk work caught up.

Late Sunday Night, December 17

Your husband has had a busy day, with five services of ½ hour plus each, besides some other things. But it's good to be kept busy thus.

Today I discovered a soldier with a box of Christmas tree decorations, so I now have them and perhaps I'll get to use them at a Christmas party for French children. I've got plans—if they work out all right.

Tomorrow will probably be another full day. I have to work hard and seem to touch so few in numbers, but I guess it's worth it. Chaplains certainly *take* the church to soldiers; maybe they won't be able to get to church as civilians but will expect front-porch services at home! Let's hope not.

December 20

Some days ago my heart went pit-a-pat. I was by myself (and, incidentally, going through a minefield—not dangerous, for the safe lane through it is clearly marked) when a shell hit way in front of me and beyond the hill's nose, but a few fragments fell close. Of course I hit the ground; and then jumped up and raced for the nearest dugout. It was the only shell that hit anywhere close. About an hour later I was telling my experience to a few of the men when—WHAM—another hit about 250 yards away and I heard the fragments whizzz. Pit-a-pat, pit-a-pat! But it was the last. And then when I was at this dance [described earlier to my wife] someone whistled with a trill in his whistling to get attention, and I almost threw myself flat on the floor, for it sounded just like a piece of shrapnel when it whirs through the air. I can imagine how some of the shell-shocked patients feel. This is not to worry you—such is a rare experience for me —just to let you share an experience with me.

The men of the 100th, along with those in several of the special units of the Combat Team, made up my parish, and I preached to them much as I would have to civilians back home; of course I kept in mind their special needs and applied the Scripture to their special situations. During these months on the border sermon themes included the following:

"The Blessed," "The Word of God," "Saints," "Parables," "Temptation." Whenever the opportunity came, I arranged special services.

During the closing days of November and the beginning of December, Kent and I were busy writing letters of condolence—I composed the messages and he typed them in triplicate. On November 28, I submitted thirty-six of these to the regimental CO to be sent to the next of kin of the KIAs of the 100th lost thus far in France, along with three to the next of kin of men of the Antitank Company. The next day we sent the letters for the five men the 232nd Engineers had lost. On December 6 there followed a letter for the technical sergeant of Regimental Headquarters killed in the Vosges Mountains. The other two chaplains of the Combat Team were doing the same for the KIAs of their battalions and the other special units; Chaplain Hiro Higuchi, for example, wrote the official letters for the members of the Medical Detachment who had lost their lives. In almost all cases the following two paragraphs were included.

> We who were the comrades of your [relative, name] want to express our sympathy for you as you mourn his loss. May the heavenly Father give you His comfort and strength in your hours of sorrow.
>
> Whenever we gather for church services we remember in prayer the loved ones of our fallen comrades. We seek to honor their memory by carrying on as they would have us do until the peace is won; in the day of victory their sacrifice will not be forgotten.

In addition, I added special thoughts, such as those in these two examples.

> A year's experience in the horror of war has not shaken my faith in the eternal goodness of God; I cannot understand why there is so much evil —I can only trust in His mercy. I pray you may feel the Presence of this Father now.
>
> From friends who were nearby at the time I have learned that [man's name] was killed instantly and did not therefore experience any pain—I tell you this to relieve your mind of any anxiety on that score.

Those of us who were quartered in Menton had comfortable lodgings. I wrote home that so far as accommodations go, I was fixed almost as well as at home. The medics used a part of the Hotel Floreal, located amid palm trees and lush greenery. Our immediate area was part of the battle zone and without civilians unless they were employed by the military, but it was a short walk westward past the army checkpoint to where civilians were living and only a brief jeep ride into Nice through Monaco. (We could not stop off at the latter place; it was "off limits" to Americans.) On December 6, I wrote Peggy that my good friend Doc Dahl had been replaced by an AJA medic, Capt. Hugo S. O'Konogi. Since Captain Kometani was very busy as our morale officer, scheduling dances among other events, I often teamed up with Etsuo Katano when I visited in French homes; Etsuo had become an officer, a second lieutenant in medical administration and in charge of the enlisted men of our Medical Detachment. We often visited the family of a local schoolteacher.

> In the evening at 7 p.m. Katano and I visited the Domine family (Christmas Eve). I had on a parka with hood; in the hood I put a bottle of shampoo, two packages of cough drops, and a candy stick, all wrapped in Christmas paper. I made Jacqueline reach in and pull the presents out, saying I was Papa Noel. And I took along the pudding Anne [Anne Slotter Yost, wife of my brother Bob] had sent. Bernard (13) and Jacqueline (12) called it "the traditional pudding" in English, for they had read of it in their English language book. Mrs. Domine served some quiche, a bacon-cheese pie peculiar to Lorraine where she was raised. (Don't think I'm there; I'm not. But Mrs. Domine was born in that locality.) We had a jolly time till 11:30 p.m. But such a visit brings homesickness. On Christmas night we visited there again. It's a fine home.

In one of the buildings near the Hotel Floreal there was a piano. Occasionally I relaxed by trying to play it. To me it was like playing the mouth organ; I could achieve only a measure of success if I transposed songs to E flat. Of course, all sorts of books were available; I even became interested in trying to learn some Russian. All of us were able to relax at least a part of the time during these days of guarding the border, for from time to time those on duty on the line were replaced by others from the rear so that all the troops could enjoy what came to be known either as the "Riviera Holiday" or the "Champagne Campaign."

Kome and I cooperated in a caroling project just before Christmas. We transported young ladies from Nice to the hotel in Menton used as a rest resort by those not on the front; this meant we actually brought our visitors through the military checkpoint into what was considered the battle zone.

> The French girl carolers came to visit us one afternoon before Christmas. It was to be only 40 but 51 piled on the trucks; a few had to be turned away. The Red Cross was in charge, but I took the trucks to pick up the

girls. Many of them reminded me of Luther Leaguers back home.[1] We arrived and the girls spent an hour dancing with a few of the soldiers. I tried to get the two groups to mix. One leader said, "Everyone must dance." I added, "Except the chaplain." One French girl who speaks English came for me—"You, too." "Not I." "And why not?" she asked. "Because I think too much of my wife"—so she left me alone. At supper the fifty-one split into three groups and ate at three different messes. At one place after the meal they cleared off everything left over—bread, canned milk—and took things home with them. That was the real reason for the large turnout—a good meal. They sang before supper—and well. When they sang "Adeste Fidelis," I had the men join in, and afterwards we sang "The First Noel" for them; I chose it because the chorus has the word *noel* in it. I thanked them in my (abominable) French. I told them that we use the French word *noel* because William conquered England in 1066 but now we are all friends. I got them all home, including three carsick ones who rode in my peep. And was I glad; the Jerries had been shelling very close to where the girls were! But it was a nice affair. It was the finest group of girls I've seen thus far overseas.

That evening a rear echelon group had a dance. I went, to look in— the group is also under my care as chaplain. Lo and behold, a lot of the same French girls appeared. I stood at the door directing folks to the cloak room. (At first I called it *salle de manteaux* until someone informed me the French word is *vestiaire*.) Inside were two trees decorated with candy. The girls rushed these and down came the trees; the girls got all the candy. And these were not rowdies but girls of good families. It's hard for us to appreciate not having candies for five years. And at refreshment time, what a mob! I finally took a hand and helped, making those already served move over for others. There was a paucity of politeness. Finally one French girl helped us, the one who wanted me to dance in the afternoon. She also helped us to get the trucks loaded after the dance.

At 11:00 I began paging people, yelling, "Camions pour Nice a onze heures" (Trucks for Nice at eleven o'clock). It took thirty minutes to get everyone ready. One young lady lost her scarf; I took her address. Another one came lamenting in English, "I've lost my overcoat and I can't go home without it." We asked everyone to check and finally she found it; I felt like spanking her. And at last all departed. *J'etais fatigue* (I was tired).

Another big event was the Christmas party held in the large pavilion overlooking the ritzy tennis courts of Monte Carlo. On my weekly trips along the border for worship services, I had been collecting candy and gifts and Christmas cards from the men and bringing them to the rear with me in my burlap sack. Although the men on the line could not be present for the gala event, they certainly were with us in spirit; their gifts

made the holiday possible. We had our party on the Sunday before
Christmas (December 24) at three p.m.

> Sunday afternoon I rounded up some men, and a fire unit, and utensils
> to make cocoa, plus two GI cooks, and we began. I discovered that one
> cook was somewhat drunk, but he finally got the cocoa made, though he
> insisted we didn't have enough cream, after opening and using almost a
> case of canned cream plus twenty liters of fresh milk. I discovered that a
> large place had been reserved for the "committee" [Frenchmen]—it cut
> into our working space. Our regimental dance orchestra got set up; they
> also had several Hawaiian numbers sung in costume and had excellent
> arrangements of "First Noel" and "Silent Night." And the people poured
> in until the place was packed—at least 700 people, half grown-ups. We
> gave cream, sugar, raisins, and chocolate with which a French baker made
> 2000 buns. I made several attempts in French to get the adults to move
> back and let the children have the fun. No good—and the "committee"
> moved in; they helped themselves. I had broken up a carton of cigarettes
> to pass out to all the men present; when I came for it about 15 cigarettes
> were left and another unopened carton had disappeared. I said in French
> what I thought of French officials! Somehow my men passed out the
> cocoa and buns without incident; kiddies brought their own cups; they
> kept the big can of cocoa moving through the crowd. Monsieur Domine
> had helped; he got the building, chairs, oranges, baker, etc. [He was the
> local school superintendent.] Whenever I made an announcement in
> French, usually trying to get adult cooperation, the band, not knowing
> what I was saying, clapped long and hard. Finally the mayor made a
> speech and M. Domine thanked us in English, with kisses on both cheeks,
> *a la francaise.* I replied in my abominable French; my pronunciation is
> really terrible but most people can understand me, so I'm told.
>
> Then began the distribution of candies. Each child up to age 12
> received a packet of biscuits (four crackers), one chocolate bar, one candy
> bar, one fig bar, several (French) oranges, and a handful of hard candy.
> What a pushing and shoving, but it was finally finished! And we had
> enough left for another party later. The small children couldn't carry all
> their things—pockets too small. Little girls turned up their dresses like
> aprons. During the party we also served crackers spread with jam or pea-
> nut butter. I was disgusted with the lack of discipline, the fault of parents,
> who shoved worse than the children, even though I kept yelling, "Beau-
> coup pour tous" (Enough for all). But it was a happy time for the kiddies.
> It was too big an affair to really enjoy oneself. Next time I'll limit the
> number of ages. Incidentally Mrs. Domine and Jacqueline stayed at the
> far end all the time; if only all could have been as polite as that family.
> Lt. Katano helped considerably.

On Christmas Day I wore vestments and set up an altar, but we had no music to accompany the singing. I sang, as a solo, "Wake, Awake, for Night Is Flying," and all joined in singing carols. Afterwards I offered communion to all who wanted to receive it; only a few came forward. I conducted three services on Sunday and two on the day before. I sent a mimeographed sheet to all the men on the line for them to use within their groups on the Holy Day.

For me the Christmas season of 1944 was blighted by a letter sent to all unit commanders of the Seventh Army by Lt. Gen. A. M. Patch on the subject "Non-fraternization" and dated 25 December. The insensitivity of General Patch was shown in the timing of the release: Christmas Day; his lack of understanding of basic human nature is evident in paragraph 5. That some such policy of restricted association of Americans with Germans in wartime was justified, I do not question; but to release any such statement on the Day of the Nativity of our Lord and to paint *all* [his emphasis, not mine] Germans as responsible for the war and Americans as incapable of any atrocities goes beyond plain common sense. Had I been in an area making possible contacts with Germans, I certainly would not have obeyed such orders to the letter, especially not where children, the aged, and known resisters were concerned. Here is the offending release in toto.

1. The most important problem facing us now is the destruction of the German army. Following the winning of the war on the battlefield, total victory must be won over Germany itself.

2. To achieve the first goal we have to kill Germans, to achieve the second goal we have to adopt a policy that we are fighting not just the German army but the entire German nation. We must make the German populace feel that we blame it as well as the German army for the atrocities that have been committed. Therefore, we must adopt a strict non-fraternization policy.

3. Non-fraternization is the avoidance of mingling with Germans on terms of friendliness, familiarity, or intimacy, either individually or in groups, in official or unofficial dealings. However, non-fraternization does not demand rough, undignified or arrogant conduct, not the insolent overbearing attitude which characterized Nazi leadership. Personnel of this command will maintain a high standard of self-discipline and so conduct themselves as to command respect. Acts of violence or pillage will not be tolerated.

4. The following restrictions are therefore placed in effect:
   a. Troops will not be billeted in homes of German people.

b. Marriage with Germans or personnel of other enemy countries is prohibited.

c. Visiting German homes, drinking with Germans, attending German social events or accompanying Germans on the street, in theaters, taverns, or elsewhere, except on official business is forbidden.

5. It is probable that the German people will not admit that they belong to or sympathize with the Nazi party. They will express disapproval of the atrocities which have been committed. Some will tell us that they were *ordered* to commit atrocities. This is not an excuse. American soldiers would not have committed such atrocities even if ordered to do so. Not only the Nazis, but *all* Germans, are responsible for the war. The Germans relish war. They respect only force of arms and a dictatorial form of government. Hitler's rise to power was not an accident. The German people have demonstrated that they can be counted on to produce such a leader whenever the time is ripe for conquest.

6. It must be made clear to our soldiers that non-fraternization is a necessity not only for safeguarding their own well-being but to make the German nation realize that only by many years of proper conduct will it merit consideration and be worthy of being accepted as a member of the family of civilized nations.

It can be seen that in such a letter, a military officer of the United States far exceeded his area of responsibility and set himself up as an authority not only within his own area and time, but beyond the bounds of his time and commission.

The above order may have been a reaction, at least in part, to American reverses in the Battle of the Bulge. On December 16, the Nazis, in a surprise attack in the Ardennes Mountains of Belgium, advanced against the Allied forces; not until December 22 could air strikes by the Allies begin to slow down the German threat, and not until Christmas Eve was the battle stabilized, and not until January 21 did Hitler withdraw from the area. During this time all forces opposing German troops in Europe were alerted to the possibility of advances in their areas; on our border with Italy we were warned of the possibility of paratroopers dropping behind our lines. Should this occur, such Nazis would want to acquire American uniforms to pass themselves off within France as Americans. We chaplains were therefore ordered to carry arms during this period whenever we were away from close contact with our own troops. I complied; on jeep trips away from Menton, Kent carried a rifle in its case on his side of the vehicle and I placed a loaded pistol beside my car seat. It was clear to me that we were armed for the protection of our uniforms and not of our persons. It was only during this short time span that I was ever "armed" while overseas.

✦ ✦ ✦

With twelve junior officers of the 442nd, I spent several days at the end of the year at Hotel Carlton in Cannes. Although the resort was pretty and the hotel accommodations excellent, I wrote home that it held no special attraction for me. When I returned to my quarters at Menton after the rest leave, a package from the sister of one of our KIAs was waiting for me. She had sent me some handkerchiefs and a Waterman pen and pencil set as a thank-you gift for my letter of sympathy to her. I was much more impressed with this gift than with the sights I had seen at the world-famous city on the Riviera coast.

In the December "Report of Chaplains," I listed a guardhouse visit to talk with one of our men. It is strange that I made no other note about this and that I do not remember whether the prisoner was of the 100th, another unit of the 442nd, or of a non-AJA outfit near us. It was unusual for any of our Nisei to get into any serious trouble. Also recorded was a visit to a military hospital to see 25 of our wounded. In January, I made four such hospital visits and contacted 89 men. In February, on eight visits I talked with 150 soldiers. In March, on four hospital trips I counseled with 70 of our men.

Like the others, both enlisted men and officers, I attended motion pictures from time to time. Occasionally Kent drove me to Nice to see a movie in a French theatre. I guess there were officers' clubs in the area, but, since I never visited any, I do not know for sure. I tried to keep my days busy with reading, writing letters, and visiting the men and holding services. Sometimes I played cribbage with the medics, or learned some new pastime from the Nisei.

Wednesday Night, December 13

Tomura just beat me in several games of Sakura—or Hanafuda, as it is sometimes called. It's a Japanese card game in which flowers, birds, and beasts are matched. It has 48 cards. *Sakura* means Cherry Blossoms. It's a lot of fun for me as I'm just getting to know all the combinations (of three cards each) for *yaku,* which means the other fellow must subtract 50 from his score. The cards are hard to shuffle since they are smaller and thicker than ours. Tomura calls the cards by their Japanese names (from the flowers on each) and often doesn't know the English equivalent.

I forgot to tell you: last week I saw a praying mantis here in France. It was busy chewing off the head of a smaller insect. I wonder if they have been imported to Europe as I think they have been to the U.S.A.

In one respect making the rounds of troops overseas is like pastoral calling in Pennsylvania. I must have a bite to eat or drink a cup of coffee, but if I accepted all the invitations to "have a bite" I'd never get all my services in.

One of the boys I baptized last November wrote to me from a Mainland hospital reminding me of the anniversary. It's encouraging to know how much the instruction and the sacrament meant to him.

On Sunday, January 15, 1944, for the first time since coming overseas, I preached in a regular church at a civilian service; even though I felt rather lost in the chancel and pulpit of this Protestant Episcopal parish, I certainly enjoyed the privilege. That same day I looked in on worship at a Russian Orthodox congregation. At this first such experience I was impressed by the beautiful chanting without any accompaniment, but offended by the lack of participation by the laity, as the clergy alone seemed to be truly worshiping. I felt that the icons were in good taste and added beauty to the church interior.

On January 18, something occurred that truly flabbergasted me. Here is how I wrote home about it that same evening.

> Tonight after supper our S-1 [adjutant, staff record keeper] handed me an official envelope and shook my hand saying, "Congratulations." I asked, "What's this, a transfer to another outfit?" Said he, "You have been awarded the Legion of Merit." I thought he was kidding, but when I opened the paper, there it was. It reads: ". . . the Legion of Merit was awarded by the Theater Commander to the following named officers for exceptionally meritorious conduct in the performance of outstanding services:
>
> Israel A. S. Yost, 0511005, Captain, Chaplain's Corps, 100th Battalion, 442nd Infantry Regiment, for services in Italy from 15 October 1943 to 8 September 1944. Entered service from Nazareth, Pennsylvania."
>
> It is dated 30 December 1944.
>
> I could have cried. I don't know who initiated papers for it. It was a complete surprise to me and made me feel ashamed of each time I've complained about my work not being appreciated. It's not a bravery medal; it's a work-done medal.[2]
>
> Last year this time my captaincy came through, also unknown to me until I received it. I'm glad for it for the children's sake. They can see that their daddy did try to do his job in the army.
>
> When I receive the decoration, whenever that is (I don't even know

what it looks like), I'll send it home to you. Put it somewhere with my Purple Heart.

A few of the men have heard of it and several have said, "It's about time; you deserved it." To hear that makes my heart sing. I hope God also has been some little pleased with any poor effort of mine. His approbation is worth more than man's.

I haven't been a very good chaplain, but I've tried to put myself out now and again for the men. That's what the award is really for, I guess.

You see that if my men and officers do think thus well of me I must stay with them so long as I can serve. Therefore we must not wish too hard for rotation. My conscience might even make me refuse it. Tell Mother but no one outside the family yet.

Whenever troops stay in one area for any length of time, some few become emotionally attached to the young women there. Occasionally even one of our older and wiser Nisei felt that he had fallen in love with a local belle.

Tuesday Evening, January 23 France

Now it's beginning with my men, too. One thinks he wants to marry a French girl. So I'm going to visit her one of these days and explain all the difficulties. I hope I can discourage them. I'd almost say the Army ought to flatly refuse to allow any marriages overseas, but that's not exactly fair, either.

Sunday Evening, January 28

In one case of a soldier wanting to marry a French girl, the father said, "No, you are too young." I also spoke to the girl of the various difficulties: religion, citizenship, customs, distance, red tape. I tried to help the soldier, too. The girl seems like a fine girl and the fellow is a quiet, fine chap, what the French call *gentil* (from which comes "gentleman"). Maybe after the war!

Every chaplain must include in his monthly report statistics of his "pastoral, educational, recreational, and miscellaneous" activities; I always listed the number of "personal conferences" I had with men who had problems, the number varying per month from three to twenty-five, except for January of 1944, when I reported that I had none of any kind. Shortly after submitting the January report, I received a phone call from a higher echelon of the Chaplains Corps well in the rear—over the field telephone. I was in the forward battalion aid station at the time, for we were still in combat in front of Cassino; I could scarcely hear the message because of the distance it had to travel. The caller demanded to know why I had not included any numbers at all in this section of my report.

My simple answer, that we had been in combat constantly during the month and men had no time for conferences, did not satisfy the inquirer; he insisted that I must have talked with somebody about something sometime during the month, but much to his disappointment I insisted that my definition of a personal conference did not cover any "conversations" during that hectic month. I could have added that as soon as we got out of combat, there would be conferences to report, but I knew that the pencil-pusher in the rear was only interested in numbers to swell his total of activities for the month.

January of 1945, the 100th was on the border and not in the kind of fighting we experienced at Cassino; I held twenty-two conferences with worried soldiers. One such concerned a problem back at the home front, brought to the GI concerned in a letter. Had he received such a letter while at the front he could not have asked for my advice very easily, but during the "Champagne Campaign" he had the opportunity to come to his chaplain. Like the above-mentioned situation of the lovesick swain who wanted to marry a Frenchwoman, the following example is of an unusual situation; our AJAs at home did not often cause any of their loved ones overseas any such personal problems.

> Monday Night, January 29 France
>
> I'm trying to advise one of the men what to do about his wife who has been unfaithful and apparently has had an illegitimate child. I'm not sure what he ought to do. Some of these men have been away three years now. It's not fair the way so few have borne so much and now others at home have taken advantage. I pity this fellow, for he still loves his wife.

In conference with my men I was always direct but sympathetic and attempted to explain what I thought was the Christian way. In the above situation I asked the soldier to examine his own life, asking him if he had remained faithful to his vows, whether he could forgive his wife, whether he still loved her. Because of his faithfulness to his vows and his continued love for his wife, I urged him to forgive her, write to his wife of his feelings, and beg that she change her lifestyle and renew her vows to him so that after the war the marriage could continue.

In January we lost one of our men, KIA during a patrol between the lines, and occasionally WIAs came through the battalion aid, as the following incident reveals.

Wednesday Night, January 31 France

A soldier was receiving plasma. His eyes were covered because of the bright light annoying him. I spoke to him, explaining that the plasma would help him. "That's all right, chaplain; I can't see you but I know you." He was an old-timer and knows my voice as well as my face. Often on the phone I say just a sentence and the soldier at the other end replies, "Chaplain—thus and so . . ." It's good to be known by voice.

In February, two members of the 232nd Engineer Company were killed while working with mines. Since this unit of Nisei was also under my care, I officiated at their burial at the American military cemetery at Draguignan as I had the previous month for our C Company KIA, the one lost on a patrol. Later on I was the official representative of the Combat Team at the funeral of a young French solider who was killed by mines as his unit was relieving our men in a position along the sea-coast.

February of 1945 might well be described as a "ho-hum" month; for most of us on the Riviera it was much like being once again in camp rather than combat. We were adjusting to a change in command; Colonel Singles left to take a promotion as the CO of a regiment, and Lt. Col. James E. Conley, a kamaaina from Maui, moved over from the 2nd Battalion to the 100th. I kept myself busy; most of the time I was my own boss, free to move about and setting my own priorities.

Friday Morn (February 9)

The ways of men—because the colonel of the regiment was to eat breakfast with us, the chow time was moved up ½ hour and everyone was to be there on time—usually a number [of the officers] slept through breakfast. I strolled in a few minutes before the regular time; everyone was just about finished. And the colonel wasn't there! I had a good laugh on the others.

About this time I showed up one day at the officers' mess wearing a new combat jacket. When the executive officer, a major, saw it, he exploded; he had been trying to requisition one for some time. He accosted the supply officer, a captain, and loudly demanded that the jacket be taken from me and given to him. The captain coolly looked the major over and replied, "Major, you don't get up on the front where the men are in the snow. The chaplain does and therefore he needs it more than you do." That settled the argument and I kept my new, warm acquisition. It improved my appearance somewhat, but I was still wearing my old combat shoes acquired from the 109th Engineers back in September of 1943. And for a muffler I had cut a strip from an army blanket. And the burlap bag I always carried on my hikes did not beautify my appearance. But, of course, the only item of any significance about my dress was the little silver cross I wore on my cap; at a glance anyone could see that I was the chaplain.

March began with a bang—on the first day I received my medal, a beauty. But I also had to have my throat painted because it was sore. At first I did not consider this a serious matter, but I was wrong.

Saturday Evening, March 3 France

Yesterday I did nothing, absolutely nothing, except take pills and gargle with salt water. Wednesday I had noticed a swollen throat and had it painted with argyrols. Thursday I took a peep ride and when I got back at 9:00 p.m. my throat was terribly bad. I went to bed and stayed there all day Friday. Katano gave me sulfa dyazine pills. Then last night I got chills and then a fever of 102 plus. But during the night it passed away and this morning I felt better. For a bit I thought I would have to go to the hospital. I've spent all of today in bed, too, but I'm not sure I'll be able to conduct services tomorrow yet. And it was my turn to take a trip to Paris just now, too. But I'll get another chance at that later. I should not have gotten sick—not taking strict enough care of myself. It is apparently my tonsils that caused the illness. But imagine—18 months of war and then in good spring weather I get laid up for 2½ days with a sore throat!

Sunday Evening, March 4

Today I spent in bed again. The swelling in my tonsils is down but they are still sore. And a lot of little glands in the back of my head and neck are swollen. However, tomorrow I think I'll get up, whether or no. Katano does the best he knows, but we've no doctor right here just now —Katano is just a medical administrative officer, MAC we say. After I'm up a while I might run over to see the regimental surgeon.

The medics have taken good care of me during the three days— juices, medicine, meals, water to gargle, mail, newspapers.

One morning while I was ill, Katano came into my bedroom and began to write out an EMT tag, saying, "Chaplain, I'm sending you to the hospital."

"Oh no, you're not," I replied emphatically. "You are an MAC officer and I don't have to take orders from you. Now if one of the battalion surgeons were here I'd have to obey, I guess."

Katano smiled and put his tags away. It's a good thing I did not listen to him, for soon afterwards in came an officer from headquarters with the news that we would be alerted for a movement within a few days and the last leave for Paris would be that of March 7. He wondered if I was too sick to make the excursion; I told him to put me on the list of those going.

On March 7, eighty of us climbed into four big trucks and headed for the capital of France far to the north, officers in the cabs with the drivers and men in the bodies. The top sergeant told me that no one was quite sure just where we would stay overnight on the stops en route. Since that was not my worry I rode merrily along all day, resting as my sore throat began to feel more normal again. Somewhat before dusk we pulled up before a hotel in a small town, and all the officers got their gear together to stay there. When I inquired where the men would be billeted, one of the louies [lieutenants] answered for all of them, "Chaplain, you are the senior officer in this group so you're the one to take care of the men. In fact, you are in charge of all the details until we get back with the regiment." I protested that I was only a chaplain, and a sick one at that, but to no avail. The junior officers disappeared into the hostelry.

From some civilians I learned that there was an unused French army barracks in the town. After the men were assigned places to sleep there, I gave all hands leave to explore the surroundings but set an hour when all had to report back that evening. Meanwhile I was approached by a citizen who invited me to be his overnight guest—the bed was a delight, soft and with pretty quilts. At check-in time only one AJA was missing. As I stepped out of the barracks to begin a search for the absentee, I spotted a group coming down the alley by the light of a single candle: a French family was escorting the delinquent "home."

Other overnight stops to and from Paris were not as memorable as this first one. In one town we found a large garage, parked the trucks in it, and then bunked the best we could in and around the trucks. Who minded such an inconvenience after the hard nights on the border? The only transport problems we experienced were several flat tires. Gas was available at the several army dumps we passed.

Friday Evening, March 9 France

This morning a French farmer's wife made me a delicious egg omelette with onions—also some home-baked bread. Tonight I had ice cream for dessert.

In some parts of France they have anchored boats where women wash leaning over scrub boards at the side extending into the river water; and everywhere, as in Italy, one sees buildings for washing clothes *(lavoirs)* with compartments through which water is always running. Thus several neighbors wash and gossip at the same time.

One still sees here and there remnants of a moat around a walled town or a castle, and old churches abound, often with flying buttresses.

By the time we arrived in Paris, I was fully recuperated. We headed for the American Red Cross, somewhere in the center of the city. At one point I slowed down the lead truck, hopped off the running board, and called out in my best French to a man strolling on the pavement, "Ou est la croix rouge?"

"Just a block ahead around the corner," answered the Frenchman in excellent English. "And you need not use French. A lot of us understand English here." At this the Nisei in the four stopped trucks burst into laughter at my embarrassment.

At the Red Cross the men and officers checked in and were assigned to quarters; after that everyone was on his own, and I was responsible during the next two days only for myself—after taking care of one "small" detail: getting the flat truck tires fixed for the return trip.

> In attempting to find a place to have our flats fixed, the four drivers and I with the trucks began a merry chase around Paris. After many twists and turns I looked behind and behold—no fourth truck. We retraced our route several blocks but found no signs of it. We concluded he would return to our parking lot, so we didn't worry any more. That evening I checked at the hotel but all the drivers were out. Next morning I found that the fourth truck had run out of gas and its driver had slept in the truck. It was noon until we [the top sergeant on the trip and I] requisitioned gas and found the truck. By this time the driver had left. So I left a note at the nearest store and drove the truck back to the parking lot myself. I had never driven one before, but the other driver showed me the gearshift, and I set off; he followed in his truck. So down the main streets of Paris I drove and got safely to our destination. These trucks are six-by-sixes with a total of ten wheels, two in front and two sets of double tires in the rear. If I had not driven, it would have meant waiting until the one driver took his truck back and returned on the subway to drive the second truck back. Later on the [lost] driver showed up; he too had gone after gas.

On the two days actually spent on leave in Paris I went sightseeing, attended Sunday worship, and contacted the head of the Lutheran Church in France. I saw no movies or shows in gay Paris.

Napoleon's Tomb at Les Invalides is the most elaborate monument I saw in Paris. Formerly it was a Roman Catholic church, built by Louis XIV's architect; it still has a replica of the high altar of St. Peter's, Rome. The stone work is magnificent. The floor was removed and later replaced at a lower level (cellar) so one enters and peers down at the Emperor's Tomb, a magnificent one of stone. Elsewhere in the place are monuments to Foch, Napoleon's two brothers—and the Germans brought the body and coffin of Napoleon's son (called "L'Aiglot") from Austria and placed it here—we saw it.

Many bronze statues around Paris were removed by the Germans for their bronze; only pedestals remain.

I passed by the Louvre, Tuillerie Gardens, the Royal Palaces, the Opera, the Church of the Madeleine (like the Parthenon of Athens) but did not get inside. I was in Paris only two days and had to do a lot of running around since I had charge of 70 men and 9 officers on pass with me.

I worshiped in St. Jean Lutherien Eglise and had dinner with Inspecteur (Pasteur) Boury who is sometimes called bishop since he heads the French Lutheran Church. Also I spent several hours one evening in his home. I had to use French.

Also I attended an ecumenical service at the British Embassy Church. Russian Orthodox priests, Anglicans (including the Bishop of Chichester, England), and French Protestants attended; there was a French sermon and one in English. The Russian bishop (I guess) gave the benediction in his language—quite an experience.

I saw also Notre Dame Cathedral, Arc de Triomphe, the Eiffel Tower (did not ascend it though), and passed by the Sorbonne University and the Latin Quarter. I bought only postcards as souvenirs are extremely expensive.

When we assembled for the return trip, one Nisei could not be located. To leave without him might have resulted in a court-martial for him; his friends fanned out in an effort to find him. He was located not far away, drinking a last toast to his holiday, already a little tipsy. For punishment I had him stand guard that night at our first stop while all the others had leave to explore yet another French town. Our convoy overnighted in Lyon and Nice; at both stops I spent time with the local Lutheran pastors, in the evenings when the rest of our group was sightseeing.

The day we arrived back at Menton, the official news came that the 442nd was leaving for a new assignment; on March 16 at night, the 100th moved out, headed for Nice and then Marseille.

Sunday Night, March 18

Today I had a memorial service for all men killed since the 100th has been in action. I spread red carnations around the cross on the altar. A bugler played church call and, during the prayer, taps. The men sat in a semi-circle on the grass.

Virgil R. Miller replaced Col. Charles W. Pence as the CO of the Combat Team, promoted from regimental executive officer. The 522nd Field Artillery was detached from us and sent north to fight against the Germans.[3] There was an urgency about getting ready to go somewhere, but no one knew where.

Notes

1. The Luther League was the youth organization of the Lutheran Church in the United States.

2. See the appendix following for Colonel Singles' letter stating the basis for the Legion of Merit Award.

3. From March 12–May 8, 1945, the 522nd Field Artillery Battalion participated in the invasion of Germany as part of Gen. George Patton's Third Army. It also participated in the liberation of Dachau, the notorious German concentration camp, and served for seven months with the occupation troops.

Appendix

The Legion of Merit Award

HEADQUARTERS 100TH BATTALION, 442D INFANTRY
APO 758, U.S. Army

7 October 1944

SUBJECT: Recommendation for the Award of the Legion of Merit
TO: Commanding Officer, 442d Infantry, APO 758, U.S. Army

1. Under the provisions of Army Regulations 600-45, it is recommended that Chaplain ISRAEL A. S. YOST, 0511005 (Captain), Chaplain's Corps, be awarded the Legion of Merit for exceptionally meritorious conduct.

2. I have personal knowledge of the services rendered by Chaplain ISRAEL A. S. YOST.

3. The entire service of Chaplain Yost since the performance of the mentioned facts has been honorable.

4. Basis for Award:

ISRAEL A. S. YOST, 0511005, Chaplain (Capt.), Chaplain's Corps, for exceptionally meritorious conduct during the period 15 October 1943 to 8 September 1944 in Italy. During the last crossing of the Volturno River about 4 November 1943, Chaplain Yost recovered all bodies in an area known to be mined before the area had been swept in order to bury the bodies before decomposition set in. In the action near Pozzili about 8 November 1943, Chaplain Yost served as an aid-man in addition to his other duties, because of the almost complete elimination of the Battalion Medical Section.

In the action near Coli, between 25 November to 11 December, Chaplain Yost, realizing the precarious state of the Battalion's morale because of the severe climatic conditions during a period of ferocious fighting, held divine services for small groups within thirty (30) yards of enemy positions in a prone position. In this fashion, and others similar, he covered the entire Battalion, holding approximately fifteen (15) services.

In the vicinity of Radicossa and San Michele, 6–15 January 1944, Chaplain Yost carried a pack weighing approximately seventy (70) pounds filled with dry socks, blankets, mufflers, lemonade powder and other items that might be of comfort to men, well or wounded, fighting in snow at elevations over 3000 feet.

In the vicinity of Cassino, 24 January 1944 to 21 February 1944, Chaplain Yost again acted as litter bearer, aid-man, chaplain, and supply-man in utter disregard of his own safety. He was found searching unswept minefields for bodies, and had to be ordered to stop his attempts to recover bodies remaining in the fields.

In the vicinity of Anzio, 24 March 1944 to 23 May 1944, Chaplain Yost continued to give spiritual guidance and make personal contacts, despite the fact the Battalion installations were wide spread and that his endeavors necessitated his staying up day and night at least three days a week. The zealousness of Chaplain Yost for the welfare of the men of this Battalion was magnificent. Despite being wounded twice by shell fire in carrying out his duties, the Chaplain was in no way deterred from his attempts to relieve both physical and spiritual suffering of friend or foe, regardless of his position on the battlefield.

This Chaplain is held in such esteem by the personnel of this Battalion that a Division Commander promised never to transfer him while the Battalion was assigned to that Division, even though his seniority entitled him to a better position.

Entered military service from: Nazareth, Pennsylvania. Home town address: R.D. 3, Nazareth, Pennsylvania

/s/ GORDON SINGLES
Lt Col, 100th Bn, 442d Inf
Commanding, 7 October 1944

TWELVE

Italian Finale

T HE 100ᵀᴴ left Marseille, France, aboard three LSTs on Friday, March 23, but the troops did not know until Sunday morning that the Combat Team was headed for Italy. After two Palm Sunday services on the LST (with a sermon about Jesus emptying himself of the powers of God and coming as a man to earth to lift us up toward God), we landed at Leghorn at noon, without any identifying insignia on our uniforms, for, as in the Battle of Bruyères, the Nisei were to be used as a secret weapon to be thrust against the German defenses in Italy. After three days near Pisa, and equipped with new arms and vehicles, on the night of March 28 we moved to San Martino near Lucca. On Holy Thursday evening, six candidates for baptism attended their third class of instruction. During our six-day stay here, battle training was rigid, including instruction about the newer and nastier Jerry mines.

Saturday Morning, March 31

Two nights, Wednesday and Friday, I took the few Jewish officers we have to Passover services in town. [These were conducted under military supervision at a synagogue in Pisa.] While they were there I visited a family nearby. Incidentally, any gifts for kiddies you think of, send, especially for little girls as I have a weakness for them. I've about run out of presents. But for tomorrow, Easter, I have some candy for the eleven or so children nearby. In fact, while writing this a soldier from our A and P platoon (ammunition and pioneer) brought me about 20 chocolate bars since he had heard that I was planning something for the kiddies.

Today I have a lot of desk work—chaplain's report, sermon to prepare, article for our unit public relations man. And I have quite a stack of personal letters to answer.

Our regimental colonel is easy to get along with. Yesterday I explained the case of three brothers, all in front line companies, who were concerned lest a fourth brother (and younger) might also be placed up front. The colonel immediately told the placement officer to make sure that brother is not put up front, and in addition gave orders to pull a second brother to a rear echelon also, thus doing more than asked for.

In the report alluded to, for the month of March, these items appear.

> Regimental Mass was arranged in order that all might make their Easter duty; Catholic devotional material was made available. Mormon men met with a chaplain of their faith under regimental supervision. The regimental commander has given splendid cooperation in arranging services and considering the recommendations of the unit's chaplain. . . . Three conferences with Regimental Commander.

Easter Monday Noon, April 2 Somewhere in Italy

> Yesterday was busy. I had a sunrise service in the mist at 6:00 a.m. with the regimental band and a sextet of singers from the band [180 attended]. Two battalion commanders were there. The altar looked thus [see below].
>
> An Italian gathered many wild flowers which were strewn over the altar around the cross. (Of course I paid him.) I wore freshly laundered vestments. We read the Easter story responsively from [a] pamphlet. Six soldiers were baptized: the font was my helmet placed in between three rods stuck in the ground. In the afternoon I had a second, smaller service. After dinner I had a party for 14 children. We played "Steal the Bacon" and "Three Deep" and had ice cream mix to drink and jelly sandwiches to eat. After the morning service about 20 men communed and two after supper. I spent some time on records and in the evening sat a while in an Italian home. So you see I am back here again. My APO is now 464.

Those baptized were Minoru Harada and Noboru Ashida of A Company, Dan Uchimoto of C Company, and George Minoru Miyama, Earl Yohey Yonehiro, and Ben Tsutomu Matsumoto of B Company. Kent Nakamura and Dan Uchimoto stood up as witnesses, except that for Dan's baptism Minoru Harada joined Kent as a witness. Some of the Roman Catholics attended Easter Mass at the nearby civilian church.

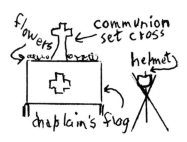

Necessarily, my letters home during the next few days in combat did not tell the story of what was happening. So that the excerpts from these letters and additional recollections of mine might fit into the total picture, here is the historical account as it appears in Shirey's pamphlet, *Americans: The Story of the 442nd Combat Team*.

[O]n 3 April, the Combat Team was . . . assigned direct to Fifth Army, and attached to the 92d Division for operations. General Almond assigned the Combat Team the sector from Highway One east to include the Folgorito ridge line, a 3,000-foot hill mass which rose abruptly from the coastal plain, dominating Massa, Carrara, and the great naval base of La Spezia.

The mission of the 92d Division with the 442d and 473d Infantry Regiments attached was to launch an offensive some time before the main weight of the Eighth Army was hurled at Bologna. It was believed that such a move would lead the enemy to divert some of his central reserve, then massed in the Po behind Bologna, to meet this threat to his flank.

Under cover of darkness 3 April, the 100th Battalion moved into a forward assembly area in the vicinity of Vallechia. The 3d Battalion detrucked at Pietrasanta, and marched eight miles over mountain trails to Azzano, a mountain village which was under full enemy observation during daylight. There the unit remained hidden until the next night, when it moved out, led by a Partisan guide, and gained the ridge line between Mount Folgorito and Mount Carchio.

This move had been a long gamble on the part of Colonel Miller, the regimental commander. It was necessary that the troops achieve this ridge line without detection since it was a Herculean task in itself merely to scale the sheer mountain walls. It would have been an impossibility to take the positions by storm. Success meant that a position which had resisted the 92d Division for six months would probably fall in two days. Failure meant that the regiment would be forced to make a costly frontal attack on these same positions. Our troops did not fail.

Gaining the ridge line, the 3d Battalion jumped off at 050500 April [5th], enveloping the enemy from the rear. At the same time the 100th Battalion attacked the enemy positions on the ridge line which ran southwest from Mount Folgorito to the coastal plain.

The attacking battalions, having moved forward toward each other for 24 hours, made contact on Mount Cerretta late the following day. They had been supported by three battalions of artillery plus a very effective air strike, and enemy casualties were extremely heavy. Exploiting the initial advantage, the 2d Battalion had followed the 3d during the night of 5 April, and at 061000 swung north from Mount Folgorito to seize Mount Belvedere. This was a long mountain top, having a knoll at each corner and forming a rough rectangle. Resistance was heavy and the mountain was not occupied by nightfall. (35ff.)

A look at a map of Italy shows that the Fifth Army had not advanced far since the 100th left for France at the end of September the year before. The 92nd Division, to which the Combat Team was now attached, was an all-black unit; two of its battalions had given ground before a German attack in December. Because of its poor showing, its best fighters were reorganized as the 370th Infantry Regiment; in addition, antiaircraft units had been retrained as infantry—they were no longer needed against the nonexistent Luftwaffe—and designated as the 473rd Infantry Regiment. Thus the 92nd Division became an effective force: one regiment of black troops, one of AJAs, and one of former AAA (antiaircraft artillery) men. Clearly, Gen. Mark Clark was depending on the 442nd to strengthen the west wing of his Allied forces in Italy. On April 3, he visited the 100th and welcomed them back to his command; he had asked for our return because he sorely needed the One Puka Puka and the boys of the 442nd Infantry.[1]

This same evening, just as we were moving out, the soldier who had wanted to be baptized on Easter but who could not be present at sunrise came and asked for the sacrament. With only Kent Nakamura available for a witness I promptly baptized Yutaka Dick Takaki of B Company.

Wednesday Morning, April 4 Italy

Italy is about the same as we left it. I never figured we would ever return, but here we are. But I guess it's better here than in Germany, for there the army has a strict non-fraternization policy which I would probably break, for children everywhere will be treated alike by me, be they American, French, Italian, German.

Yesterday I composed a letter to a disappointed girl in Nice. If she pressed matters she could bring a real case of breach of promise against one of our soldiers; and then I translated it into French—a nice little exercise. I must also write to the Domine family soon. Katano and I miss their fine hospitality.

At any rate we missed active campaigning during the winter months. From now on the weather will at least be livable. The nights are still cool but the days are sunny and warm.

Capt. O'Konogi is our battalion surgeon. He's Japanese-American—don't let the "O'" fool you. We get along fine. I'm glad that all the surgeons we've had have been congenial gentlemen: Kawasaki, Kainuma, Dahl, Mastrella, Shapiro, O'Konogi. Capt. Kometani and I have seen them all come and go.

On March 23, 1945, the 100th Bn returned to Italy to participate in the last series of battles before the German troops in Italy surrendered on May 2, 1945. In the Ligurian coastal area, General Almond assigned the 442nd RCT the sector from Highway One east to include the Folgorito ridgeline. The 100th moved into a forward position at Vallechia and then attacked the enemy positions on the ridgeline, which ran southwest from Mt. Folgorito to the coastal plain. In two days the 100th and the 442nd broke through a German line that had held up the Fifth Army for six months.

Thursday Noon, April 5 Italy

The conditions under which I am writing this are certainly far from the best. But I am still all right, thanks be to God.

I dropped the Domine family a letter, but I dare not tell them where I am—to civilians except in the U.S. and Britain, the country where I am dare not be mentioned.

This innocuous note above (and its continuation a bit later) covers the horrible facts of this initial day in our last battle of World War II. April 5 is the date of the death of Pfc. Sadao Munemori, who was awarded the Medal of Honor posthumously for the actions leading to his heroic sacrifice.[2] In addition, at least thirteen others of the 100th were KIA and many more WIA; during the intense American barrage our own shells fell short, causing eight casualties just in the 1st Platoon of A Company. By April 25, letters concerning the death of these fourteen KIAs as well as of two DOWs of this date were written. For six who died of mortar shell fragments I wrote, "I saw him shortly thereafter" or "twenty minutes after." For another who died of the same cause I wrote, "Lieutenant [man's name] of Co. D was nearby," so that the loved one would not picture her loved one as alone when dying.

In each case the exact cause of death was given: "enemy rifle grenade, died instantly" for three, "enemy bullet in forehead, killed instantly" for another, "enemy artillery shell" for another, and "mortar shell fragments, killed instantly" for two whose bodies I did not personally see after death. In every instance the statements were entirely authentic. For the two who died of wounds the letters of condolence read, "He was given medical attention at the aid station and sent back to a hospital; there he died." I did not say that I saw either of these two; it is probable that I was out with the litter squads when they came through the battalion aid.

My memory of the incidents of this final battle are not as vivid as those when I first joined the 100th, but the April report sent to the Office of the Chief of Chaplains attests that I was still functioning in the same manner as previously: "Because we were in combat or on the move most of this month [April] it was not possible to hold the normal number of services. However, I was with the men all the time, either at the battalion aid station, or in the march column, or with the ration detail, or with the litter bearers."

Same Day, At Supper [April 5]

Pretty soon I'll open up a package of K rations for supper, though I'm going to eat the breakfast menu since I like it better. (I traded my supper unit for it.) And Lt. Katano just gave me a Hershey bar for dessert—I've a sweet tooth for chocolate.

I finally got a chance some time ago to see the Leaning Tower of Pisa though I didn't get to climb up it; also I spent about ten minutes inside the cathedral which is quite artistic and the same time examining the three bronze (I guess that's what it is) doors with scenes in bas relief. The baptistry was closed, but I examined its exterior. These three monuments are a credit to Pisa. They were not damaged by the war, though many buildings in the city are in rubble and ruins.

Friday Night, April 6 Italy

This is written by flashlight, which at the moment is the most available light here. Several of us at the aid station here are talking before falling off to sleep. Mostly we are discussing treatment of the wounded.

What a time I have with my languages; once it's Italian, then French, then German. It's getting so I mix them all up. Again I must use any one of the three acting as interpreter. I don't always like the experience.

For those on the line, April 6 was a continuation of the day before. The letters of condolence sent out on April 25 were specific about our KIAs: "He was brought to the forward aid station and I helped give him plasma. He was very weak, and we eased his pain as best we could. He was sent farther to the rear and died on the way. He was given the best care possible; but his leg was too badly wounded." "While participating in an attack he was shot by an enemy sniper, and death came quickly." (This second comment for two men.) "He was killed instantly by enemy shell fragments. I tell you this so you know he did not suffer." (This third comment for three.) "While moving to a new position with his fellow soldiers some enemy mines were set off and the resulting explosion caused [his] death. An aid man was present but your son was mortally wounded." ". . . died soon after, even though first aid was given to him."

One day when we were in the hills, I was walking by myself up the mountain on my way forward to the battalion aid when shells began to fall uncomfortably close; I ran ahead to take cover behind a knob on the slope. There I encountered an enlisted man of the 92nd, a black man, who like me was waiting out the shelling before proceeding forward to his unit. In the course of our conversation I discovered that the soldier was not really an infantryman but a truck driver.

"If you're a transportation man, how come you're up front today?" I inquired.

"Man, I'm being punished. I screwed up my job in the rear, so now they put me up on the line." He did not appear to be very frightened by the shelling, and when it stopped he continued up the mountain with me.

Even though we were attached to the "Negro"[3] 92nd, I had almost no contact with any of their men or officers. A black litter squad was attached to our battalion, and they did their work well and were respected, but in general their reputation was poor. Gen. Mark Clark has been criticized for his derogatory remarks about their unfavorable combat record, but many are unaware of the mitigating factors Clark added to his judgment of their conduct in Italy. In *Calculated Risk* he wrote,

> At the same time, it would be dishonest and unfair to future Negro soldiers to overlook the serious handicaps which they had to overcome. Leadership was one of the biggest problems. There were many illiterates among the Negro troops; hence it took longer to train them, and there was, in general, a reluctance to accept responsibility for the hard, routine, discipline that is essential in wartime. This failure I view not as a reflection on the Negro soldier or officer, but as a reflection of our handling of minority problems at home. The Negro had not had the opportunity to develop qualities of leadership. Most of all, perhaps, the Negro soldier needed greater incentive, a feeling that he was fighting for his home and country and that he was fighting as an equal. Only the proper environment in his own country can provide such incentive. (414)

Unfortunately, the close proximity of the Nisei and the blacks in this last Allied push in northern Italy led to comparison of the records of the two groups in World War II, to the praise of the Nisei and the disparagement of the black. The remarkable performance of the 100th and the 442nd justifiably illustrates the best in those we call Japanese Americans; unfortunately, there was also a small group of AJAs in the U.S. Army that illustrates the worst of the same ethnic minority. Tamotsu Shibutani, in his book *The Derelicts of Company K, A Sociological Study of Demoralization,* wrote of Nisei soldiers whose military record was the opposite of our Nisei in Italy. (Note well: he is not writing of our K Company.)

> The aim of this study is twofold. It is a chronicle of one of the most disorderly units in United States military history, and one objective is to learn just how it deteriorated to this point. . . . The second objective is the formulation of sociological generalizations concerning the process of demoralization. (vii)

Sociologist Shibutani notes as a participant in the activities of this unit how his fellow soldiers became undisciplined under conditions quite different from those experienced initially by the 100th and then also by the Combat Team. In contrast with both the Nisei of K Company and the blacks of the 92nd Division, the men of the 100th and of the 442nd were exceedingly well trained, led by proficient and understanding officers, motivated to the highest degree, better-than-average educated, supported within the ranks by close friends and relatives, certain that their record would benefit all the survivors of their ethnic group. Furthermore, the Nisei are a far more closely knit group in spite of differences between generations and residence than those we designate loosely as American "blacks." It is grossly unfair to compare the 92nd Division with the 442nd Regimental Combat Team.[4]

About this same time a distraught buddhahead talked with me at the forward aid about the death of a close comrade. He expressed his frustration by remarking, "I will not take any more prisoners. From now on I'll shoot every German I can." A day or so later I stood just outside the aid station watching a long line of enemy POWs being led to the rear. I was surprised to recognize that the armed guard at the rear was my distraught friend. He tried to pass by without looking up at me, but I walked up to him.

"I thought you said the other day that you were not going to take any more prisoners," I remarked.

My friend looked up, his face reflecting his inner sadness, and softly replied, "You can't kick a man when he's down, Chaplain." And he continued shepherding the captured enemy back to the safety of an American prison camp.

One of our tall, lanky Caucasian officers was carried into the aid station; a mine had blown off his foot. Because both legs stuck out over the end of the litter, it was difficult for the carriers to keep from jostling him, and he was crying out in pain. Knowing that he would feel better if I helped transport him, I took the leg-end of the stretcher as we continued on to the rear. That's all I remember of the incident, and I did not see the officer again until 1983 on a visit to the Los Angeles area. It was then I heard the rest of the story: he recalled that when artillery shells began falling and all of us had to take cover, I stretched my body over his to protect him since he could not move off the stretcher. I did not contradict him, but I have no recollection of such an act.

✶ ✶ ✶

In two days the Combat Team had broken through the defense line that the Germans had occupied for six months. The battalion later received an Oak Leaf Cluster to the Presidential Unit Citation for its success on April 5 and 6, coupled with its accomplishments in the Biffontaine-

Bruyères sector. As the Combat Team consolidated its forces and moved after retreating Germans, the 100th suffered no KIAs until April 13.

Monday Noon, April 9

Sometimes I think I'm just kidding myself by being a chaplain in the army. I ought to be a line officer, taking my chances and leading men. Actually I'm without tangible responsibilities, just so I take care of myself and get a few services in a week. The rest is mostly convincing men that men of the cloth are brave, happy, gentle, and generally good-skates—mostly a lot of bilderwash. Even in civilian life much the same is true; clergymen do lead sheltered lives for the most part. Their salaries are paid and there is little tangible responsibility, no business to manage with losses to stand, etc. Of course, there is an intangible responsibility, but that is easily evaded.

I am almost tempted after two more months to ask for a transfer to another unit, if by that time rotation does not send me home, and for that there is only a slight chance. For one thing the unit is not the same one it once was, and for another thing I'm getting fed up with some of the mannerisms of the men, though on the whole they are a superior lot. We shall see. Of course you know me so well and will see herein the pattern of dissatisfaction working. When I become restless I try to change, as in my first parish I sought an outlet into the chaplaincy. However, we'll let time decide. Maybe at the moment I'm only a bit too griped and the mood may pass by. Part of it all is, of course, the army, which is full of things to irritate any and every man.

Today I saw some fine violets beside a mountain trail. They were hard to see and I suspect not many soldiers passing by noticed them, for there were things besides violets on that trail.

Katano is here with me at the moment. We just had our dinner. We made lemon powder drink to go with our canned spaghetti.

Tuesday Noon, April 10 Italy

The Stars and Stripes has been featuring the 442nd the last few days, so no doubt the newspapers at home have something to say about our present combat with the 5th Army near the Ligurian Sea. It's the same old experience though for us old-timers. I'm quite all right.

Last night I slept all of ten hours. I was nice and warm; one blanket and a raincoat underneath and two blankets and a Jerry shelter half on top. I was lying on a farm door so it was not too soft, but good enough. And this morning I've stuffed myself with cocoa and canned ham and eggs and potatoes (a C ration menu of the newer type).

Goma of the medics says that right now I look like one of Mauldin's GIs, except that I wear glasses and officer's insignia; he's referring of course to my several-days' beard and unkempt hair. But I did wash my face this a.m. and even washed out my extra pair of socks.

Wednesday Night, April 11

Yesterday I shaved but left on my moustache. I think I'll leave it grow until I get home; no doubt it will be pretty long by that time.

Thursday Evening, April 12

I had three women carry water to some of the boys, and I paid them in candies and C rations. Today one of the women wanted to give me some cow's milk, in return, I guess; but there's too much danger of getting "Maltese" fever from dairy products, so I had to say no.

On April 13, the 100th passed through the marble-supplying city of Carrara and continued on to Gragnana, where at noon an artillery barrage began just as they started to eat their first kitchen-cooked food in many a day. Two men of B Company, one from Maui and one from Denver, Colorado, were killed instantly by shell fragments, as the letters of condolence indicated. (For one I added, "I saw him shortly afterwards, since the medics and I were nearby at the time.") However, my letter home makes no mention of the six-hour shelling, which we waited out within the town's houses.

Friday Night, April 13 Italy

Today we received the bad news of the president's death. Only one thing struck a wrong note in the account: the statement that he had warned his friends not to mention his illness of the several past months. I hope Truman will be able to carry on creditably.

The next day, during a counterattack by the Germans near Castelpoggio, several of our men were killed and wounded, but the enemy was repulsed with many of their soldiers KIA or WIA or made prisoners.

Sunday, April 15

Sunday morning and all is well. I'll have to visit the companies today and have whatever little services are possible. But first I'll read the New Testament a bit before beginning.

Recently we had some Italian women come through the aid station; two were young. One of about 17 was dying when brought in; the other was badly wounded, one leg almost off and the other badly torn, and left abdomen and thigh pierced; but we gave her plasma and sent her to the hospital. She has a slight chance of living; she was 19. It's bad enough to see wounded men, but to treat wounded women is worse. These folks were at home eating supper when a shell or mortar came through the roof and through several floors into the ground floor room.

Two different soldiers at two different times have told me that I talk in my sleep. That's a new one for me but could be so, for I dream terrifically and seem to thresh about in sleeping. Probably it's a part of my homesickness. Could be!

Monday Morning, April 16

War news is hardly interesting—just gruesome. Yesterday I was able to have a very few services for a very few people. In the evening I censored a lot of mail for our Japanese-American engineers. [At this time members of our 232nd Engineer Company were serving as infantrymen up front.]

On this day and on April 18, we lost several men while patrolling in enemy-held areas. To the mother of one I wrote at the end of April, "While on patrol with other members of his company he was hit by enemy machine gun fire and died instantly. I went up with the party that carried his body from the hill to the rear."

Tuesday Night, April 17 Italy

Here's a humorous incident. Doc O'Konogi and I were staying in an Italian home, using a big bed with sheets. We noticed a pot under the bed, but of course we didn't use it. In the morning the old lady came in saying, "Permess" (Pardon), and stooped down, pulled out the pot, and then looked up with a toothless (or rather, to be exact, a two-teeth) grin, and said, "Niente!"—just the one Italian word (it means "nothing")—and out she walked. Doc and I decided that we should have used it just one night so as not to disappoint her, but we haven't.

In one village there hasn't been any formal school for almost two years.

Wednesday Night, April 18

Can't say as there's much to write about tonight. Chaplains Yamada, Higuchi, and I just had a little talk-fest, mostly about Chaplain's School.

Some time ago my jeep was hit by shell fragments, but not bad. Anyway, I can point out some holes in it. But I was safely in a house and my driver also, so no one was hurt.

Friday Noon, April 20 Italy

Lately I've been as irritable as a wet hen. I've been with one group too long. And I miss some of the old standbys like Doc Dahl. Now some of the officers seem to try to cut each other for this or that. Maybe it was always so, but when I was new I didn't notice it. So it goes!

I've been writing this as we've been talking about the war as we know it close-up, local settings and local boys. Not much fun.

The Germans have retaliated against partisan actions here in Italy. Last August they burned out a number of mountain villages. Evidently the Italian patriots thought we would be pushing through then and so harassed the Germans, but we didn't. So the German S.S. troops punished whole towns thus. The people are glad to finally see us. "We've waited a long time for you" is their greeting.

April 21 Italy

Just recently on the phone I heard that the Russians and Americans have linked up and that in Italy Bologna has fallen. That's good news, but with us we still have a war going on.

This is being written by imperfect candlelight in an Italian home. Near me someone is snoring away.

Tomorrow is Sunday, but I don't expect to have more than one small service with a few medics.

At this time I was having an unusual experience: I was in charge of a battalion aid station. Our companies were moving fast over the hills and were spread out so that the medics decided we should set up three separate centers through which to evacuate casualties. I agreed to take some ten aid men and litter bearers and establish a post in a village along the advance route least likely to need medical aid. A telephone wire was run from the main station through my post forward to an infantry group. At night we barricaded our small group inside a house and I slept with the field phone cradled on my chest—just like Captain Dahl used to do. No wounded came back through our sector, but at least we were ready if they had. This explains the mention of a phone in my letters of April 21 and 23. During combat I had no "private" access to any telephone.

Monday Midmorn, April 23

Yesterday I did not get around to writing. I was busy at the phone relaying messages. The only service I held was brief devotions for about 10 men here at the one aid station. Since Easter I've not been able to hold a real service. Looks like they want to end the Italian campaign by the time they mop up Germany. That suits me—and here there was an interruption for breakfast and a mad dash to contact some men.

One morning while in these hills I met a teenage girl leading a flock of sheep up the mountain toward new pastures; daily life continued for these poor peasants even with the war going on around them. After greeting her and pointing to my chaplain's insignia, I said, "Tu sei pastora" (You are a shepherdess).

"Si," she answered with a smile. (Yes.)

"Io sono pastore anche," I continued. (I am a shepherd, too; but *pastore* also means "pastor.")

"No," she replied, with a shake of her head, indicating that I certainly was not a shepherd.

"Si," I insisted. "Sono pastore d'anime; sei pastora d'animali" (Yes, I am a shepherd of souls, you are a shepherdess of animals). Slowly the light of understanding broke into a smile on her face, as she led her sheep forward and I turned back to my parishioners at the aid station.

At the time I did not know of it, but it was on April 21 that Daniel Inouye, who later became the senior senator from Hawaii, was severely wounded; units other than the 100th were meeting stiff resistance here and there as the Combat Team continued fighting up the boot of Italy. His *Journey to Washington* is worth reading. He was awarded the DSC for his heroic conduct on this day.[5]

> Friday Morning, April 27 Northern Italy
>
> Because of much moving and work I've not gotten around to writing to you. Last night I lay down without supper since my head was aching; now I'm rested and feel pretty good. You will of course have received the news of the breakthrough and the resultant fast moving.
>
> Right now I would enjoy a good hot bath, a shave, and then more sleep. You should see how dirty I am.
>
> The Italians have a greeting that sounds to us like "chow." As we go along the crowds keep yelling "chow, chow, chow," and it's like being called to eat. We get a good laugh out of it.
>
> And now we are moving again.

During this campaign I had not put off the writing of condolences. Already most such letters were written and in the hands of the rear echelon. We lost one more man on April 28, but that was not a combat death. On May 3, I wrote the soldier's mother at the Heart Mountain, Wyoming, Relocation Center, "In taking off his pack he accidentally set off a grenade he was carrying, and fragments of it severely injured him in the abdominal region. He died immediately and so suffered no pain; I talked with the company commander who was right there at the time."

> Saturday Afternoon, April 28 Italy (Northern)
>
> This a.m. it rained, and when it rains in Italy, it rains! From the knees down I was soaked, for besides hiking I did some wading.

Last night I had fried eggs and bacon, both Italian. And this a.m. I carried some hardboiled ones in my pocket. This part of Italy has cleaner villages and people, and also (maybe because) it is not much destroyed. Last night we heard a radio in an Italian home. And also we've had some white Italian bread today. Here there are many chestnut-haired folks, and a few redheads, and blondes. But of course we still see many dark-complexioned Italians. Most of the young girls have heavy and long braids.

Just had a shave by an Italian barber but left the mangy growth under my nose as it is.

The Italian partisans have saved us many lives by capturing many prisoners and liberating towns. In the north here people seem to take their politics more seriously than in the south.

Monday Morn, April 30

Yesterday I had three services, two of over 100.

You are much ahead of me in Bible reading, but in the next few days I intend to catch up. At the present I am not rushing around as much as I've had to this past week. And today's the end of the month—another chaplain's report to type and send in.

All of a sudden things moved fast in this Italian campaign and the 442nd had its share in the drive. Aunt Reta wrote of hearing us mentioned on the radio, and *Time* mentions us under the Italian War News. Belonging to such a unit makes it easier for folks at home to know where I am and what I'm doing.

Hiking along through liberated towns is something: crowds, flowers, eggs, nuts, wine. And flags hung everywhere. Often the American flags are homemade. I saw one with the 13 stripes running the wrong way [up and down, with some under the blue field], but the folks meant well.

Last night I had a shower, a bit cold, but nevertheless a treat, for it was the first time I washed completely this month. Once before I had the opportunity but was too busy to take time off.

In one place Katano and I walked to a little village on a hill; the Italian call such *paese*. I passed out cigarettes to the smokers and candy to all. One man said, "The Germans burned our village; the English give us cigarettes." It had been partially burned out because of partisan activity in the section. And to many, English and American seem the same.

In another place we met a man who had proof he is an American citizen. He came back to visit his home some years ago and could not get out of Italy again. During the war he kept his passport hidden and is now anxious to get back to the U.S.A. There are a number of such persons.

Last night I saw a part of the movie *Music for Millions*. It was not particularly interesting. Lately I've eaten a lot of rice. Up north here they have it, and we trade some of our rations for it.

Tuesday Night, May 1 Italy

Tonight I had a real Italian meal: rabbit, fried artichoke leaves, pasta (like thick noodles), doughnuts, nuts, wine, bread. The people said it was real Tuscan cooking—in oil—and it was excellent indeed. Now the women folks are all at another home and Kent and I are sharing the bedroom with the father and son. It's the Antichi family.

While the 100th was resting at Genoa, I drove back to visit our WIAs in the hospitals. As the above excerpt indicates, my driver and I spent the night just outside of Pisa with the family whose nine-year-old daughter I had swept off the street during enemy shelling there many months before. Most of May 2 was spent at hospitals and driving back so that I was not aware of the end of hostilities in Italy until the next day. My first thought was, I wonder where we go next. On May 4, our troops settled in at Novi Ligure to clean up, relax, and don garrison clothing. We stayed here until May 16.

Saturday, May 5 Italy

I'm sitting here trying to organize my thoughts for the battalion memorial service on the morrow. Now there will set in a wave of immorality since this campaign is finished. So many of the officers set a bad example with their drunkenness and lewdness. But of course the good are not affected by such conduct anyway.

Yesterday I did not get to writing at all. Just laziness, I guess. Already the higher-ups are bearing down on the enlisted men for military courtesy and the usual garrison rot. I don't like it at all.

It's a month now so I dare write that on April 5 Lt. Maehara[6] was killed in action. He was killed instantly. . . . He was a fine man all around. We lost too many of his type.

On Sunday, four hundred attended the memorial service for the One Puka Puka's honored dead. Colonel Miller attended, and of course our own CO, Lieutenant Colonel Conley. The regimental band added to the solemnities. Unfortunately I preserved no record of the details of this service, except that the altar was covered with red peonies.

Monday Night, May 7 Italy

This p.m. came news of the end of the European War. It doesn't affect me much since we knew it was coming. However, here I am away from my unit for several days visiting hospitals, so I won't be there for a service tomorrow—not until Thursday.

While on the tour of hospitals I visited old friends in Volterra. During May I made four hospital trips and counseled with 299 of our AJAs. I was back from this particular journey in time to hold a combined Victory and Ascension Day service on Thursday evening, but only a few attended since the main service would be on the following Sunday.

Sunday Morning, May 13

Today the division general has scheduled a parade for 11:00, so I must squeeze my church service into a half hour just after breakfast. Some of these leaders are not worth the space they take up, and the 92nd Div. General is one of such so far as I am concerned. He has declared today his VE Day—wouldn't give the men a day off before and instead of prayer schedules a parade! That's what I don't like about our army system; too many such can get near the top too easily.

Sunday Night, May 13 Novi Ligure

For some reason the parade was held this afternoon. It was an impressive ceremony, but I don't warm up to such things anymore. Many men received citations, a few posthumously. I was glad for the recognition the men thus received, though some of the reasons for citing seemed poor. Nowadays medals are given away with very little cause.

At the service [for the battalion, in the morning] I had a long prayer for the world, a shorter one for our nation, still shorter for our ideals, and finally a short one for our mothers. We knelt and the stones were hard, but I thought it good to thus humble ourselves. [We used a mimeographed sheet with the words of the hymn "Come, Thou Almighty King" and "Psalm 46" printed out; the meditation was on the scripture reading and concerned "prayer"; the title proclaimed this a "Service of Prayer for our Nation." Attendance was 550.]

Tonight Katano and I visited a Protestant family. I had met one of the men two days ago and had wanted to get to one of their services today but didn't. . . . We stayed a bit over an hour and enjoyed ourselves.

✯　✯　✯

Someone suggested that pictures ought to be taken of the graves of each of our men here in Italy. A captured German camera was given me, and I began visiting our American military cemeteries, beginning on May 14. At this time the graves had only a triangular wooden marker in place with the soldier's dog tag tacked to the top; the ground was neatly raked at each site but as yet no grass had grown. After much time and effort had been spent in the project, when we tried to send the photos home, the censors would not give us permission; not until proper markers were erected and grass covered each grave could such pictures be taken! By Saturday, May 19, Kent and I had traveled over 850 miles. On May 17, at the cemetery near Granaglione, I held funeral services for four of our men interred there.

While we were away the Combat Team (on May 16) was detached from the 92nd Division and trucked to Ghedi Airfield,[7] a distance of 125 miles. The Nisei were given a new task: processing prisoners of war.

On Saturday, May 19, I wrote a long, official letter to the chief chaplain of the Fifth Army; I felt that his office had harassed me too long.

Subject: Correction of Monthly Report for April 1945

1. Your office has called attention to the fact that on the monthly report under 7b only one witness was listed for the last baptism recorded there. If you will notice carefully the date of that last baptism is different from the others; at times conditions do not permit the exact fulfillment of the letter of the law. In this case it was not forgotten; if you desire the second witness for matter of record it will have to be the one who performed the baptism: Chaplain Israel A. S. Yost. If you desire me to add my name to this particular baptism, please advise.

2. Great pains have always been taken even under trying combat conditions to present reports that are accurate and complete, and in conformity with the ever-changing regulations of higher echelons. It would be greatly appreciated if consideration were given to men in the field in this matter of memoranda; at least indication might be given in such matters to the effect that reports in question might be perfectly accurate, and that the one correcting reports might be the one in error, not being fully aware of pertinent facts.

3. It is pointed out that baptisms are strictly ecclesiastical in nature, and that all rules governing the performance of the Sacrament are to be made only by the church of which the individual chaplain is a pastor. Because a directive from the Chaplain's Office requires two witnesses for such a thing does not bind me in the least, and I am perfectly free to perform this Sacrament without any witnesses. (Performance of marriages is a different thing, and for that rules are binding.) I do not mind listing witnesses for baptisms; but I point out that when I am called in question on this matter I insist that *no* witnesses are necessary. For convenience I comply with directives; but when my conduct of strictly ecclesiastical matters is called in question I shall in no uncertain terms remind you of my freedom as a pastor.

4. If this were the first correction of this nature it would be too insig-

nificant to bring to your attention. However, in twenty months of service with combat troops I have been again and again harassed in this matter of monthly reports. And from conversation with other chaplains I find I have not been alone.

I never heard anything further in this matter except that rumor has it that the matter was discussed at some length among the members of the top chaplain's staff.

Saturday Afternoon

I have 112 points officially. We have five battle stars. I might have gotten twelve more points by including Alberta [our foster child] but didn't think it fair.[8]

Service	27 months	27 points
Overseas	21 months	21
Battle Stars	5 x 5	25
Purple Heart	2 x 5	10
Legion of Merit	1 x 5	5
Children	2 x 12	<u>24</u>
		112

But I don't think it will apply to me at all, being an officer and a chaplain. I wouldn't be surprised if your intuition about the South Pacific is right. We'll see, though, and I'll be home before going to the Pacific, I'm sure. We were asked to indicate our preference: discharge immediately, after [the] emergency, reserve commission, regular army. Of course I asked for discharge as soon as possible. But I don't think this will affect me much yet either.

I've seen so many German prisoners I'm tired of seeing them.

Tomorrow I'm receiving one of our men into the Methodist Church of Ely, Nevada. I baptized him on Easter and now he's being received through me into this church as a full member.

Incidentally, last month I was alternate on the rotation list, and this month I probably would have been on the list, but you know they've stopped all that. At least I almost got to come home.

Sunday, Almost Dinner

At the regimental service this morning I had the sermon; I spoke of the Trinity and the Holy Spirit—not very well. But before, I discovered a company of another battalion having a physical exam; the officer who scheduled it said it had preference over church, so I hiked off to the colonel who backed me up.

Tonight we have a regimental song service scheduled. Chaplain Higuchi is in charge of that. At 1:00 I have a short service for those who were on duty this morning. Right now a soldier is coming in to check up on some records.

The Ghedi Airfield was near Brescia. We lived in tents in the midst of the dirt and the heat of summer; thankfully, the nights were cool. Kometani set up his dentist's tent and saw patients. I invited Katano to share mine. Our unit band played some evenings. After dark there was usually a movie to see. Books were available for reading. Off-duty men got passes for Milan and the 442nd had its own rest camp. High-point men anxiously awaited orders to go home.

Wednesday Morn, May 23 Near Brescia, Italy

Yesterday I met a few other 5th Army chaplains and the general consensus is that we chaplains are tired and want to get back home soon.

Just now a boy came in, worried about his family. He lost his brother in the last push and his mother died some months ago. His oldest brother and his father are sickly and his youngest brother is only ten. So.

Recently I got to talk with several German chaplains. They wear a Red Cross brassard with a purple stripe around the arm. However, many pastors and priests are in the army as enlisted men, not chaplains. I met one such who once had a Lutheran Church in Hartford, Conn. . . . But I have little desire to talk much with them. I'm sick of Germans, war, regimentation.

Thursday, Morn, May 24

In the army I must learn to mind my own business. I looked in on the prisoner of war camp and found the German chaplains needed some things. So I reported it to a higher office and now the higher-ranking chaplain has appointed me to coordinate the work at the POW camp in addition to my other duties. I have no stomach for the job and at the earliest opportunity shall ask to be relieved of the responsibility.

The area chief of chaplains arranged with me for him to visit with all POWs in the Fifth Army enemy concentration area who claimed to be pastors or priests in civilian life; he intended that they should be recognized as such and begin to serve within the POW camp as clergymen. I discovered that there were some such also among the officers—one major in the artillery said he was a Lutheran pastor. After they were assembled, the American chaplain asked me to introduce him to the group. In my best German I explained that Chaplain ———— was in charge of all American chaplains in the area and wanted to meet with them. However, I used the general term for a military chaplain in German and not the rank of our chief. He may not have known much German, but my superior did know that I had not used his military rank. He interrupted me; he requested that I tell them that he was *Colonel,* not *Chaplain* ——————. With an innocent face I turned to him and answered, "Chaplain ——————, I don't know the German word for 'colonel.'"

That was the only time he ever used me as an interpreter. Even had I known the word (or did I?), I would have introduced him as a chaplain, for in the U.S. Army we always address chaplains with their own title. He soon appointed someone else in the Corps of Chaplains to take over the responsibility of supervising religious work among the POWs.

Saturday we spent working on a certificate to be printed and sent to the next of kin of each of our men who died overseas. These 13 x 10¼-inch memorials listed, in addition to name and rank, the awards presented to each and were inscribed with the words of John 15:13: "Greater love hath no man than this, that a man lay down his life for his friends." The certificates for those who died after the 100th Battalion became a part of the 442nd were signed by Lt. Col. Jack E. Conley; certificates for those who were KIA when the 100th was still "Separate" were signed by me. There was one other distinction: those for men of the "old" 100th bore the patch of the 34th Division and the crest with the words "Remember Pearl Harbor" instead of the 442nd "Statue of Liberty" patch and the "Go for Broke" crest.

On Sunday I held nine brief services, playing "Jesus, Lover of My Soul" and "Savior, Like a Shepherd Lead Us" on the field organ as the men sang. For some reason I did not list these meetings in my May report. Apparently I forgot about them; it is possible that this happened other months and means that, if anything, my monthly reports recorded minimum numbers rather than inflated figures.

On Memorial Day, Chaplains Higuchi and Yamada took groups to cemeteries for religious ceremonies; I conducted the service at our bivouac with one thousand attending. Our band played a prelude and accompanied the singing of "America" at the opening of the hour and of the national anthem at the close. The message was based on John 15:13, the verse on the certificates mentioned above. A rifle squad fired a volley and taps was sounded. All company guidons and the regimental and national colors were displayed; a cross of greens formed a backdrop behind the altar. Because of rain at ten a.m., the activities were postponed until two p.m. I dressed up for the first time overseas, wearing an Eisenhower jacket and all my decorations. I had to borrow crosses from

Higuchi, captain's bars from O'Konogi, and US's [a brass pin that stands for U.S.] from Katano. A number of officers commented favorably on the day's observance.

> Thursday Afternoon, May 31 Italy—near Brescia
>
> This a.m. Kent worked on what will be his last monthly chaplain's report, for he's slated to go home very soon. Just before dinner Capt. Kometani replaced a filling of mine; he's due to go home very shortly, too. Both have been away for over three years.

On this date thirty-eight enlisted men (no officers) with the highest Adjusted Service Rating scores left Ghedi to go home; at least thirty-four of them were of the 100th. On Saturday I wrote that Kent was scheduled to leave with the next group (in fact he did leave on June 4) and that by the end of the next week I'd probably be *the* old-timer. All of this was quite depressing, most of all because I had no idea what rules applied to chaplains. At least for the time being, both Doc Kometani and Etsuo Katano were staying—but I felt that they ought soon also get orders as they deserved. Meanwhile I had unfinished work that had to be attended to: services to conduct, memorial certificates to complete and send, letters to write; and I could visit old Italian friends and seek out new ones. The first duty was to prepare for my own services and those of one of the AJA chaplains who would be away the coming Sunday.

The Combat Team remained at Ghedi Airfield until June 14. My attitude during these days was summed up in a letter: "Report for the Day on the Home-Going Situation: Policy of watchful waiting being pursued since no information is available." One day I spent eleven dollars for a ValPack (army suitcase), my first such in two years and five months in the Army of the United States; I put the Eisenhower jacket and most of my clothing in it and remarked, "I carry a lot less now than I used to." One evening I viewed the orientation film *On to Tokyo;* its message that some of the men in the European theater would go directly to the Pacific fighting without a furlough at home almost made me volunteer for duty in the Far East. Softball games in which I either umpired or pitched for the officers' team were great fun. In Brescia I visited the Waldensian pastor and the Salvation Army, learning that the latter was banned by Mussolini in 1939.

Since an electric wire had been strung to my wall tent, I had light for reading and writing after dark. PX rations kept us supplied with chocolates and candy, and the army chow was good except that we had no fresh milk—chocolate milk was the drink I missed. Showers were available at the bivouac or in town; though the sticky and dusty weather should have prompted me to a daily bath, I managed to go unwashed for a week at a time, and I never got to the nearby swimming facilities. Packages with their gifts for children kept arriving and letters crossed the Atlantic in good time. An officer hospitalized in the States wrote his thanks for my helping him get to the aid station quickly and for my prayer for him there. I was still collecting souvenirs and sending them home, including a set of German field telephones. Most important, I made an important decision about the future.

> Wednesday Evening, June 13 Brescia, Italy
>
> I cleared out a few more letters today. And instead of answering some I simply disposed of them, because from now on I'll gradually sever my ties with the Japanese-Americans. Of course where an answer is expected I am polite enough to answer. But I'll be plenty busy with the church in years to come and won't be able to keep up too much correspondence with the old 100th men. So I might as well start now.

This decision reflected my philosophy of life: as a called and ordained minister of the Gospel I felt I had to apply all of my energies to the Christian responsibility at hand insofar as this would be possible. During the war years my responsibility was to the 100th; now that the conflict was ended I had to look forward to a different call to service.

The June 13 letter also stated what was what with the unit I was still serving: "Rumors are flying fast but as yet there is no clear picture of what will be done with the Regimental Combat Team. Time will tell. The army keeps some things secret until the last moment."

Notes

1. With World War II nearly over, there was some question as to why the 442nd was called back from France and given the assignment of attacking a nearly impregnable castle on the Austrian border. The initiative was that of Gen. Mark Clark. Clark wrote in his memoir that he personally asked Generals Marshall and Eisenhower for the 442nd so as to include them in his spring offensive (Clark, 419). Fearful that the Germans would use their twenty-five divisions and the six fascist Italian divisions in a stronghold in the Bavarian Alps to prolong the war, he resolved to destroy the remaining German divisions before they could move into a defensive position (18).

2. During a horrendous battle, Pfc. Sadao Munemori threw his body onto an enemy grenade, saving his comrades (Murphy, 257). A statue of him now stands as a memorial to the 100th Battalion in Pietrasanta in northern Italy. Although eight thousand members of the 100th Bn and the 442nd RCT were decorated during World War II, none received

a Medal of Honor until after the war, and it was given posthumously. Fifty-two of the men received the next highest award, the Distinguished Service Cross. Later, thanks to the efforts of Honolulu attorney Ed Ichiyama, veteran of the 442nd RCT, legislation was introduced in Congress for the records to be reviewed and the medal awards upgraded. On June 21, 2000, twenty new congressional Medal of Honor awards (fifteen posthumously) were made by President Bill Clinton to AJAs in the 100th and 442nd.

3. The name used at that time.

4. The use of the 92nd Infantry in combat was an experiment to see if an all-black regiment with some black officers could do as well in an integrated army as an AJA unit. In contrast to the 442nd, which was made up of highly educated young men, the 92nd had an illiteracy rate of 13 percent. The men had different motivations. "In contrast to the black soldiers who had little hope of any gain from proving themselves in battle, the Japanese-Americans believed they could demonstrate they were loyal Americans by shedding their blood for their country" (Duus, 228).

5. His Distinguished Service Cross was upgraded to a congressional Medal of Honor in 2000.

6. Lt. Saburo Maehara.

7. Ghedi Airfield was a Fifth Army enemy concentration area for POWs.

8. While Yost was overseas, he and his wife welcomed a teenage foster daughter, M. Alberta MacKenzie (now Whitman), into their family. Yost did not meet her until he returned home after discharge from the army.

THIRTEEN

Three More Months

O N JUNE 14, 1945, the 442nd, relieved of all POW duties, folded up its tents and in American and confiscated German vehicles moved to Lecco, sixty miles away. While the regiment settled in, I took a jeep ride up to a hill overlooking the city and lake; the view was delightful. After the evening meal I strolled through the streets, handing out gifts to the children I met. One little three-year-old was shy of me, until I gave her a doll and some candy. Apparently my walrus moustache scared some of the kids. In the morning I discovered that this was an industrial center as well as a resort town: long before I wanted to get up, whistles and bells awoke me. One plant's siren made me think of air raids. A half hour later the same racket started up again.

The first letter home from Lecco revealed discouragement.

> Thursday Night, June 14
>
> Watchful waiting is still my theme; I've heard nothing for or against an early return for me to the States. I'm still sweating it out, as they say in the army. But I have definitely made up my mind that I'll ask for a transfer if I'm not sent home this month, for I no longer care to stay with the 442nd.

Old friend Kometani had left for home. Our regiment was now designated a Category I unit for continued service under the Fifth Army in the Mediterranean theater. On our first Sunday in our new vacationland, only 124 turned out for the three services. On my twenty-ninth birthday, June 18, I wrote, "This organization is so different from the old 100th. Now you speak to boys and they don't even answer; they seem surprised when I greet them on the street. Usually they salute but say nothing. I want to get out of this outfit as soon as possible. I'm fast losing my sympathy."

On June 19, new orders classified the Combat Team as a Category

II unit to be transferred to the Pacific or Asiatic theaters, and a full training program began for combat against Japan. That same day I met Father Richard Newman, a Free State Irishman in charge of a boys' school in nearby Pusiano; he agreed to hear the confessions of our Catholic men on Saturday afternoons in my tent. I tried to be patient, keeping busy with such details as sending out the memorial certificates, visiting with Katano among civilians, enjoying the Italian lake country, and just being with our men and officers.

GI movies were shown in the Lecco theater. One night along with the feature *Thunderbird, Son of Flicka,* a short film about the 100th was shown; it included scenes of the communion service at Orciano a year before. We all went swimming at the GI beach on Lake Como and rowing across it. As always I had free use of the chaplain's jeep, with Henry Nakasone temporarily filling in as my driver—I told myself that I would soon be leaving the One Puka Puka and did not need a regular assistant.

June 22, at a meeting of the Fifth Army chaplains, we were briefed as to the future: because of a shortage of seven hundred chaplains, none now in the corps could hope for discharge for many months; low-point padres would see Pacific service soon; high-pointers would remain in Europe for some months; and, of course, there were loopholes in the prediction. I reacted thus: "Of course I'm disappointed, but I'll get over it, if past experience indicates future reactions. But I am so tired." That I did not apply the general statements to myself was indicated by my note on June 29: "Today I cleaned up my things—it's amazing how few things I have left—just in case I ever do get orders to go home." On July 1, the rumor spread that high-point officers would leave in the next ten days, but whether this included chaplains no one knew. On July 3, the regimental CO informed me that he was willing to release me but wanted the two AJA pastors to stay. On July 6, I learned that the Fifth Army had to approve all transfers of chaplains. I knew that I was by no means a secret weapon, but nevertheless the military was keeping my future veiled in mystery.

Association with Father Newman helped to take my mind off the uncertainty of my status. I enjoyed conversing with him; his viewpoint was so civilian and Italian. He inquired if I took a nap most afternoons as he did! His life story was simple: he had come to Rome as a student for the priesthood, was ordained, and continued living in Italy as a member of the Rosminian Order, but kept his Irish Free State citizenship. Because he insisted upon visiting some captured English fliers early in the war, local authorities had wanted to treat him as an enemy; only with difficulty had he been able to convince them that although he spoke English, he was loyal to his Ireland, which had chosen neutrality when World War II began. He was as fine a Christian minister as I had ever met.

One day Brother Newman and I had tea with the Italian lady who had suggested that I ask him to hear the confessions of my Nisei. She and I had previously discussed the differences between Protestants and Roman Catholics. Upon this occasion she asked Father Newman how the chaplain could be a true pastor since he was married and had children. The question was posed in Italian, and the reply was given quickly, also in Italian: "My dear woman, it is not for you to question whether Chaplain Yost is truly a pastor. Do you not know that in the early church priests were married?" Then without any comment to me about the query, my Irish friend turned to me and asked quietly in English, "Chaplain, would you like some more tea?" He, of course, knew I had understood the verbal exchange.

Lecco is located in a beautiful area of Italy. The mountains frown majestically down upon the lakes. Of an evening, one cannot get one's fill of looking at the truly picturesque green and brown mountains. By jeep I got to see Lake Maggiore and the towns of Stressa and Como and the farming country all around. Once we drove to Milan on business and took time to go sightseeing. This would have been a real vacation if my wife had been with me. Katano and I often visited the Bodega family, where Mrs. Bodega was the perfect English hostess. The days passed, with irritations and surprises. Only eight men responded to the eighty invitations to meet with Father Newman for confession, but the Irish priest did not mind. On July 1, worship was poorly attended, but the CO, the executive officer, and several lieutenants of the 100th were on hand, and Lieutenant Kodama played the organ as he had so often done before.

On the Fourth of July, we paraded through Lecco (in itself a good event and one I usually enjoyed), but our band had been detached from us, and without music the exercise resembled a funeral march. Afterwards decorations were awarded, for the most part to noncombatants, but many of us had become disappointed with the manner in which decisions were made concerning medals and felt that the honors had been cheapened for the recipients.

Then on Saturday afternoon, July 9, when I was "just sitting around," I received a phone call: Chaplain George Aki, a third Japanese American padre, had arrived from the States; I was to bring him to Lecco from

Verona whither he had flown by plane from Naples. Driver Nakasone and I set off immediately over the fine *autostrada* Mussolini had built in northern Italy; within three hours I would meet my replacement, the first real step in the process of getting home.

After a while I decided that Nakasone was not driving fast enough. Since the war was over, speed limits were again in effect, and my driver was keeping to the law. We stopped and exchanged places. The miles sped by with me behind the wheel, driving in excess of the military limit. I breezed by a soldier lying in a ditch by the side of the highway, apparently enjoying the fine summer day. Then we slowed down for a posted checkpoint, an ordinary procedure for the MPs to scrutinize travel orders to prevent unauthorized use of military vehicles.

The driver of the jeep in front of us was a British officer; I pulled up close behind him. It dawned on me that we had just gone through a speed trap, for the Limey was loudly protesting the speeding ticket the American sergeant was handing him. I realized that the soldier in the ditch was part of the system of clocking how fast traffic was moving! When the MP approached our jeep and asked to see our travel orders, I exchanged places with Nakasone so that he could resume driving. I expected to be censured for driving, for technically I had no permission to do so. But instead the lawman noticed my chaplain's cross and said, "We shouldn't arrest a chaplain, should we?"

"For what?" was my response.

"For driving in excess of the speed limit. You were clocked at forty-nine miles per hour." The MP began writing out a ticket in my name as the Britisher, still sputtering, drove off with his. The fine would be fifty dollars, I learned from the smiling policeman. He seemed friendly enough, but he gave no indication that he would tear up my ticket. I would be informed later on where to settle the matter.

Henry had begun chuckling as soon as he became aware I was being fined. As he drove off with me seated properly in the passenger seat, he burst out laughing and said, "Chaplain, if I had still been driving, I would have gotten that ticket." With my approval he drove the rest of the way to the airport at a more modest pace.

My replacement, Pastor George Aki, was among the West Coast Nisei who were swept up and placed in relocation centers early in the war. That he was an American by birth and an ordained Christian pastor gave him no special consideration in the eyes of the bigots who had pressured for the removal of all persons of Japanese ancestry from their homes in the Western Defense Command area. He had volunteered with the Corps of Chaplains from his confinement and was eventually sent overseas to take my place in the One Puka Puka. He had his orders to take over, but as yet I had not received any indication where I was to go or when.

Naturally the new chaplain assisted me at the Sunday services the day after his arrival. I expected that within the week I could fully orient and train him to fill my shoes. He met Father Newman, my Lecco friends, and the personnel of the 100th. On Tuesday I turned all my battalion records over to him and packed all my belongings in anticipation of receiving travel orders. On Thursday, July 12, our battalion moved in truck convoy south to the Pisa area. Here the new chaplain and I toured nearby towns and I introduced him to my old friends among the local civilians. On Sunday, July 15, I preached for the last time to my AJA buddies—to men of the separate companies only, because all the men of the 100th were busy militarily that last day. My parting word to the men was that I hoped they would remember me as an evangelical Christian.[1] Although the men of the 100th could not attend worship on my final day with them, they had surprised me that morning. At six a.m., an enlisted man walked into the tent Chaplain Aki and I were sharing; he held an upturned helmet in his hands. "Chaplain," said the soldier, "we men of the 100th don't want you to go home broke because of your reckless speeding. The boys have taken up a collection that should take care of paying your fine."

"But," I spluttered, not yet fully awake, "you know I can't take money from enlisted men. It's against the regulations."

"Well, you can do as you please, but here's the money." He dumped the helmet full of Italian paper money into my lap and promptly left. I had not even recognized just who it was that brought the money, nor did any individual admit donating any of it to me. I counted the bills and they more than covered the fine I expected to pay. In my letter home I gave credit to the medics for a gift of twenty-five dollars and to a group of old-timers for eighty dollars.

The arrest never was reported through channels, for I never heard anything at all about it. In my mind's eye I could picture the MP watching me leave the checkpoint and laughing at me as he tore up the part of the form he had kept. After all, it was not often that a chaplain could be caught in anything that was very wrong; how could anyone, even an MP, act disrespectfully toward a chaplain when in Italy the chaplains were probably the most highly thought of among all the military groups.

Sunday afternoon, after signing over the tally-out sheet transferring the "¼-ton 4x4 and ¼-ton trailer" to Aki, I reported to the 432nd Anti-aircraft Artillery Automatic Weapons Battalion (Separate) in Florence. To Peggy on that day I wrote,

> The *AW* is for automatic weapons, the *AAA* for antiaircraft artillery, and note that the APO is the same as for the 442nd Inf. Seems funny that after two years I'm back in the AAA, just like back in [Camp] Davis. So far as I can figure out this is a break for me, so just have patience. . . . All these men have been overseas a long, long time. But it will seem strange to be in an outfit other than the infantry. . . . The 442nd certainly treated me well. . . . This present one will be up to par too, I know. I've been fortunate in my army assignments thus far.

The Special Orders No. 189, which included my transfer, were from Fifth Army and dated July 8 and effective July 11, but I did not get to the new unit until July 15. I suspect that because the 100th was the last of the Combat Team to leave Lecco, these orders were not delivered until we were settled in at Pisa.

The next day I visited the batteries of my new unit—batteries instead of companies—and introduced myself to the first sergeants. Since most of the men—all with enough points to go home—went out of bivouac on passes each day, this was like a replacement depot and I had little work to do. On Tuesday I went to the PX to buy some clothing; I had only two pairs of pants and two shirts at the time. I met chaplain friends in the area around Florence and a number of buddhaheads. I found the officers of the 432nd quite congenial. In the evenings GI movies were free to all. In Florence were many cultural and historic spots to visit.

By Wednesday I learned that chaplains were being flown to the Holy Land before being sent home. On July 19, my name appeared on the list of eighteen padres ordered to Palestine on temporary duty for a period of seven days, excluding travel time, on or about July 20. On army transportation we chaplains went by way of Bologna to the airport at Verona. That night we swam in the clean, blue, warm waters of nearby Lake Garda. Friday, the 20th, after watching planes take off for several places but not Palestine, we chaplains hitched rides to Venice and managed to squeeze in three-quarters of an hour of sightseeing.

Saturday, on a C-47, we bounced our way to Athens, Greece, where we stayed overnight. Sunday, beginning at Tel Aviv, we began our tour of the Holy Land: that is a story in itself. By the end of the week we were flying around the pyramids, and after a short stop at Cairo, proceeded to Athens for our overnight stay—one dollar at the King George

Hotel. The entire holiday cost about ninety dollars—just about the amount of my farewell gift from the men of the One Puka Puka.

Monday Morning, July 30 Italy

Here I am in Italy again and compared to Greece and Palestine it seems like home. While waiting for transportation back to the unit I visited the 100th and had breakfast with the officers. Afterward I spoke with Chaplain Aki. He's getting along well with the 100th. Tomorrow my chaplain's report is due. It won't look so good since I've done very little work this month with transferring to a new unit and the trip to Palestine.

The first half of August, I continued as the chaplain of the AAA Battalion: two Sunday worship services, one Sunday hymn sing, a stockade service that reached 115 GI prisoners, three visits to hospitals to see 39 men, seven personal conferences. On August 1, I conducted the funeral of a soldier killed in a traffic accident. Most of what I did was for transient soldiers since the AAA unit was almost depopulated. As always I had a jeep for transportation and an assistant, T/5 Julius B. Papa. I kept in touch with Chaplain Harold C. Koch, with whom I had spent most of my time while in Palestine. Chaplain Aki visited me, and now he was the one who provided the transportation on our visits to old friends. On August 8, I wrote to Peggy, "Right at the moment I know less about getting home than I did three weeks ago." On August 10, I wrote, "Everyone is praising the atom bomb; it makes me shudder! Of course it will save American lives, but what a thing to be set loose on the world! But all of war is inhumane, unreasonable, and unchristian."

On August 15, the extra edition of *The Stars and Stripes* (Mediterranean) carried eight and one-quarter-inch headlines, "PEACE AT LAST." That same Wednesday, the Florence Redeployment Training Area Headquarters Special Orders No. 63 listed my name as attached to the 27th Replacement Depot for transshipment to the United States. This indicated that ever since I had been assigned to the AAA Battalion, I was actually no longer under the Fifth Army but in the process of being sent home. All 150 officers and men on these orders had over one hundred points ASRS [adjusted service rating score]. Effective August 17, I was in line to board a ship to cross the Atlantic. I was number eight on the list, one of the twenty-five officers, and the only chaplain. One of the majors was designated troop commander.

The day I learned of my good fortune, August 17, was also the date of the Service of Thanksgiving for World Peace in the Florence military area. It was not much of a service: prayers by two chaplains (one, my friend Harold Koch), remarks by a full colonel, two numbers by an army band, and the singing of "America the Beautiful" and "The Star Spangled Banner" by the audience.

On August 18, I reported to the 27th Replacement Depot and was assigned to Battalion 114, Company 562; I signed that I objected to traveling by air—probably because I thought surface transportation would get me home sooner. This day's letter home instructed my wife to stop writing to me and to tell others in the family the same. On August 20, I visited the 100th for the last time, saying good-bye to CO Mitsuyoshi Fukuda—the One Puka Puka finally had a buddhahead as its leader. August 23, I posted my last letter home from sunny Italy. Water Movement Orders RN934-21-45, dated 21 August, were in my hands, and my destination was Indiantown Gap, Pennsylvania, the discharge center closest to my home in Nazareth, Pennsylvania.

> Shipment will move on or about 25 August from present overseas station to a reception station or Separation center in the United States to be named by indorsement [sic] to this order by the commanding general of the port at which shipment is debarked.
>
> Upon receipt of these orders each unit commander will immediately have the Class A Agent Officer obtain the necessary United States currency at the Finance Office. It is mandatory that all Lire notes be exchanged for United States currency prior to departure from this theater and that a proper certificate be carried by each individual.

On August 25 at Leghorn, 713 enlisted men and 33 officers, including 66 men and 6 officers bound for Indiantown Gap, boarded the SS *George Handley,* a 441-foot-long Liberty ship of 10,920 tons. During the 4,330-mile voyage to Norfolk, Virginia, this cargo vessel, built in 1943, laid over at Oran (Algeria) for six hours on August 28, for twenty hours at Benisaf (Algeria) on August 28 and 29, and broke down for several hours in the middle of the Atlantic Ocean. The passengers resented each delay, especially the one at Benisaf, which rumor said was caused by some sort of Arab holiday during which the North Africans would not load our ship. We high-pointers were anxious to get home. Many got seasick and stayed topside during most of the crossing; each day fewer diners came to the officers' mess.

As the only chaplain on board, I had two duties: conduct worship on the three Sundays and be available for personal conferences. An average of 172 attended the general Protestant service each week, and a total of 60 turned out for the two Sunday-evening devotional gatherings. Each

Lord's Day a Roman Catholic officer led his co-religionists in the recitation of the rosary. No one asked for any Jewish rites. About ten fellows consulted me officially, but only one of them had a serious problem; it involved conflict with an officer who had charge of a work detail to which the soldier concerned was assigned. In part the problem reflected the circumstances of the voyage: just about all of us were veterans detached from our units and coming back as strangers to the others accompanying us.

The GI on the work detail had objected to the profanity used by the junior officer in command of the motley group. He explained, "When we were in combat we never had officers who swore at us as this one does. When I told him that, he got mad and swore even worse at all of us. Some of the others agreed with me but were afraid to speak out. I don't know this officer, and he doesn't know me. But he has my name and serial number, and I'm afraid he'll wait and try to have me court-martialed after we reach the mainland and all my witnesses have scattered to their homes. Can you help me, Chaplain?"

I assured him that I could. I told the story to the lieutenant colonel who was serving as the troop commander; he was a high-pointer like the rest of us and a stranger to each of us, as each of us was a stranger to him. He called in the foul-mouthed lieutenant, verbally reprimanded him, and warned him not to act in such a manner again. In a normal situation, all involved would have considered the matter settled.

However, the next morning, while I was shaving in the lavatory, the reprimanded officer came in and began griping out loud about the poor discipline on the transport, speaking to no one in particular but making sure that I heard him. After ignoring his pettiness for a while, I addressed him directly and ordered him to be quiet or I would take him to the troop commander for his lack of military courtesy. He shut up.

Later, at mess, he began again in my hearing, this time stating that he would like to meet some of the enlisted men on board when everyone was out of uniform, implying that he would beat up a few of them. Lt. James Williams, unaware of the mixed-up situation, glared at him and spoke up sharply, "Lieutenant, I know some guys who would like to beat you up after we are out of uniform; you'd soon learn who's going to beat up whom." The other officer had nothing further to say.

Jim Williams was the only one I really got acquainted with on the *Handley*. He was from Philadelphia and, like me, headed for the Gap [Ft. Indiantown Gap military base]. As we chatted day after day I discovered that this tank commander had high ideals. Later on I officiated at his wedding and stood as the sponsor at the baptism of his only child, Charles Arthur. Even though we lived too far apart after the war to visit back and forth, we continued corresponding through the years.

After eighteen days on the sea, our tired Liberty ship reached Norfolk, where we read the message, "WELCOME HOME WELL DONE," painted in large, white letters on the ocean side of the dock. After a night at Camp Patrick Henry, on September 11, we boarded trains to proceed to our several destinations. Williams and I shared a seat as we headed for eastern Pennsylvania by way of the Delmarva peninsula. I remember so well how he turned from gazing out the window and said to me, "Look at all those fields, miles and miles of them, and not a single mine in one of them." He summed up my own feelings of thankfulness at finally arriving back home. Here it was safe to walk anywhere at all without fear of being blown to bits by a careless step.

On September 14, by Special Orders No. 228 of the Third Service Command at Ft. Indiantown Gap Military Reservation, eight of us officers were transferred to the separation center. I inquired about the status of returning chaplains and was assured that all officers except certain medical specialists were eligible for mustering out. On September 16 and 17, we were "processed" from building to building, going through "Records," "X-ray," "Medical," "Finance," "Counseling," "OR Branch" (was this "Officers' Reserve Corps" or what?), and finally "Signing Papers."

I was informed that I would revert to inactive status on December 3. I signed a financial settlement paper by which I agreed to pay the United States for seventy-five meals in August at 25 cents a meal ($18.15) and the government allotted me $6.80 for travel home (at 8 cents a mile). After I was home in Nazareth, I received Special Orders No. 234, dated September 20, in which my date for becoming a civilian was changed from December 3 to November 30.

The homecoming must have been wonderful, probably occurred on September 18, 1945, and involved the shaving off of the handlebar moustache, but no one recorded any of the details—after two years of writing down events! Our two-year-old son had to get used to having a father around; the three-year-old daughter apparently adjusted easily. In addition, a teenage foster daughter had joined the family while I was overseas.

The possibility of being called back into active service because of bureaucratic mismanagement in the separation procedure kept recurring in my thinking. Therefore my wife and I, after visiting her folks on

Maryland's Eastern Shore, journeyed to Washington, D.C., to consult with personnel of the Office of the Chief of Chaplains. There, officials assured us that I was free to accept a civilian parish and to forget the chaplaincy.

By the end of November, the Lutheran parish consisting of St. Paul's in Tower City and St. Peter's in Reinerton, both in the Pennsylvania county of my birth, called me.[2] The chaplain of the 100th became Pastor Yost again, explaining to parishioners that he had been named "Israel" since that had been his grandfather's given name, received in accordance with the Pennsylvania German custom of using Bible names, many of them from the Old Testament.

Notes

1. By "evangelical Christian" he meant a person whose life is centered on the Gospel of Jesus Christ. He was not referring to a fundamentalist theology or a political movement.

2. "Called" means that the parish contracted with him to be their pastor.

Epilogue

ECHOES OF the military reached me in my parish from time to time. From the Office of the American Provost Marshal, Headquarters Florence Command in Italy came a copy of a letter dated September 15, 1945, praising Japanese American soldiers for their exemplary behavior in the previous months.[1]

Then a personal letter from an officer in Italy, dated November 23, 1945, spoke of the problems cropping up among the men still serving overseas.

[T]he moral state is not so good. . . . We are way down in strength, approximately 2000 at the most and so you can see what handicaps we are having in our work of guarding PWs. The men are being worked very hard and they are complaining, but they are getting used to it and so we needn't worry about it. They have no complaints in comparison with the men who have seen real combat.

I saw the 66–70 pointers (enlisted men) off this morning. I think they are going to catch the aircraft carrier now in Naples. They were stuck in the Staging Area in Pisa for over a week and a half and you can imagine their disgust at their predicament. . . .

Getting many letters stating the difficult time the evacuees are having in the relocation centers since they are being kicked out of the centers in a very high-handed manner. I wish I were there to stop some of the dealing some of our people are getting. It makes my blood boil when they tell us that they are going to take extra care of servicemen's families and relatives. We have written to Mr. Dillon Myers but it doesn't seem to do any good since he is just the big shot and not in direct contact with the people in the relocation centers. Hope the people do not have to suffer too much. . . .

The many marriages which are coming in for our men is appalling. So many of them apply and many of them are rejected but there are enough that come through to make me worry about the future status and problems that shall be theirs too soon. . . . The most pitiful cases are those in which the women are pregnant. They take the responsibility and wish to marry, but still, it may have been someone else's fault—and so you could imagine the problems that grow out of this status of occupation.

The ordinary citizen back on the Mainland had little idea of the problems caused when troops trained for combat, composed largely of young men, had to remain overseas to serve as occupation troops. In addition, Nisei soldiers were worrying about the resettlement of their families in the continental United States; it was not proceeding as humanely and smoothly as the authorities would have everyone believe.

One day a package arrived from overseas. Inside was a dainty demitasse china service (cups and accessories) decorated with silver.[2] It came from some of the Nisei still on duty in occupied territory.

The letter from the War Department, dated June 5, 1946, remains an enigma to this day. It was forwarded to me from Nazareth, Pennsylvania.

> There is transmitted herewith the decoration awarded you by the Italian Government. The citation relating to this award is being forwarded under separate cover. The acceptance of this award has been approved and the approval made a matter of record in the War Department.
>
> BY ORDER OF THE SECRETARY OF WAR
>
> s/ Edward Fox
> Adjutant General
> 1 Incl
> Military Valor Medal

The citation reads thus.

> No. 2370
> WAR DEPARTMENT
>
> Humbert of Savoy, Prince of Piedmont, Lieutenant General of the Realm, by His Decree under date of September 15, 1945, in view of Royal Decree No. 1423 of November 1932 and successive modifications; upon the suggestion of the Secretary of State for War, has conferred, on his own motion, the MILITARY VALOR CROSS upon Capt. Yost, Israel A. S.
>
> In the Italian Campaign he distinguished himself by valor and a splendid spirit of self-sacrifice. The Secretary of State for War therefore issues the present document as proof of the honorific insignia conferred.
>
> Rome, October 5, 1945

With the blue-ribboned cross came the original citation in Italian, bearing the impression of the seal of the Ministero della Guerra at the bottom.

Precisely why such a decoration was sent to me, I do not know. In the "Battalion Records" printed at the end of *Ambassadors in Arms* (Murphy 1954), only five recipients of it are listed: Farrant L. Turner, Young O. Kim, Irving M. Akahoshi, Masao Awakuni, and Kaoru Moto. Since the recorder did not know of my award, it is probable that others, too, were omitted from the list. That I am named only as a captain and not as a chaplain adds to the mystery. Perhaps the medal really belongs to someone else, for all the soldiers honored by Prince Umberto were highly respected by their buddies in the One Puka Puka.

When, in 1946, the Combat Team returned to the United States, President Harry S. Truman reviewed the troops at the White House and presented the Presidential Unit Citation to the men. Although someone telephoned me an invitation to participate in the march down Pennsylvania Avenue to attend the ceremonies, I decided there was not enough time to arrange for someone to take over the Sunday duties in my parish. Of course I would have liked to again be a part of the old unit, but, in keeping with my basic philosophy, I had to set priorities: my first loyalty at the time was to my parish.[3]

Even though adjustment to civilian life gradually crowded out thoughts of the war, from time to time vivid memories surfaced. The many souvenirs sent to the Mainland had arrived safely, including a German helmet with the former owner's unit insignia colorfully painted on it, but I regretted that my own helmet was no longer in my possession; somewhere along the route home an overzealous official had insisted that it was government property and had to be turned in. Of all the paraphernalia of war, the American helmet was the GI's best friend: for protection, like the one from which a bullet sheared off most of the rim but left the wearer unscathed; for carrying water as well as serving as a wash basin; for digging a foxhole when no shovel was available; for cooking, especially among buddhaheads, who liked to steam local vegetables with their army rations; for sitting on during the ten-minute hourly break on a march, or during a worship service; for a baptismal font in the hands of a chaplain; for an overnight container for glasses, wallet, personal effects —to be grabbed up quickly on orders to move out.

Some reminiscences had lost the tags of time and place: the premonition of danger one dark night, the soldier who worried about breaking God's law, the combat infantryman's feeling of kinship with the enemy, the heartaches of displaced AJAs, and the uniqueness of the men with whom I had served.

Kent Nakamura and I had spent a long day visiting buddies in hospitals and had misjudged the time required for the return trip to the 100th. It may have been that we lost an hour or so waiting for our turn to cross a river on a pontoon bridge. Darkness came while we were still on a narrow, winding route in the mountains. The jeep's cat's eyes provided no light to see the course ahead. Because a stone barrier marked the outer edge of the road, we felt reasonably safe as we inched along, both of us wide-awake and trying to sense each turn in the road. Suddenly I yelled for Kent to stop, not knowing why but aware of some danger ahead; the mountain fell away on the passenger's side—my position. I got out of the jeep and took a few steps directly in front of our vehicle. There, the protecting wall on the roadside had been knocked down; if we had proceeded straight ahead we would have driven through the gap and off into empty space. Somewhat shook up I returned to my seat and told Kent to turn sharply to the left. Were there other breaks in the safety barricade? We never found out; for the rest of the descent Kent hugged the side of the mountain on his left, driving even more gingerly than before. Both of us were thankful for the premonition that saved our lives that night.

★ ★ ★

After a service of worship during a lull in the fighting in Italy, an infantryman stayed after his comrades had left. "Chaplain, that was a good service," he said. "I always feel better after worshiping as we did today. I like your messages."

"I'm glad to hear that, soldier," I replied. "I feel better after worship, too."

"But, Chaplain, I have a problem. You know that when we sight down our rifle at a Jerry and then pull the trigger, we see a man fall back dead. We are different from those in the air force; they drop bombs and never see the people they kill. Now with us, we see the men we kill. And that's what's getting me. I know what the Bible says: 'Thou shalt not kill.' But that's what I'm doing—killing. I don't know what to do about it, but every time I go back into combat I'm more upset about what I'm doing. But—that's not your problem, Chaplain. You never have to kill anyone."

"Wait a minute, soldier. What do you mean, it's not my problem?

Didn't you just tell me you always feel better when you come to worship?"

"Jeez, Chaplain, I sure do. And I'm glad you're in our outfit."

"Well, if I make you feel good, doesn't that make you a better soldier? And doesn't that mean you become a better killer? And doesn't that mean that I'm helping you pull the trigger?"

"Chaplain Yost, I never thought of it that way," responded the Nisei. "But I guess you're right. You help me be a better killer."

"Yes, indeed, soldier, and I know that. The army has me here so you do your work better. When I build up your morale, I'm guilty of whatever you do wrong because I help you do a better job of it. And think of that little old lady back in the States; she saves tin cans and helps the war effort. Isn't she a part of the whole system that backs up our war? The difference between her and you is that you are a young man who can take physically what is necessary in combat, but there is no difference in what both of you intend to have happen. And the only reason I don't carry a gun is because I'm a chaplain and can do more for morale with my prayers and sermons than I could with an M-1."

"Chaplain, I never thought of it that way," replied the Nisei a second time.

"Well, I thought the whole thing through before I volunteered. You know, chaplains are not drafted. I could have sat the war out at home. I didn't, because I look at this war not as a right thing to do, but as the lesser of two evil things. If we do not fight the Nazis they will kill off more and more innocent people and that would be wrong. So we are forced to kill off the Nazis, even though killing is wrong, to stop them from continuing to do a greater evil."

"Thanks, Chaplain. I'll have to think about what you've told me."

"You do that, soldier. And the next time you get upset about what you are doing, just remember I'm in this with you, too."

★   ★   ★

The combat infantryman often has a quite different outlook on the war he is engaged in from many other members of the armed forces. In the front-line foxhole he is often wet and muddy, tired to the point of exhaustion, hungry and thirsty and cold, and often scared. If the fighting is stalemated, he may spend several days cramped in his burrow, aware that not too many yards in front of him enemy infantrymen are in the same condition. He knows that many of the enemy wanted the war no more than he did—that they were drafted and forced into combat. In contrast, he thinks of those in the rear echelon, who are eating well, getting an opportunity to sleep on a cot with blankets, perhaps even making money on the black market, and whose military service is only occasionally interrupted by the extreme danger he lives with almost constantly. Is it any wonder that he sometimes feels greater kinship with the man facing him only a stone's throw away, one whose life is exactly like his? This is not a matter of disloyalty, for when the time comes he will kill or be killed, and he will not shrink from his duty, but . . .

The 100th took many prisoners, and they treated them well. Often our combat veterans were appalled at the extreme youth or the poor physical condition of the POWs they herded to the rear. Many came through the battalion aid, where they were given the best treatment possible under the circumstances. Was this not in accordance with our American ideal of fair play?

✶   ✶   ✶

One day, when the newspaper carried a story about the inhospitality—even persecution—shown to an AJA family who had relocated in the Harrisburg area,[4] only an hour's travel time from my parish, I recalled the letters I had written to the next of kin of the Nisei who had given their lives in Italy and France. Some of these were answered by families still languishing in relocation centers, and they revealed a continuing sadness and sometimes anger that our democratic country had betrayed its ideals in its treatment of AJAs. Whenever I was invited to tell of wartime experiences to local civic and service clubs, I witnessed emphatically to the amazing loyalty and sacrifice of the Japanese Americans within our borders.

Perhaps the 100th Battalion was composed of a rare breed of men, different from all other Americans. I doubt it. I am of the opinion that my comrades were real men, reflecting the high ideals of their centuries-old ancestral culture as well as those of the land of their birth, and screening out the base elements of both heritages. In addition, they seized opportunities and used them to write a remarkable chapter in the history of our times.

As a Christian who accepts the premise that God works all things together for good for those who love him (Romans 8:28),[5] I suggest that all things worked for good in the experiences of the 100th, of which, by the providence of God, I was the chaplain.

Notes

1. See the appendix following for this letter and supporting letters written by other commanders.
2. The Yost family still has this special demitasse set.
3. The parade was made up mainly of replacement soldiers from the 100th Battalion. Only a "handful" of the soldiers who had been with the battalion from the beginning were in the parade. (Duus, 232).
4. Harrisburg is the state capital of Pennsylvania.
5. Yost referred to Romans 8:28 as "the Bible verse which I used as the motto for my life." It meant to him that a person's life is in the hands of God and that those who see with the eyes of faith know that out of the discouragements and pains of life can come great blessings.

Appendix

Letters of Commendation for the Japanese American Units

Office of the American Provost Marshal
Headquarters Florence Command
A.P.O. #534, U.S. Army

15 September 1945

SUBJECT: Conduct of Japanese-American Soldiers
THROUGH: Commanding General, Peninsular Base Section,
                     APO #782, U.S. ARMY
TO: Commanding General, Mediterranean Theater of
                     Operations, United States Army, APO #512,
                     U.S. Army.

It is the desire of this office to express its deepest appreciation to the officers and men of the Japanese-American Units serving in the Mediterranean Theater for their splendid conduct during the Italian Campaign. This officer has, for the past 15 months, been Provost Marshal of the cities of Rome and Florence. During that entire time, a delinquency report has as yet to come across my desk on these fine soldiers. Their combat record is one for which only the greatest admiration can be expressed. In the areas behind the lines when on leave or rest, they have conducted themselves in a manner reflecting credit upon the highest traditions of the service. Their appearance, courtesy, and personal actions as soldiers have been superior. It is with a feeling of pride that I look over the record of these young Americans. For a job well done in the service of their country, the thanks of this office.

/s/ DAN S. McMILLIN
Lt. Col., Cavalry
Provost Marshal

HEADQUARTERS PENINSULAR BASE SECTION, 21 Sept 45.

TO: Commanding General, MTOUSA, U.S. Army

I concur fully in the statements made in basic communication. The conduct, military bearing and attention to duty of both officers and enlisted personnel in these units have been exemplary during the entire period in which the units have been stationed within PBS territory or have been under my command.

/s/ FRANCIS H. OXX
Brigadier General
Commanding

Hq MTOUSA, U. S. Army, 30 September 1945

TO: Commanding Officer, 442d Infantry Regiment.

I am pleased to add my commendation and praise to the officers and men of Japanese-American Units in the Mediterranean Theater of Operations for their exemplary military conduct.

/s/ JOSEPH T. McNARNEY
General, USA
Commanding

HEADQUARTERS 442D REGIMENTAL COMBAT TEAM, US Army, 10 Oct 45.

TO: All Organizations, 442d Regimental Combat Team.

I have noted with pride and satisfaction the contents of the basic communication from the Provost Marshal, Headquarters Florence Area Command and the indorsements [sic] of the Commanding General, Peninsular Base Section, and Commanding General, MTOUSA. May I add my appreciation for your excellent conduct and the record you have made for the 442d combat team.

/s/ V. R. MILLER
Colonel, Infantry
Commanding

Col. Farrant Turner leads the men of the 442nd RCT and the 100th Bn from their troopship through the streets of Honolulu on their return from the war. (Courtesy of Bert Turner.)

Yost in his clergy vestments in front of St. Peter's Lutheran Church, Reinerton, Pennsylvania, after the war, 1946.

Yost's arrival in Honolulu to conduct memorial services for 100th Bn soldiers killed in war, September 1947.

A MEMORIAL SERVICE

in honor of

THE COMRADES OF THE
100th INFANTRY BATTALION

who fell during

WORLD WAR II

Pastor Israel A. S. Yost Officiating

sponsored by

The Oahu Chapter of "Club 100"

at

McKINLEY HIGH SCHOOL AUDITORIUM

HONOLULU, T. H.

SUNDAY, OCTOBER 5, 1947   2:00 P. M.

Program for memorial service at McKinley High School auditorium, Honolulu, October 5, 1947.

Yost and other speakers at memorial service, McKinley High School, October 5, 1947. The text of Reverend Yost's address appears on pp. 293–297.

Audience at memorial service, McKinley High School, October 5, 1947.

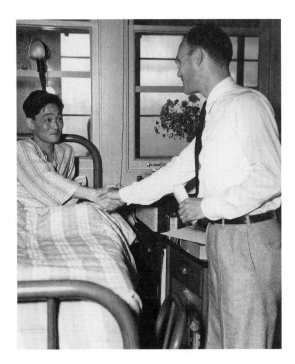

Yost with convalescing veteran of the 100th Bn, 1947.

Yost with 100th Bn veteran Kenneth Kengo Otagaki, 1947.

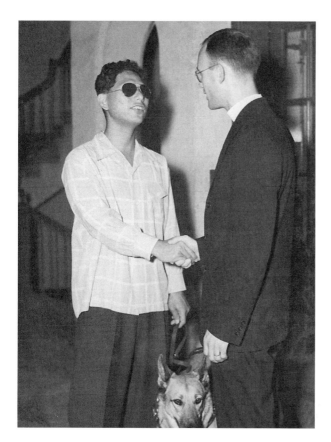

Yost with 100th Bn veteran Yoshinao "Turtle" Omiya, 1947.

Yost with 100th Bn Gold Star Mothers who lost sons during the war, 1947.

Yost with relatives of 100th Bn soldiers killed during war, 1947.

Yost at picnic with 100th Bn veterans, 1947.

Yost enjoys meal with 100th Bn veterans, 1947.

Yost and 100th Bn veterans at World War II memorial in downtown Honolulu, 1947.

Yost at 100th Bn honor roll memorial, Maui, 1947.

Stanley Y. Nakamoto, Dr. Kenneth K. Otagaki, Peggy Yost, and Reverend Yost with memorial to American soldiers of Japanese ancestry killed in World War II at the National Memorial Cemetery of the Pacific (Punchbowl), 1983.

Peggy Yost (in 2005), at her home in Maryland, looks over the letters her husband wrote to her almost daily during the war. (Courtesy of Homer Yost.)

AFTERWORD

Monica E. Yost

WHEN ISRAEL A. S. YOST enlisted as a chaplain, I was the infant daughter in Nazareth, Pennsylvania, he said good-bye to for over two years. I have no memory of the war years or of my father's return after the war. However, as I was growing up, I heard stories about the men of the 100th Battalion and sensed my father's deep respect and fondness for them. The stories he told were not about strategies of combat, but about cherished memories of the character of the men, especially their kindness to him, their bravery, and their sacrifice for each other and their nation.

In 1984, three years after he retired from the ministry, he went through the journal pages and daily letters to my mother that he wrote during the war and produced this manuscript, which he titled "Chaplain of the 100th." He dedicated it as "my gift to my children that they might have some understanding of their father's experiences and feelings while he served in the military." I believe he also wrote it as a tribute to the men of the battalion and hoped that some day it might be published to add to the historical record of the remarkable character and accomplishments of the 100th.

I appreciate the hundreds of hours he spent first going through his letters and making typed copies of them, then writing the manuscript on an old typewriter (without benefit of a word processor), and then finally standing at a copy machine to make multiple copies, one for each of his children.

Twenty years later, preparing the manuscript for publication has prompted me to read many of the original letters themselves, giving me the privilege of seeing both my parents as young adults before my memories of them begin. I have come to know them as a young couple in their twenties who were very much in love, shared a strong Christian faith, and had the courage to risk the death or serious injury of one of them in order to serve a larger good.

My father's letters reveal the depth of his love for his family. I have been touched by his many references to me, the daughter he tried to picture in his mind as she grew from an infant to a three-year-old, and to his baby son whom he had not yet seen. They speak, too, about his dreams for his family's life after he returned home, including the children he hoped to have in the future.

The memoir Israel Yost wrote offers its readers a picture of the war, the 100th Battalion, and the life of a chaplain who is a stranger to most of them. For me, it is the gift of knowing better who my father was as a young man. I see his joys, his discouragements, his friendships, his commitment, his bravery, his soul searching, his compassion for the enemy, and his ability to see the beauty of the countryside around him despite the horrors of war.

★　★　★

Who was this twenty-seven-year-old chaplain who became a beloved member of the 100th Battalion? What influences in his life made him the man he was? Here is a glimpse at his life, both before and after his time with the 100th.

Israel A. S. Yost was born in Schuylkill County in eastern Pennsylvania in 1916, the third child of Ammon Henry Adam Yost and Lillie May Sassaman Yost.

Six generations earlier, in 1738, Israel's ancestor, Peter Jost, emigrated from the Palatinate in Germany to eastern Pennsylvania, fleeing religious persecution and the devastation caused by war. In all probability, Peter's ancestors were Swiss Mennonites.

In America, the Josts originally settled in Montgomery County, then moved to Schuylkill County, where they were farmers and owners of farm-related businesses. As members of the German Reformed Church in America, they gave their children biblical names such as Daniel and Sarah. Although they learned English, they also continued to speak a dialect of German interspersed with English words that came to be known as "Pennsylvania Dutch" (or as they called it, "Pennsylvanisch Deitsch"). To guarantee that English speakers pronounced their name correctly, they anglicized the spelling from "Jost" to "Yost" (the German letter "j" is pronounced like an English "y").

In 1905, Israel's father, Ammon, married eighteen-year-old Lillie Sassaman, the oldest child in the Lutheran family of Ida and George Sassaman, a master carpenter. They began their life together on Ammon's parents' farm. Upon Lillie's arrival at the farmstead, her father-in-law decreed that from then on the language used at the dinner table should be English, as Lillie did not understand Pennsylvania Dutch. Within a year, daughter Ida was born, followed by another daughter, Elva, three years later. At age three, Ida died of scarlet fever while her father lay insensibly ill with the same disease. When Elva was seven years old, Israel Ammon Sheldon was born. He was named Israel for his paternal grandfather, Ammon for his father, and Sheldon for a popular preacher of the time. Two years later Robert was born.

By the time of Israel's birth, Lillie and Ammon had moved off the farm into their own home, and Ammon's parents had died. Ammon, after teaching school briefly, had a business selling farm equipment and managed the Yost family farm, which marketed butter and eggs. Often he took his two young sons with him, one at a time on alternating days, as he made his business rounds in Schuylkill County. Israel had many fond memories of spending the entire day accompanying his father to farms, sometimes falling asleep on the way home with his head in his father's lap beneath the steering wheel of the pickup truck—after they had stopped to get his favorite treat of rice pudding.

In their home the family said prayer before each meal and at bedtime. Every Sunday morning they worshiped at their church, and often on Sunday afternoon or evening gathered in the front room for a hymn sing, sometimes accompanied by his dad on the violin and his sister on the piano. His parents liked old Gospel hymns, and at an early age Israel learned many of them and continued to enjoy them throughout his life.

A week after Israel's ninth birthday, his life was suddenly torn apart by the death of his forty-two-year-old father. Years later, this is how he described that tragic day.[1]

> Dad's death came without warning. On a June day he and Robert set off in the morning—it was my turn to stay home. As usual Dad drove toward Tamaqua on back roads from Frackville. . . . He was heading toward the farm at New Ringgold. En route he stopped at the bottom of a hill called the Vulcan, to talk with one of his friends who owned a gas station there. He parked his pickup beyond the pumps which were just off the side of the road. A car came down the highway hill, veered toward the gas pumps, knocking down Dad's friend and somehow catching Dad and dragging him along, bumping the pickup and then veering back across the highway to stop at the embankment on the left side of the road. Bob was sitting at Dad's seat in the pickup and grabbed the brake so that nothing happened to him. Dad's lower torso was badly crushed; evidently he

knew at once that he was seriously, perhaps fatally, hurt. The man who climbed out of the car was intoxicated—at nine o'clock in the morning! The Tamaqua fire company was phoned and an ambulance dispatched. We learned that Dad began to sing "Abide with Me, Fast Falls the Eventide" in spite of the pain.[2] One bystander reported that he sang verse after verse of the hymn. He was taken back through Frackville to the State Hospital at Fountain Spring. Someone had telephoned Mother. She took me along and drove to the hospital. I wanted to go along in to see Daddy, but she insisted I stay in the car. When she came back after what to me seemed like hours, she reported that Dad was very, very sick. She took me home and then returned to stay with Dad until he died early the next morning.

Dad was conscious only part of the time. When conscious he tried to explain to Mother all the important details of his business. He was so badly crushed that even his spleen was affected. . . .

We three children were inconsolable; Mother was, too, but she was also angry. "To think that Ammon never took a drop of liquor and now he has been killed by a drunk!" There was truth to her bitterness. Our Dad was a gentleman of the old school—clean of speech, without bad habits, well liked by all, always going out of his way to help someone else, active in community affairs, easygoing. . . . After his death the most effective control of our conduct was Mother's often repeated saying, "Your Daddy never did that." . . .

The driver of the car that killed my father was arrested and jailed. Mother attended the trial in the county court house at Pottsville. She had little to say but what we heard was bitter. The man was convicted and sentenced; within a few months he was released. . . .

Pastor Gallenkamp had services at our house . . . in Frackville. Then began the slow and solemn ride . . . to McKeansburg. Father's coffin was again opened for viewing as he lay in state in the Sunday School room of Christ Union Church. We all went upstairs for the funeral service in the sanctuary. Of course he would be buried in Christ cemetery, close to the grave of his oldest child Ida. Just a few paces from the side door of the Sunday School room where his body lay was the monument covering the graves of his father and mother and several siblings. In this same graveyard were buried his grandfather and grandmother as well as his great grandfather and great grandmother.

I remember nothing about the service, but that was of no great importance. Mother had carefully explained to us that Daddy was not dead, that he was in heaven with Jesus, and that we should not think of his dead body as being the real Daddy. We knew from her words that Daddy was all right. We understood that the body he had used would be put into a grave, but Daddy would not be put there. Because of such careful preparation I remember myself as being calm during all the formal proceedings. I was prepared for the walk through the graveyard to the burial plot.

When we came down from the church nave, Daddy's coffin was still open for viewing. One of the undertakers came over and stooped to Bob and me and whispered, "Do you want to kiss your Daddy goodbye?" His well-meaning but entirely inappropriate words broke my calm. I remember that I became hysterical; I think Robert did, too. I remember nothing more about the proceedings. [For a long time afterward] day after day I punched myself after awaking because I thought Daddy's death must certainly be only a dream.

Lillie often said that she saw her husband "buried on our wedding day —exactly twenty years later." She was left with a sixteen-year-old daughter and nine- and seven-year-old sons. Her husband's business affairs were in disarray. Ammon had been known for being a very kind, good man, but not a good businessman. Apparently many of his "records" were kept only in his head. When he died many who were indebted to him simply forgot about what they owed. Lillie had no way of knowing even where some of the farm equipment had gone. The Yost farm had to be sold.

Lillie herself had a keen sense for business. She had given up her dream for education when her father refused to permit her to attend high school. As the oldest of eleven children, she had helped raise her brothers and sisters. When she married into the Yost family, her father-in-law recognized her business sense and gave her responsibilities with his financial affairs. Even before her husband's death she had worked outside the home, as the manager of a clothing-store branch. Now after Ammon's death, as the sole supporter of three children, she moved her family to a nearby town, where she opened a butcher shop. Her teenage daughter did not return to high school but instead got training as a beautician and began working.

Life after his father's death meant major changes in Israel's life besides losing the companionship of his dad, who was the more easygoing of his parents. Just before the tragedy, he had taken two piano lessons; now financial constraints squelched any plans for music lessons. He no longer heard his father's voice singing the beloved hymns. He no longer heard the Pennsylvania Dutch dialect that his father spoke with many of the farmers on his sales rounds. Israel had been intrigued by it, listening intently to the conversations and keeping a little notebook listing comparisons of English and "Deitsch" words. His mother had learned the dialect when she lived in the Yost household and could use it effectively, but when Israel ventured to speak in the dialect at home, she forbade it, saying she did not want his English speech to become "dutchy." He did, however, acquire the local Pennsylvania Dutch way of speaking English with its distinctive intonation of English words, interspersed with German words.

Money was tight in the Yost household now that Ammon was gone. At age ten, Israel helped in his mother's butcher shop, slicing meat and cheese, plucking feathers from steamed chickens, and delivering orders within walking distance. The next year (1927) the meat store business failed.

Israel, now eleven, experienced another big change in his life when his mother married William Clayton Lord, a widower with a daughter and three sons. Despite the fact that as an orphan W. C. Lord had been forced to quit school in the third grade, he had worked his way up from ash boy to supervisor of the power plant of a silk mill. The marriage meant not only a stepfamily, but also a move to Phoenixville, a town twenty-seven miles from Philadelphia, outside the Pennsylvania Dutch area. Israel was not ready to accept a new father. In his words, "I can recall telling myself that I would never call my stepfather 'Dad' and I carefully avoided addressing him by any title, but after a while I began to think so well of him that 'Dad' would slip out, and finally I had to admit to myself that he was the kind of a man that deserved to be called 'Daddy' even though he was not my real father."[3]

Junior high school in Phoenixville began as a challenge for Israel. He had no difficulty with the academic work; however, the other children made fun of him because of his "dutchy" speech pattern. "I learned to my amazement that I did not talk like the other children. They made fun of the way I pronounced some words and used other words that they had never heard before. I soon decided to do as little talking as possible until I was better accepted by my schoolmates." Within a year he felt accepted, and over time his speech lost its "dutchy" flavor.

Perhaps remembering how his speech was perceived as different, even odd, made him more easily accept the pidgin speech of the Japanese Americans from Hawaii when he first met them in Italy. Because of his unusual first name, Israel also knew what it was like to feel different because of a "funny" name that others mispronounced and misspelled.

Israel's life in Phoenixville also brought interaction with peers of more diverse ethnic backgrounds than he had encountered previously. He enjoyed the friendship of a vivacious Jewish girl, and two of his male buddies were a Jewish boy whose father had a delicatessen store and a

Roman Catholic boy whose parents were Hungarian immigrants. Junior high school brought an awareness of social class distinctions as well. Israel coped with feelings of inferiority regarding his social status and was motivated to excel academically in order to prove himself. In his words,

> I was aware that in our town there was an upper crust to society. Through the Lutheran Church I came to know [a boy whose father was a partner in a meat-packing company]. . . . I got invited out to the W—— home in the wealthier part of town. In my heart I knew that the W—— family was no better than the Yost family, but my father had died and my mother had remarried. I knew that my stepfather was as good a man as any other, but he had only a third-grade education and his job as power boss at the Eagle Silk Mill did not qualify him to move in the country club set. . . . Subject matter in school came to me easily, but I was also motivated to work hard because I wanted to prove myself better than others who came from the old established families in town.

Pushed by the desire to prove himself, at graduation from junior high Israel ranked first in academic standing. As valedictorian of his class, he read his essay titled "Justice." Etched in his memory were incidents of religious and ethnic intolerance that he had witnessed earlier in his life.

> I attended grades 3 and 4 in Frackville [in Schuylkill County]. It was here that I became aware of the hatred in America between some of the older immigrants and the more recently arrived families from non-Anglo-Saxon countries of the Old World. At least three times crosses were burned close enough to where we lived to be seen by the people of Frackville—one of the crosses blazed on the lawn in front of the Ukrainian Church right in town. This was a part of the program of the northern KKK [Ku Klux Klan] against Roman Catholics and foreigners. One morning I discovered little KKK signs on the store windows of my mother's place of business. When I came crying to my mother (we lived in the same building) she comforted me by explaining that the KKK was not after us but was against the owner of the building.

His own experiences of feeling different and his awareness of groups who were treated unjustly helped to shape the man he was when he met the Japanese American men of the 100th Battalion. He accepted them as equals though their backgrounds were different from his, and he understood their drive to prove themselves.

His early years also prepared him for the physical rigors of combat life and taught him skills that were valuable on the front lines. As a youth he bicycled long distances, played basketball, and was a long-distance runner on the high school track team. As a Boy Scout he participated in hiking, swimming, and camping and learned first aid and the use of a compass to create maps.

At age fifteen, Israel was confirmed in the Lutheran Church. The next year he was inducted into the National Honor Society and completed his junior year in high school, ranked number one in his class. He skipped twelfth grade and, in the fall of 1933, enrolled at Muhlenberg College, a liberal-arts college in Allentown, Pennsylvania, affiliated with the Lutheran Church. Through his mother's advocacy, he had been able to take courses during his junior year that qualified him for admission to college.[4]

With his pastor's help he was able to procure scholarship aid. That, coupled with waiting on tables in the college dining hall and whatever summer jobs he could get during the Depression (including digging with a pick and shovel at a construction site), paid for his tuition and room and board at the college. As a language major he studied Latin, Greek, German, French, and Spanish and was involved in many extracurricular activities. In 1937, he graduated magna cum laude and headed for The Lutheran Theological Seminary at Philadelphia. While completing the three-year course of study there, he also took graduate courses at the University of Pennsylvania, participated in a clinical program at an inner-city Philadelphia hospital, and did volunteer work with youth at settlement houses in the slums.

In 1940, Israel graduated from the seminary, was ordained a Lutheran pastor, and began his ministry in the Hecktown-Farmersville union parish in the Lehigh Valley, between Easton and Bethlehem, Pennsylvania. He served two country Lutheran congregations that worshiped in church buildings located several miles apart. A "union" parish meant that each Lutheran congregation shared its church building with an Evangelical and Reformed congregation that had its own pastor.[5] Such a situation was fraught with problems for which his seminary training had provided no preparation.

On top of his problematic vocational life, his fiancée (whom he had met the summer before and to whom he became engaged shortly after coming to this parish) abruptly broke off the engagement. Israel was distraught by this second great loss in his life. Years later he reflected, "Without doubt the two tragedies I experienced early in my life have greatly affected the way in which I have related to the world. . . . If indeed I have had any success in working with people, in part that has been the result of the two sorrows that have made me somewhat empathetic to others and their tragedies."

Then into his life came a young woman who made him realize that his broken engagement opened the way for the most precious blessing of his life. "One member of the choir and the Luther League I could not ignore, and not only because she was president of the League. She was vivacious, bright, popular, pretty." She was twenty-year-old Peggy Virginia Landon. Soon he began visiting her at the farmhouse her family rented near the cement mill where her father worked as a machinist foreman.[6] Before long, Israel and Peggy were engaged, then married in September 1941.

The following September, their first child was born. Several months later, disappointed with how little he thought he had accomplished in his first parish and having seen so many young men of his parish leaving to fight in the war, he felt he, too, should do his part in the war effort. He enlisted in the army as a chaplain and after several months of training shipped out to Europe, leaving behind his infant daughter and eight-and-a-half-month pregnant wife, entrusting his young family to God's care.

✱   ✱   ✱

After the war, Israel returned to his family in Nazareth, Pennsylvania. They were now a family of five: wife Peggy, three-year-old daughter Monica, two-year-old son Christian, and teenage foster daughter Alberta, who had joined the family while Israel was overseas.

Returning to his role as a parish pastor, he moved the family to Tower City, Pennsylvania, a small town in the mountains of Schuylkill County, where he served a two-congregation parish. Here two sons and two daughters were born: Israel J., Nathan, Faith (now Faith Northrop), and Hannah (now Hannah Finnley).

In 1947, the 100th Battalion's veterans' organization in Honolulu, Club 100, invited Israel to come to Hawaii—all expenses paid—to participate in memorial services for those killed in the war. His friends of the 100th presented him with gifts, including a large, beautiful, hand-carved chest, which Peggy still has in her living room. To Peggy at home with the children, the men sent boxes of lovely, exotic Hawaiian flowers.

In 1951, the Yost family moved to Phillipsburg, New Jersey, a town along the Delaware River on the New Jersey-Pennsylvania border, where Israel was pastor of St. John's Lutheran Church. In addition to his pastoral work, he also taught Latin and English at the local high school. During their eleven years there, the family added four more sons and a daughter: Reuben, Homer, Peter, Maria, and Luther.

In the summer of 1962, the family moved to Oahu, Hawaii, where the men of the 100th and their families graciously helped them get settled and extended friendship to them. During their three and a half years in Hawaii, the Yosts lived in Honolulu and Makaha, and the two oldest children received degrees from the University of Hawaii. Israel taught at Kailua, Radford, and Waianae High Schools, began a new Lutheran congregation named Maluhia in Waianae,[7] and served as pastor of St. Paul's Lutheran Church in Kaimuki.

Life in Hawaii gave the children the broadening experience of living in a natural and cultural environment quite different from that of northwest New Jersey. They had the opportunity to interact with and learn about the heritages of people of Asian and Polynesian backgrounds, as well as enjoy the beauty of a tropical climate, including the fun of living just off the beach in Makaha.

In early 1966, the Yost family returned to the East Coast, where the four oldest children were already attending college and working. Israel served as pastor of Prince of Peace Lutheran Church in Baltimore County, Maryland, where he provided leadership in building a new church facility and with Peggy's help began a day-care center. Here, as in other communities, he also taught in a public high school and took graduate courses at nearby universities. Following his seven-year ministry in Maryland, he served an urban congregation in Jersey City, New Jersey, and a country church in the Kutztown area of Pennsylvania.

In all of his parishes, Israel was active in social ministry. He led his congregations in the resettlement of refugees: German ethnic families from Eastern Europe after World War II and an Indian family exiled from Uganda in the early 1970s. Remembering the role that Boy Scouts had played in his life, he was an ardent supporter of scouting. During the civil rights movement he organized a community fair housing council and prodded his parishioners to confront racial discrimination. His own children were not permitted to swim in a community swimming pool until it was integrated. By word and example he taught his children to be concerned about the less fortunate in society.

In 1975, Israel, Peggy, and their youngest child, now a teenager, began a new adventure. They moved halfway round the world to the mountains of Papua New Guinea, where for two years Israel was a literacy developer for the Wabag Lutheran Church, training leaders of the Enga Stone Age tribe how to teach members of their clans to read.

When they returned to the East Coast, Israel again served country churches in eastern Pennsylvania. After retirement in 1981, he was a high school substitute teacher, a member of the board of directors of the county Red Cross, and a volunteer chaplain at the county jail, where he and Peggy held services and Israel prepared inmates for their GED exams. Both he and Peggy, as trained literacy teachers, also tutored adults in reading.

Over the years, wherever they were living, Israel and Peggy kept ties with the veterans of the 100th and their wives. In 1983 and 1992, they returned to Hawaii as guests of Club 100 for memorial services and other anniversary events. On these occasions, Israel gave memorial addresses at the National Memorial Cemetery of the Pacific (Punchbowl) on Oahu and at cemeteries on Maui, Kauai, and the Big Island.

In 1994, Israel and Peggy, now in their seventies, moved to Frederick, Maryland, where three of their children live. Parkinson's disease slowed Israel down and finally took his life in June 2000, at the age of eighty-four. As he suffered from the dementia caused by the disease, memories of the war burst into his mind, causing him to awake at night, calling, "Medics, medics." Throughout his illness, as in all of their fifty-nine years together, Peggy was his steadfast support. His ashes are buried in the Yost ancestral cemetery at Christ Church in McKeansburg, Pennsylvania, next to the graves of his parents.[8]

The eleven Yost children all graduated from college and most went on to earn graduate degrees. Though they are scattered across the country, on both coasts and in Alaska, they are a close-knit family, frequently gathering in Maryland. Israel's beloved wife Peggy, in good health, enjoys her family, which now includes fourteen grandchildren. This book is now a gift to them, providing a lens for viewing a special part of their grandfather's life so that they, too, may know of his faith, courage, and commitment as a young man.

Notes

1. The first-person narratives are from autobiographical material Israel's family found in his files after his death.

2. The same hymn was sung at Israel's funeral seventy-five years later.

3. When Israel was in college, W. C. Lord, who had a bad heart, died at the age of forty-three; after his death, Israel lost contact with his stepsiblings. Several years later, Israel's mother married Arthur Sterner.

4. She had a voice with the principal because she had gained respect in the town by joining the hospital auxiliary and impressing some of the socialite women with her ability to purchase supplies for the hospital.

5. The Evangelical and Reformed Church was created by a merger of the German

Reformed and the Evangelical denominations; a more recent merger of this church body with the Congregational Christian Churches resulted in what is known today as the United Church of Christ.

6. Dewey and Hilda Landon, both of English heritage, moved their family to Pennsylvania when daughter Peggy was fourteen years old. They were both from Crisfield, Eastern Shore, Maryland, where Dewey, like many generations of his family dating back to the 1600s, was a waterman who harvested fish, crabs, and oysters from the Chesapeake Bay with the boat he built himself. Hard economic times during the Depression brought them to Pennsylvania for work. While Israel was with the 100th, they returned to their way of life in Crisfield.

7. "Maluhia" is the Hawaiian word for "peace." This church, still active today, is on the outskirts of Honolulu on the leeward coast of the island of Oahu. Peggy Yost stays in touch with this congregation.

8. See the appendix following for the condolence letter Senator Inouye, veteran of the 442nd RCT, wrote to Peggy upon learning of Israel's death.

Appendix

Senator Inouye's Letter to Peggy Yost

UNITED STATES SENATE
WASHINGTON, D.C.

Daniel K. Inouye   July 19, 2000
Hawaii

Dear Mrs. Yost

I was most saddened to learn of the death of your beloved husband, Reverend Israel Yost.

The men of the 442nd Regimental Combat Team were truly blessed to have had Reverend Yost's spiritual guidance on the battlefield to help the troops through their darkest hours.

You and your family should be proud of Reverend Yost's accomplishments over the years on behalf of our nation, in the ministry, and as an educator and advisor. His legacy will live on for generations to come.

I realize that mere words are not sufficient to lessen your burden of grief. However, I hope it will help you to know that your burden is shared by many others. Reverend Yost will live on in the hearts of all who knew and loved him.

With much aloha,

/s/ DANIEL K. INOUYE
United States Senator

Memorial Address—100th Infantry Battalion

September and October 1947

"Step Off the Road, and Let the Dead Pass By"

The Reverend Israel A. S. Yost, former chaplain of the 100th

Comrades and friends and parents:

I regret that I am not able to address you parents of our fallen comrades in the language with which you are most familiar. If I could I would gladly speak to you in Japanese about "Stepping off the Road to Let the Dead Pass By."

This day has been set aside lest we forget the sacrifice made by our fallen comrades of the 100th Battalion. For many of us it is not necessary that a special day be set apart for such remembering; some of us think often throughout the year of old friends or relatives who are no longer with us. In fact, at times even the nights are filled with memories of deceased comrades as we dream of the battlefields of Italy and France. Furthermore as we meet the prejudice against race and color still loud in its cry and strong in its injustice, many of us cannot but remember the brave soldiers, living and dead, who proved so nobly that in one generation real Americans can be made from any racial background. In addition, as some of us look into the faces of our own sons and daughters we are reminded of other little boys and girls who are orphaned because their fathers died both for the sake of our nation's existence and for ideals of equality for all Americans. For us who were close by blood or comradeship to these three hundred-odd dead of the 100th Battalion, there is no need for a special memorial day, except as such an occasion is used to strengthen us in our resolves to live in a manner worthy of the dead, and as such an occasion serves to remind the world around us of the splendid achievements of the Americans of Japanese ancestry.

All of us here present have reason to be thankful for what our dead have done. Because of such soldiers the war was kept away from America; because of these men our homes were not invaded, nor our loved ones endangered, nor our property destroyed. We who were over there have seen what war does to a country; because of the courage of our comrades, even unto death, we at home have been spared such ravages of war.

Some of us have even greater reason to be thankful for what the dead have done. A great many of us would not now be living were it not for the sacrifice of brave friends. If, for example, three men had not stayed at their forward post until enemy action killed them, many of us might never have come away alive from the Pozzilli area of Italy. There are present here today some of us who owe our very lives to the dogged determination of comrades who would not give ground, but who fought valiantly on to win security for the rest of us of the battalion.

There was never any fear at the battalion aid station that the enemy would suddenly appear to threaten us; we knew that the line up front would hold or advance, and we were conscious that it would be at the cost of the lives of good friends. I, for one, want to thank, in the name of my wife and family, the parents here present whose sons were killed overseas—I want to thank them for giving their sons that I might live.

And, while speaking of giving thanks, there is something else for which I want to publicly thank the members and friends of the One Puka Puka. Never once in the long months that I served as a member of the battalion did any member of the outfit discriminate against me because I was of a different color and creed and race. Americans everywhere ought to be thankful for such a living testimony of the practicability of the idea that "God hath made of one blood all nations of men for to dwell on all the face of the earth" (Acts 17:26). My experience was that of countless other Americans who had contact with the members of the 100th.

Today we step off the busy road of life to let these our dead pass by. They bring us a message as they parade by in review, and we are proud of them— and pray God, may they be proud of us and the way we are carrying on their traditions.

Once, over there, four men came slowly up a trail along which was strewn the debris of war. Our soldiers had fallen, wounded or dead, along that path, dropping rations and arms and equipment in agony or haste. The four were carrying a dead comrade on a litter. It was not so much the weight of their burden as it was the weight of the sorrow in their hearts that made them tread so slowly on their way. Toward them came a lone soldier, of a different division and of a different race (though American). When he noticed the funeral procession he stopped, stepped off the path, removed his helmet, and stood with bowed head as the men bore the dead past him. I shall never forget how that white soldier of the 45th Division took time to honor one of our dead AJAs; in reverence he stepped off the road to let the dead pass by.

Once again today, as is our custom, we step off the road to let our dead pass by. Each of us will be thinking especially about his own dear son, or husband, or brother, or relative, or friend. Look with me at some that I see passing by.

There goes a sergeant of the medical corps. He was well known in our outfit, especially by those who fell with legs blown off or holes ripped into their sides, for he was the liaison man of the battalion Medical Detachment. He saw to it that litter squads got to the wounded, and often he was the one to creep up to give encouragement until the carriers came. Then one night enemy shells interrupted his errand of mercy and he fell mortally wounded. As we watch this sergeant of the medics pass by he bids us remember that he has a son living in America, and he wants us to see to it that his boy gets a fair deal in life.

There goes another lad in the line of march. We found him alongside the road just across the Volturno River in Italy with a large picture of his son lying near his body where it had fallen from his pack or out of his hands. He, and all the others who have left orphaned children behind, are beckoning to us from the ranks of the dead not to forget their loved ones. When we feel we have no time for other people's boys and girls—no time because we need all our time and money and energies for ourselves—let's step off the road and allow our honored dead to pass by, reminding us of the debt we owe to their children and to the youth, all the youth, of America and the world.

There goes, in the ranks of the dead, one who was university trained, adept in languages, a student of world affairs, interesting to chat with, eager to meet the future, one of whom a friend could always be proud. He had plans for his life and visions of serving his fellow men. But one day up front a mortar shell cut off his visions, his future, his hopes; when I brought him back for burial his face was so changed that at first I did not recognize my friend. He was not cynical as are some Americans; he really believed that the American way was worth fighting for, worth dying for. When we feel like giving up our ideals, or when we grow weary of trying to arouse interest in the apathetic, when we are tempted to stop fighting for liberty and freedom and justice, let's step off the road to allow the dead such as this one to pass by, reminding us to keep faith with the dead.

Ah! There marches our major. He was a man among men, tall, broad, and tough. Back home all sports lovers knew him for his prowess. With us he was a favorite, with both officers and enlisted men. I recall how once he mercilessly lashed out with a torrent of words at an incapable officer who had a habit of endangering his men by bluffing, and how he turned, and with the same breath gently urged a private to take better care of his sore feet. Our major flowed with health and strength and that sense of fair play for which all real Americans are known.

When I as the chaplain was having a difficult time evacuating the dead for burial this kindly comrade said, "If I am killed, don't go to so much trouble about me; just bury me where I fall." When an officer higher up blundered, our major calmly walked into a zone of machine-gun fire in an attempt to straighten out the battalion. We did the best we could for him at the battalion aid station, for we loved him very much, but there were too many oozing bullet holes in him, and by the morning he had died. When we forget our sense of fair play, when we try to cheat our way through life, or try to get by, by being something less than our best, when we feel we can't take being the loser, or in victory feel like lording it over the beaten, let's step off the road to let this beloved officer and others like him pass by, reminding us to keep faith with the dead.

Look intently at all the three hundred and some as they file past. Short, swarthy, Oriental warriors they, of Japanese parentage, but Americans of Americans, with lives gladly given for their country's welfare. They sought nothing for themselves, but strove instead to make this a land where free men of all colors, creeds, and origins might live at peace, an example to the world. While living they said, "We do not expect to live through this war, but we will die bravely so that our children, our wives, our parents might have a place in America." When mouthy men of godless "isms" preach to make us hate the other color, the other creed, the other race, and say that men of other lands have not souls like unto our own, then let's step off the road to let these Japanese Americans pass by, reminding us to keep faith with the dead.

Now, you who were members of the 100th, pick out from the ranks of the dead, your own beloved friend. You knew him as a lad, you played with him, and hiked and swam and schooled. He marched with you and sailed with you across the seas. He knelt with you in prayer and joined his voice with yours in praise of God. He had the same dislikes and loves as you. He showed you pictures of his girl, or wife and child. He wasn't always sure the higher-ups directed right, but he believed in God and in his most sincere of hours he thrilled at all the things for which our nation stands. He planned for all the things we now enjoy, and often said he knew that we would carry on if he should not return. Oh, comrade of our honored dead—or wife, or Dad, or Mom, or sister dear, or brother—all you who are his kin or bound to him as friends—

> when you begin to slide through life instead of climbing,
> when you begin to harm instead of helping,
> when you begin to curse at God instead of praying,
> when you begin to feel that life is for the one who thinks of self
>   alone . . .
> then pause a while, step off the road, and let the gold-starred soul
>   of your beloved pass by.
> Then, can you break faith with the dead?

Where these dead now are they see eternal truth. Our honored dead from their side of eternity know that God is on the side of right and compassion and justice. Not all of them in life were quite so sure that God is kind and good and much concerned about his sons on earth. But now they see with eyes undimmed by human doubt. And as they pass before us all today, I believe they bid us look at that dear One who years ago was cruelly hanged upon a tree. Not all our dead were Christians, that I know; but now from out the grave they cry that we have faith in God, the loving Father whom we know alone through

Christ. They long for us to learn to know the God of love so clearly shown to all the world by our Lord Jesus Christ.

When we lose faith in God above and doubt that love can conquer all the world, when we deny the Christ and worship things of earth, then let us step down off the road to allow our dead to pass by, reminding us that they can see that God still rules the world with love.

Those worthy soldier-dead need not our words of praise today. They need none of our gold for statues to their fame. They only ask that we keep faith with them, that we shall ne'er forget that they have died with hopes of making this old world a bit more like the place of peace God planned it for.

What if we fail, and live for self, and oft forget to champion right against the powerful wrong? What if we break the faith with these our dead? Then they would beg that we forget mistakes and try again. They know, and we know in our hearts, that it was easier to die upon the battlefield for right than to live day in and day out according to the best within us. That's why it is good for us to hold such services year after year—to bolster up and encourage us to live up to the standards they set by their deaths.

I believe they would even bid us not to mourn for them, for they know that we the living have the harder task of daily fighting on for what is right and good and kind. I know they will forgive us when we fail, if only we will try again to quit ourselves like men in fighting for that for which they gave their lives.

> When soulless men our high ideals defy,
> When our fond hopes and visions start to die,
> When selfishness engulfs, let's, you and I,
> Step off the road to let the dead pass by.
>
> When human wrongs for right to heaven cry,
> If for ideals you e'en may have to die,
> To keep your aims in life clean-cut and high,
> Step off the road to let the dead pass by.

WORKS CITED

Bimberg, Edwin L. *The Moroccan Goums, Tribal Warriors in a Modern War.* Westport, Conn.: Greenwood Press, 1999.

Blumenson, Martin. *Mark Clark, The Last of the Great World War II Commanders.* New York: Congden and Weed, 1984.

Clark, Mark W. *Calculated Risk.* New York: Harper and Brothers, 1950.

Duus, Masayo Umezawa. *Unlikely Liberators, The Men of the 100th and 442nd.* Honolulu: University of Hawai'i Press, 1987.

Hillel, Marc, and Clarissa Henry. *Of Pure Blood.* New York: McGraw Hill, 1976. (French title: *Au Nom de la Race,* trans. Eric Mosbacher. Librairie Arthene Fayard.)

Inouye, Daniel K. *Journey to Washington.* Englewood Cliffs, N.J.: Prentice Hall, 1967.

Murphy, Thomas D. *Ambassadors in Arms.* Honolulu: University of Hawai'i Press, 1954.

Puka Puka Parade. Honolulu, July–August 1982.

Shibutani, Tamotsu. *The Derelicts of Company K.* Berkeley: University of California Press, 1978.

Shirey, Orville C. *Americans: The Story of the 442nd Combat Team.* Washington, D.C.: Infantry Journal Press, 1978.

The Story of the 442nd Combat Team: Composed of 442nd Infantry Regiment, 522nd Field Artillery Battalion, 232nd Combat Engineer Company. Information-Education Section, MTOUSA, 1946.

Yamane, Stuart. *Journey of Honor* (a film). Hawaii Public Television, 2001.

Yank The Army Weekly, vol. 3, no. 10 (August 25, 1944).

Production notes for *Yost / Combat Chaplain*

Cover and interior designed by Liz Demeter
with text in Bembo and display in Trade Gothic

Composition by Josie Herr

Printing and binding by Sheridan Books, Inc.

Printed on 60 lb. Accent Opaque, 500 ppi